High Schools, Race, and America's Future

What Students Can Teach Us About Morality, Diversity, and Community

Lawrence Blum

HARVARD EDUCATION PRESS
Cambridge, Massachusetts

Library of Congress Control Number 2012937487

Paperback ISBN 978-1-61250-465-0
Library Edition ISBN 978-1-61250-466-7

Published by Harvard Education Press,
an imprint of the Harvard Education Publishing Group

Harvard Education Press
8 Story Street
Cambridge, MA 02138

Cover Design: Sarah Henderson
Cover Photo: Brand New Images/Lifesize/Getty Images
The typefaces used in this book are ITC Stone Serif for text and
ITC Stone Sans for display.

To all of the thoughtful and wonderful students
in my four Race and Racism classes at Cambridge Rindge and
Latin High School. And to the memory of Wolf—his brilliant mind,
his open heart, his yearning to make a better world.

CONTENTS

FOREWORD

Teaching high school students requires special talents of which most of the general public has no idea. It requires balancing the demands of subject matter knowledge with knowledge of adolescent learning and development as well as how to teach that subject matter to those learners. Teaching high school students when you are not normally a high school teacher is quite a feat. In this lively and thoughtful book, philosophy professor Larry Blum invites us into the classroom as high school students grapple with the historical and moral aspects of race and racism.

Blum's book joins the work of distinguished scholars committed to teaching—and learning from—young people. Carol Lee's (Northwestern University) beautifully narrated journey over three years in one of Chicago's lowest-performing high schools benefited both the students who studied English with her for those three years and those of us who attempt to prepare teachers for an increasingly diverse student body. Yolanda Majors's (University of Illinois–Chicago) work shows scholars how to make use of adolescent learners to teach teachers. David Stovall (University of Illinois–Chicago) continues to teach in Chicago Public Schools, where he helps students understand what it means to be critically conscious. Many other scholars do this work to varying degrees in regular K–12 and afterschool settings. Scholars like Elaine Richardson (Ohio State University), Dawn-Elissa Fischer (San Francisco State University), Greg Michie (Illinois State University), and Mica Pollock (University of California–San Diego) all find great intellectual challenge and reward in working with precollegiate students.

In *High Schools, Race, and America's Future*, Blum tells a compelling story. He offers an insightful analysis of the development of students' understanding of race, based on a carefully planned syllabus that includes both historical and contemporary material, and describes the animated, sometimes unexpected, and unfailingly revelatory classroom exchanges based on this reading. He also raises important questions about the ways we frame issues around race and achievement, and makes a powerful case for the value of diversity in education.

Blum's work is important because it engages some of society's more difficult social concepts—race and racism—in intellectually challenging and honest ways. Blum finds ways to make the discussion of these concepts academically rigorous without robbing them of the emotion students already feel in a racially asymmetrical society. His willingness to make himself vulnerable is an important part of this project.

Blum sought to teach his high school students how to understand the intellectual underpinnings of the emotional and psychic pain they experience as a result of race and racism. What he proves in this effort is that our young people are sophisticated enough to handle difficult topics like race and racism—indeed, they seem to thrive when they have the opportunity to delve into challenging intellectual material. Despite being immersed in a popular culture that is global, multiracial, multiethnic, and highly technological, students of color continue to suffer from the sting of racism. The students are still aware of a racial/ethnic hierarchy by which they are measured. They realize that to be a member of some groups is still to be debased and denigrated. They know the playing field is not yet level.

Blum's respect for the students' intellectual capability is refreshing and speaks to his integrity as a teacher. I am currently working with a younger, more eclectic group of students and enjoying it immensely. The twenty students enrolled in this course are among the best and brightest I have ever taught. They do not necessarily fit the typical mode of class valedictorian or honors program students, but they bring a wealth of knowledge and experience to the classroom—not to mention energy! Each week I am eager to both teach and learn. They bring fresh eyes and perspectives to some of the classic education research in which I have been immersed for many years. Readers will see the same process of discovery unfolding in the pages of this book.

While Blum set out to teach the students in his high school class about race and racism, they have a great deal to teach us in turn, as we listen to their frank and sometimes poignant conversations. Such powerful learning experiences are exactly what we need not only for our students, but for all of our colleagues who engage in work that helps prepare teachers. To begin to mitigate some of the racial disparities among our students, we need teachers who have a firm grounding in the nature of race and racism in our society. They need to know both the science and the history that have shaped our understanding of race. They need to know how profoundly the concept impacts students' daily lives and life chances. And they need to know how to teach this complicated material to students who are grappling with its implications in their daily lives.

Blum's work with this high school class represents the willingness of a scholar to step out of his comfort zone. By openly examining his own practice, he provides us with a window into the complexities of adolescent thinking about difficult topics and teenage life in a rapidly changing world. He weaves an intricate narrative like a beautiful tapestry. It is made of up many tiny details, forms specific and sometimes minute patterns, but ultimately results in a powerful and coherent piece. I hope that this revelatory account will inspire others to be more daring and courageous as well, and will put courses like Blum's on the curriculum of high schools across the country.

Gloria Ladson-Billings
Kellner Family Chair in Urban Education
University of Wisconsin–Madison

INTRODUCTION

Why I Taught a High School Course on Race and Racism

As the kids straggle in, I'm pretty nervous. I'm in my sixties; they're seventeen. I've been a college professor for thirty-three years; they're high school students. I'm a white guy and the class is mostly students of color. Hoping my nervousness doesn't show, I smile and greet them. "Just sit anywhere. We'll work out a seating plan later.

"I'm Larry Blum. I'm a professor at UMass Boston. This is a course on race and racism. I teach a course like this at UMass. This course is going to show you what college work is like. You'll have to work hard. Some of the reading will be different from anything you've had before in high school, and you may find it hard going at first. But I'll help you, and if you keep at it, you'll be able to understand it.

"My assistant, Justine, is going to help me with the class. Justine is planning to be a high school teacher. She was also a student here at Rindge and took this same course with me a couple years ago. So she'll really be able to help you and help me with the class.

"You'll notice that the class is very diverse. That's on purpose. I wanted to teach a class that reflects the diversity at the high school. I think you'll all get a lot more out of studying about race if you are doing it with students of other races. And I'm really interested in what you are thinking about the subjects we're going to study together."

Bernadette, a black student, raises her hand: "About that diversity. I'm surprised any white students would sign up for a course called Race and Racism. I thought we were going to sit around and talk about how oppressed we are."

Uh-oh. Does this mean the black students aren't going to buy in to my wanting a racial mix in the class? Are they going to resent the white students? Am I going to be able to make the class work as a group? Will I have to be a referee between different racial groups?

I reply: "I'm glad you raised that issue, Bernadette. This course is based on the idea that racial issues are important for everybody to learn about, not only black students. And I guess some white students think that too, along with Asian and Latino students, since that's who we've got here today. I'll go over the topics we're going to learn about later, but I hope you all will be willing to share your own experiences and ideas about race and racism, including experiences of discrimination."

Antonine raises her hand: "I thought you'd be a black guy, Professor."

Ten years earlier I would have been undone by a comment like this—an implied challenge to my credibility and perhaps my authority, right at the starting gate. And, sure, I'm worried whether I will ever achieve a sense of real authority with the students of color because I am white. But there is also something refreshing in how "out there" Antonine is, and her tone does not sound defiant or resistant. More just surprised. I suspect that some of my college students who sign up for Race and Racism think the same as Antonine when they see me on the first day of class. But they'd never say it. I'm going to have to get used to how, well, uninhibited these high school students seem to be. It's scary, but also refreshing.

"Well, I hope you're not disappointed, Antonine. Race and Racism is a subject, an area you can study, just like English literature or chemistry or American history. People of any race can learn about it and become a kind of expert in it. White people included. When I say 'expert,' I don't mean I know everything there is to know, and I'm sure you will be teaching me things I don't know. I just mean it is something you can learn more and more about and be able to teach to other people."

This book chronicles the life of this semester-long course, which I taught for four years at Cambridge Rindge and Latin (CRLS), the public high school in Cambridge, Massachusetts. You'll see why it is important to teach high school students about racial matters, and we'll deal with some of the challenges of teaching this kind of volatile material to diverse students. You'll see the students grappling with the intellectual, moral, and emotional challenges of difficult material. And we'll learn a lot about what young people today—the citizens of tomorrow—are thinking about such vital issues.

—⁊⁊⁊—

I didn't set out to teach high school. I have taught moral and social philosophy at the University of Massachusetts, Boston since 1973. I first got interested in race and precollege education as a parent. Between 1982 and 2005 at least one of my three children attended a public school in

Cambridge, where I live, from kindergarten through high school. Their schools were much more racially and ethnically diverse than the ones I attended as a kid. The diversity fascinated me. I became active in their K–8 school, teaming up with an African American parent to organize a committee of parents and teachers to try to make the school more inclusive of the racial, class, and cultural differences there.

As Ben, Sarah, and Laura moved to the high school, I became somewhat active there also. With about 1,900 students, Rindge—at the time the only public high school in the city, drawing students from every neighborhood—was amazing in its ethnic, racial, economic, linguistic, and religious diversity. This is not the image everyone has of Cambridge; most people associate the city with its intellectual resources, high housing prices, liberal voting patterns, and especially its two prominent and distinguished universities. But the Cambridge of the public school system, and the single public high school in particular, is very different. A large number of professional families avoid the public schools, especially after their kids reach the eighth grade. They have many options: the Boston/Cambridge area offers a wide array of high-quality private schools, including Catholic schools.[1]

Cambridge has very generous public housing policies in the form of housing projects and subsidized housing. That is why low-income people can afford to live there. And before 1994, the city had a strong rent control ordinance that enabled many working-class people to live in Cambridge. Although the public school population has shrunk considerably since 1994, the schools, and the high school in particular, still have a remarkable range of incomes, ethnicities, races, and languages. The city is also immigrant-friendly, contributing to this diversity. So while Cambridge is in some ways unusual, its mix is the new face of America, with its growing Latino and Asian populations, blacks from the Caribbean and Africa, and mixed-race people. More communities across America will look increasingly like this one.

As a parent, I got to know some of the teachers at the high school. One day, I was talking with Jane, a social studies teacher at CRLS who had taught my older daughter, Sarah. I asked Jane if students were learning how to communicate effectively across the various divides. Did she think the school was making good educational use of its diversity? Jane thought for a moment and said, "No, or anyway, not as much as it could." I thought this might be an opportunity for me to engage with the high school, to learn more about the world of high school kids, and to facilitate some cross-racial conversation with a different population than my college students. I proposed to Jane that I organize an after-school discussion group with a mixed group of kids on racial topics.

This seemed like a good idea to Jane and she suggested I call the social studies coordinator, Nancy, whom I also knew slightly. I called Nancy the next day. She said my proposal would not work, because students don't have free time after school. They are working, doing extracurricular activities, or doing homework. But she suggested I offer a whole course on race and racism the next semester. A whole course? The thought had never entered my mind. Nancy said she would consult with the principal and get back to me. I don't think she asked me if I actually wanted to teach such a course. She was just running with the idea. By reputation, the wheels of bureaucracy in city school districts move slowly. But Nancy called me back the very next day and said the course was now official, starting the following spring. I suppose I could have said no, but the whole idea was starting to intrigue me. Without any training, and without planning for this to happen, I was going to be a (temporary) high school teacher.

The school did not want me as a white person to teach the course by myself, and suggested that I find an education student of color at UMass to be my teaching assistant. The high school administration in no way believed that racial topics should not be taught by white people, or that white people should not be teaching students of color about race. A white teacher about my age had taught an African American history course at the school for many years. The school folks just thought it would help both me and the students feel more comfortable and facilitate communication if I had a young student of color to help. I thought this was a good idea, and over the years I've always found a UMass student of color to work with.

Although high school would be a completely new setting for me, I think my thirty or so years teaching at UMass Boston better prepared me for this particular high school challenge than many other colleges would have. My university is the most diverse four-year public college in New England. I have students from many different backgrounds—racial, ethnic, economic—and of extreme differences in academic preparation. The diversity of the high school would not be entirely foreign to me. Fortunately, the university was also very supportive of the endeavor, releasing me from one of my college courses so I could teach at the high school. Instead of thinking that a college professor had lost his marbles trying to teach high school, the administration saw it as serving the campus's "urban mission" of service to local communities of color. And giving a

UMass student an internship to work as my teaching assistant enriched the partnership between the university and the school district.

—⁘—

When I finally had time to think it through, I formed some definite goals for the course. I wanted black and Latino students to be its main beneficiaries. One reason black and Latino students at the national level do not get as good an education on average as their white and Asian peers is that they are not enrolled in as many intellectually demanding courses. I wanted to do what I could to respond to this problem by offering a very demanding class. Nancy and I agreed that we would try to get the class to reflect the demographic of the wider school population, and this was a way to keep the white population of the class in the minority. (Whites were then about 35 percent of the school population.) We put the sought-after diversity in the course description in the school catalog. We couldn't guarantee that every group would be proportionally represented, since students had to choose to sign up for the class and we didn't have much control over that. Blacks tended to sign up much more than their percentage of the school population, which was 36 percent at the time. So the class always had a higher percentage of blacks, and I had to turn away a lot of black students and a few white students, and take every Asian, Latino, and Middle Eastern student who signed up. I wanted to offer a challenging course that more black students would choose, so that was fine. I was sorry not to have more Latino students, but I did have their percentage in the general school population (then about 14 percent).

Students who signed up for the class were not necessarily deeply interested in the subject matter. For some, it was the intellectual challenge of a "college-like" class—or perhaps the thought that such a course would look good on their college application—that provided the draw. For others, a nudge came from a guidance counselor who pushed the student in this direction, thinking he or she would benefit from the intellectual challenge. But the fact that CRLS was itself so ethnically and racially diverse meant that all of my students would bring to the class forms of racial experience that students in less diverse settings would not have.

The only achievement standard I imposed in the course description, and in my communication with school counselors who helped find students for the class, was that the students intended to go to college—any college. The high school saw this as a central purpose of the class—to give a "taste of college" to students who may not have grown up taking for granted that they would attend college, or whose families would not have been able to give them a sense of what college was like. In fact, I always ended up with a few students who did *not* end up going to college, even if they might have aspired to, and it was great to have that kind of diversity in the class also.

The colleges the students hoped to attend, as well as the ones they ended up attending, spanned a wide range, with a small number of students going to the very top tier, others to community college, and the rest to everything in between. I was especially interested in this "in between" group, to which most of the students in my classes belonged, because the national discussion about education is so focused on the very top end—who gets into the Ivy League and other selective colleges and whether there are enough low-income and minority students at those places—and on the bottom end, those at risk for dropping out of high school altogether. The in-between group represents the vast majority of college students, and they deserve more attention in the national conversation about college education. They were more like my UMass Boston college students, and I was interested in what they were like as high school students.

I wanted my class to give the students of color a different classroom experience than they would have in other honors and Advanced Placement courses in the school. In those classes, blacks and Latinos comprised about 28 percent (while their percentages in the school as a whole were about 52 percent), but in my class, they would be a solid majority. (Asians were about 17 percent of the advanced classes and 11 percent of the student body.) When we discussed this issue in the class itself, many of the students of color talked about their lack of comfort in the advanced classes. This discomfort included some of the Asian students, who because of their low proportion of the overall student population were still distinctly a minority population in these classes. I wanted the students of color to feel that my class was an academic space that belonged to them.

Dealing with the achievement gap between blacks and Latinos compared to whites and Asians was not my only goal for the class. I did not want the class to be *only* black and Latino students. (I doubt the school would have permitted this restriction anyway.) I wanted a racial mix. I wanted to create a setting where students would be talking about racial issues across racial lines. I hoped to show that high school students could become informed about racial issues and capable of discussing them knowledgeably and intelligently with people of all races. Adults so often clam up about race when members of other racial groups are around. Eric Holder, President Barack Obama's attorney general, said, "We, average Americans, simply do not talk enough with each other about things racial."[2] He got a lot of flak for saying this but I think he's right. I wanted to help my students become adults who *could* talk intelligently, responsively, and productively about race.

I also thought this arrangement would be a good experience for the white minority. Sheryll Cashin, an African American law professor, makes a profound point when she says, "I believe a lot more integration between the races would occur if whites experienced being outnumbered more frequently and were therefore forced to adjust to and learn about people who may or may not be very different from them."[3] Whites seldom have a chance to experience what it is like to be a racial minority in an important social setting. I thought the class demography might help my white students to better empathize with the more usual situation of racial minorities. And I tried to make sure I was sensitive to how the white students were feeling in this unaccustomed situation for them.

Many high schools do not have a student demographic that readily allows for such a racially diverse class. But I would encourage teachers who want to try teaching this sort of course to work within their school's way of operating to make the classes as diverse as they can—for example, by encouraging students of color to sign up and leaving a significant number of places for them. However, I would also emphasize that teaching the material about race described below can still be a valuable experience, even for an all-white class (or for an all-black or all-Latino class).

I know some teachers may be uncomfortable with all this attention to students' racial identities. Some teachers proudly say, "I don't see race, I just see kids." Aren't we supposed to see students as individuals, not as members of groups? Shouldn't we be color-blind, or at least, in Mica Pollock's coinage, "colormute" (meaning even though we can't help seeing race, at least we can choose not to talk about it)? Anyway, since Obama was elected, aren't we "postracial"?

Well, no, we weren't then, when I taught the class, and we still aren't. Color blindness might be an ideal to strive for in the future. But we can't just jump there. Our students are indeed individuals, but they are also members of groups, and their racial identities affect their experiences as well as their opportunities in life. Their race is *part* of their complex individuality. In this sense, color blindness means *not* seeing our students.[4]

—〰—

What should the course be about? I decided to make the idea of race itself the centerpiece of the course. The curriculum would incorporate science, history, current events, and students' reflections on their own lives.

I wasn't sure the students knew prior to the class that race could be a subject you study in school, not only something you experience and have feelings and opinions about. One white graduate of the high school once said of the school in the period I taught there that race was "a discourse of blame and excuse." I was looking for something completely different. I wanted the students to see the intellectual challenges and rewards of a serious study of race as an academic subject. CRLS did have some race-related courses, perhaps more than many high schools. There were courses in African American history, African American literature, Caribbean literature, and even (more recently) a sociology course on the achievement gap. But a whole course on race and racism was new to the school, and is still unusual. I hope it won't always be this way and that some teachers will read this book and want to try it; I also hope more teachers can find ways to incorporate racial material into literature, social studies, and biology courses, once they see how important and exciting teaching about race is.

I wanted the class to be a place where the students felt comfortable voicing their opinions and speaking about their own experiences. Their diverse backgrounds would enrich their joint learning. But I did not want the course to be mainly about experiences, either their own or those of authors we read. I wanted the academic study of race to anchor the course, and to be a framework that would help the students understand what they were experiencing. When they got to college, I wanted them to see in retrospect that my course had prepared them for college's intellectual demands—historical thinking, developing an argument, analyzing ideas, recognizing and respecting expertise in a field, and other elements of higher-order critical thinking and academic study.

I thought of the subject matter of the course in another way, too. High school subjects are generally seen as building blocks, defining a basic level of knowledge every citizen and worker must have to contribute to society and to understand the world around them. I thought of my course the same way. There is a basic level of knowledge about race, and specifically race in American history, that every American should have— a kind of racial literacy—even though most of them don't. The philosopher Martha Nussbaum says, "All citizens, not only African Americans, need an education in African American history and culture."[5] I absolutely agree. My course was intended to be part of the basics. It did not tell the students how to think about affirmative action, racial profiling, reparations for slavery, or any other controversial topic. But it provided an important part of what anyone who wanted to think about those issues seriously and responsibly would have to know.

First, I wanted students to know that contemporary scientists have generally rejected the pseudoscientific idea of race that has come down to us from history and still informs the way we think about people as being black, white, Asian, and so forth. The scientists think those populations are very alike genetically, with much more genetic diversity within the racial groups than between them. Over the four times I taught the course, I experimented with different formats for conveying the scientific critique. By the last offering I had found some accessible scientific writings and an excellent PBS special, *RACE—The Power of an Illusion*, to explain the scientific critique. (See appendix 2 for a detailed description of the syllabus and course assignments.)

I began the course with the science, though it was quite challenging intellectually, in order to shake up the students' acceptance of race. (A very few of them were already somewhat familiar with the idea that race is not a scientifically valid idea.) That unit led us to what would constitute the bulk of the course, the historical study of where the U.S. idea of race comes from. I lifted a text from my college class, *Race in North America*, which synthesizes the history of European exploration of the Americas, including Portuguese, Spanish, and finally English involvement in slavery and the slave trade; an account of scientists of the eighteenth and nineteenth centuries who developed the (false) idea of race; and changes in the character especially of U.S. slavery over time that affected the development of the race idea. *Race in North America* masterfully conveys a sense that race is a particular way of thinking about human biological and genetic diversity that came on the scene at a particular period in history and was not really there before. There were people who looked different, had different skin colors, and were from different cultures, but were not thought of as different races. The author, Audrey Smedley, conveys a sense of adventure about the changes in and development of the false and pernicious idea of race over time. It is an intellectually challenging book and I knew it would be difficult. But I wanted to stretch the students intellectually, and I decided to provide detailed reading questions to guide them through the text.

At the same time—and I got clearer about this over the years—I needed to have some less academic readings as well. Each week that we worked on the history from the main or supplementary texts, I also devoted one day to more experiential readings. For example, we read a slave memoir, *The Story of Mary Prince*—the first slave narrative written by a woman—about a British slave in Bermuda, one I didn't think the students would know, and that would help with my desire for them to understand something about slavery in the Caribbean (and in Latin America), not only in the United States. The last time I taught the course, I also used some wonderful personal stories from a collection of *New York Times* articles, *How Race Is Lived in America*, which covers topics such as multiracial friendships, race differences between the United States and the Caribbean, and teaching tourists about slavery at plantations that are now national park sites.

The students talked about racial incidents in which they were involved. They also did research, in interracial groups, about issues in their own environment—such as racial stereotyping, racial self-separation in the social life of the school, and racial separation and inequity in education within the school and the nation as a whole. I approached all these matters, contemporary and historical, with a moral slant, going beyond looking at what happened and why it happened to whether it was good or bad, right or wrong, and why. If students tended to sit with peers of their same race and ethnicity in the cafeteria, was that a bad thing or a good thing, or some of both? Race was a morally fraught area for the students, as I would learn over and over. I wanted to discuss the moral angle more systematically, as I would in my moral philosophy courses at the university.

—⁂—

I imagine some of my readers, perhaps especially white teachers like me, may be as uncomfortable with such a strong curricular focus on race as they are with the insistent attention to students' racial identities—especially when teaching this material to such a diverse group. Won't it degenerate into saying how bad white people are? Won't it fan the flames of racial resentments in students of color? Won't it make the classroom an emotional train wreck, or at least be counterproductive, not a space for learning?

I was worried about all these things. But after teaching the course four times I can see that with the right approach, a class like this *can* be a terrific, engaged, respectful place for kids of different races and backgrounds to learn things that will make them better citizens, enhance their personal growth, and contribute to their intellectual understanding.

I had a very particular hope for the class that is the flip side of these fears. I wanted it to show the distinctive value of integrated education—education in which kids of different backgrounds, experience, and heritage learn to respect each other and discover how to learn from one another. Julia, a student in one of the classes, once said, "In this class, everyone cares about what everyone else has to say." That is what I was hoping for. It is an ideal that has taken a backseat in the current discussion of "school reform." But I think there is as much of a need for it now as there was when I taught the course—and indeed more, as the country becomes increasingly diverse, with students of color comprising 42 percent of the school-age population.[6]

The diversity I wanted in the class was not only racial. I was also interested in ethnic diversity within the black racial group, and there was a good deal of that at the school. The largest black, non–African American group was Haitian American.[7] Most had been born in the United States ("second generation") or immigrated at a young age (the so-called "one-and-a-half generation"). Over the time that my own children entered the high school, in 1992, until the last one graduated in 2005 the Haitian students seemed to me to rise in prominence in the school, often becoming class officers, prom king and queen, and leaders of clubs and after-school activities. With the help and guidance of some Haitian staff at the school, the Haitian students put on schoolwide assemblies and programs featuring Haitian culture and history, had a Haitian Pride Day, and formed Haitian student organizations.

The school had other English-speaking Afro-Caribbeans, mostly but not only Jamaicans, as well as a few black students of African origin. Although the Boston area has an unusually high percentage of these non–African American blacks (a third of the city's total black population in 2003), they are part of the face of America's racial future, along with the steadily increasing number of Asians and Latinos. Down the road, Ohio, Wisconsin, Maryland, and even Iowa, Kansas, Montana, and Wyoming will have non–African American blacks. I had a good number of Haitians, a few other Afro-Caribbeans, one African, and generally one first- or second-generation African in each of my classes. How these different groups related to one another and learned from one another was an important part of the learning from diversity that I was looking for, and it would tell us something important about possible futures for the diverse black population of the United States.

Besides ethnic diversity, each racial group contained a good deal of internal economic diversity. The school was officially 46.4 percent low income in 2009–2010 and probably a roughly similar percentage the years I taught there.[8] The black and Latino students tended to fall into this category more than the whites, though there were plenty of exceptions, and I generally had some low-income whites in my class as well as a small number of blacks from middle-class (as distinguished from working-class) backgrounds. The Latinos seemed about equally divided economically. In a way, the economic diversity was *part* of the racial and ethnic diversity, since your economic resources so affect the way you experience your race. These factors are not easily separated.

I also hoped I would have in the class another group that is part of the growing racial diversity of the country—mixed-race persons. Barack Obama is only the most prominent example of a rapidly growing portion of the population. I always had one or two mixed-race students. In the class I focus on in this book, I had one student with a black and a white parent, another with an Asian and a Hispanic parent, and a third with a Hispanic and a white parent.

These were my hopes for the class. But the reason I wrote this book is something I did not anticipate—how extraordinary the experience of teaching the class was. Every day was an adventure. The students were remarkably willing, indeed eager, to discuss these charged racial topics. I have the impression that very few high school teachers give racial material such sustained attention, and I hope some of you will see that it can be done, that you don't have to be a scholar to do it, that students benefit greatly from a course like this, and that it can be an intensely rewarding teaching experience. I also hope the account of the class will encourage other college professors to consider making an arrangement with a local high school to teach such a course.

It was exciting just to be part of these conversations with the students. I wasn't used to their level of uninhibitedness compared to my college students. Their frankness wasn't always easy either. The students would say, "This is boring" or complain about how much work I was giving. These remarks would rattle me. At the same time, other students would express irritation at the students who were complaining. The sixty-two-minute periods were often electrifying—and exhausting. Usually I would have to do some serious decompressing after class, as I walked the twelve minutes from the school to my house or to the subway.

But most of all, these students had incredibly interesting things to say about race and racism, while engaging with the academic material I provided for them. Deborah Meier, in her classic book *The Power of Their Ideas*, says, "All kids are indeed capable of generating powerful ideas."[9] Mine certainly were. I think all Americans have something important to learn from these kids. They are tomorrow's citizens. And we can also see from them that there are certain conversations maybe we adults should be having—but aren't. That is the most important reason I wrote this book.

I should say that it wasn't until the fourth time I taught the class that I really felt like I knew what I was doing. I had tried different readings and assignments, changing them a bit each time, and the class seemed to come together the fourth time. Each time I got a bit better at bridging the age, race, cultural, class, and other divides between the students and me. It was very challenging. It was hard to get to know the kids as individuals, since I couldn't hang around until after school (my class was early in the morning), had no classroom of my own to meet students in, and the students all had classes immediately before and after mine. This was very different from the college arrangement, which makes it much easier to talk with students outside of class.

Although I had taught college for almost thirty years when I started the high school course and could draw on that experience, there were important differences. I came to have incredible respect for full-time high school teachers who face that challenge every day. I did not have the confidence to write this book the first three times I taught the class. But experience and practice paid off. I got better at connecting with individual students and learning what each one needed. I learned how to keep better control in the class through humor, firmness, and consistency. I got better at combining attention to my material and attention to the class dynamics. I now feel—after the fourth outing—that I am in a position to share this remarkable adventure.

At the same time, I am very aware that my being a white teacher may well have affected the dynamics in the class in all kinds of ways, given the predominance of students of color, especially black students, and the racial character of the material. I tried hard to listen well to all the students, and especially to let the students of color know that I recognized their experiences with racism. I tried to create a trusting atmosphere in class that would enable all the students to feel they could say what they actually thought and felt. But at the end of the day my own racial identity certainly played a part in what happened in my classroom.

The book is a series of "snapshots" from the class—particular discussions, writing assignments, exercises, curricular developments. I drew on my (admittedly incomplete) notes on the class, and in that sense I was limited in what I could write about. (Appendix 3 has a fuller description of my methods and the research material I drew on for the book.) But something happened almost every day in the class that would have been worth writing about! Most of what you have before you occurred during a single semester; occasionally I bring in something from a discussion from another class, and I note when I do so. To help you keep track of the students, I provide their names with a brief description in appendix 1.

All the chapters have three elements—the students' voices or writings; my reflections on the students' thoughts and the class interactions; and my commentary as a moral philosopher and race scholar on issues of particular importance to teachers, but really to all Americans, concerning racial or educational issues. The chapters have these three elements to differing degrees. (Appendix 2 has a description of the syllabus, course readings, and the assignments I gave the students.) Some chapters also reproduce lectures I presented to students. In two chapters I step back to discuss background or topics related to race and education.

The chapters mostly follow the course chronologically, though one (chapter 11) is based on a class discussion in an earlier offering of the course. I have used pseudonyms for all students and adults and have taken care to protect students' privacy wherever possible; occasionally I have slightly changed a biographical detail to further protect anonymity.

In chapter 1 I ask the students to introduce themselves to each other by telling stereotypes of their racial or ethnic groups that they object to. This helps us start to think carefully about what is wrong with stereotyping.

Chapter 2 opens with an explanation of contemporary scientists' rejection of the traditional idea of race, which still persists. I introduce the students to the main textbook whose author, Audrey Smedley, presents the question whether race is a natural or a constructed idea. The students engage with the issue of whether it is natural to be afraid of people who are physically different from you and in the process reveal aspects of themselves and their family backgrounds to each other.

In chapter 3 we discuss Smedley's argument about the historical origins of the idea of race, comparing the English, Spanish, and Portuguese colonization experiences in the Americas. The students are surprised to discover that Smedley is both female and black, and they discuss their surprise. I try to get them to see how important a scholarly, academic book like Smedley's is in giving them a broad understanding of race that they cannot get only from their own experience, or from looking only at the present.

In chapter 4 the students confront issues of moral symmetry that reappear constantly in discussions of race and racism: Is it equally wrong to make fun of or exclude a white student as a black student? Does the student's race matter from a moral point of view? The students discuss a racial incident typical of ones they face and think proactively about how to intervene in such situations. We discuss whether your racial identity should affect the rights or wrongs of intervening.

Chapter 5 takes up an issue increasingly important in American classrooms (including mine)—how teachers should think about African American students in relation to immigrants (first or second generation), especially black immigrants. Providing background that draws on important contemporary research on this issue, and bouncing off a brief student discussion and some postclass interviews, I also talk about how we can (and must) revise our understanding of "racism" to take account of these ethnic differences (Haitian Americans, African Americans, Africans) within race-defined populations (black).

In chapter 6 the students continue their morality-focused conversations, this time about the role of Africans in the slave trade to the Americas. This is the first of several chapters to deal with slavery, a central issue in the course and in the development of the American idea of race. The students discuss how much we should blame Africans who sold slaves to the Europeans in Africa—looking, for example, at whether it should matter from a moral point of view that the slave trade was an economic institution, rather than a conspiracy of white people to oppress black people.

In chapter 7 we bring our study of slavery up to the late eighteenth and early nineteenth centuries. This requires us to confront the notion that blacks are intellectually inferior—an idea stated by Thomas Jefferson and central to the American notion of race. I introduce the students to two critics of Jefferson, Benjamin Banneker and David Walker (an important black abolitionist in the Boston area), and explain their historical context. The students do an assignment in which they analyze Walker's arguments that essentially challenge the stereotype of black inferiority, thereby enhancing their higher-order thinking skills while also dealing constructively with the stereotype of black intellectual inferiority.

In chapter 8 I step back from the classroom to focus closely on five students who present different learning challenges. And I discuss the issue, central to educational thinking these days, of the importance of "high expectations." I look at the five students in connection with that idea and see that high expectations are neither a panacea nor always the important issue in helping students grow academically, personally, and morally.

In chapter 9, the students engage in an unplanned conversation about skin color, sparked by a statement by David Walker about blacks being proud of the color that God gave them. The students engage with the asymmetry issue in discussing the view shared by many of them that "white pride" does not seem as morally acceptable as "black pride." The students are remarkably open about discussing various skin color issues they and some of their family members have experienced.

Chapter 10 returns to the discussion of slavery. The students reflect in a written exercise on how the study of slavery has affected them, their sense of values, and their connection to their racial group. White, black, and Latino students have differing views, but there are differences within each group also.

Chapter 11 recounts an interesting discussion (again unplanned) about the n-word, drawn from a previous year's class. The dynamics in this discussion show the complex ways that a class and groups within it can work (or not) as mini-communities.

Chapter 12 revisits the students' last day of class, when they write about and discuss how they think they have been affected by the racial and ethnic diversity in the class. The conclusion pulls together what we can learn from the class about the value of racially integrated education, which has been pushed to the sidelines in recent "reform" efforts as well as by court decisions, to students' intellectual, personal, moral, and civic growth as future citizens of the United States.

For now, back to the first day of the class.

1 The First Day

Stereotypes and Their Consequences

After introducing myself, I begin with an exercise. "Before I describe the course," I say, "I want to hear from you and have you hear each other. I am going to put you in pairs. Tell your partner your name, your ethnic or racial group, and one stereotype about your group that you think other people have and that you don't like."[1]

I thought stereotypes would be a good vehicle for this ice-breaking exercise, and a good entrée to the topic of race. Students care about stereotypes and do not want to be typecast. Of course, minority kids are generally more vulnerable to stereotyping than whites; they are forced to be conscious of how they are seen by others more than white kids are. But at a mixed school like CRLS, this difference is not as pronounced. White students are also aware of unwanted stereotypes that other groups have of them.

So the exercise put the students of color and the white students on the same plane. I thought it best to start with a racial issue with which everyone had some experience. As teachers we want to give the clear message early on that everyone is welcome, everyone is important to the class, and everyone will be listened to.

Stereotypes are also a good topic because many adults as well as high school students are pretty confused about stereotypes, more so than you might expect. They are not really clear what exactly is wrong with stereotyping. Some may think stereotyping is unavoidable, that it's just part of how our mind works—we generalize and oversimplify in using broad categories—and either isn't really something to worry about too much or isn't something we can do much to prevent.[2] Others are not sure whether it is all right to make generalizations about groups—for example, "More Latinos than whites speak Spanish," "More professional basketball players are black than white"—because they aren't clear whether or when this counts as objectionable stereotyping. And many adults who do think stereotyping is wrong aren't sure what exactly is wrong with it. They may tacitly assume all stereotyping is wrong or bad for the same reason—because it denies individuality, or says something false about a group. I wanted to get some stereotypes on the table so I could start exploring these issues.

The exercise had two other purposes also. One was to establish that this was a class in which I expected the students to participate, that they wouldn't be able to just sit back and let me do all the talking (not that their behavior so far suggested this would be much of a problem). Second, I wanted the students of color to know that I realized they probably had experienced being discriminated against or stereotyped because of their racial or ethnic group. If you're a white teacher, this is an important and fairly simple way to acknowledge students of color and their experiences.

—ɯ—

The students immediately turn to their partners; few are at a loss for words. After several minutes, I reconvene the class and ask students to share what their partner told them.

> *Norris*: Marissa says she is white and black. She says a stereotype of white people is that they smell like wet dogs.
> *Behar*: Ebony says she is black. She says black people are perceived as being lower class.
> *Antonine*: Anna is white. She says white people are perceived as preppy.
> *Jacques*: Leila is African. Her stereotype is people think Africans are not civilized.
> *Leila*: Jacques is black. He says that because he is dark-skinned, people think he's African. He is also Haitian and people think Haitians all shoot darts.
> *Sherilyn*: Esteban is Dominican, and says people think all Dominicans are dark-skinned, which he isn't.

I don't comment on what the students say. This is touchy material, they don't know each other yet, and they are no doubt looking for signs from me as to what is and isn't acceptable to bring up. If I even ask for clarification, some students might let that inhibit what they might say. As teachers, we don't want self-censoring so early in the class. The students need to feel they can express their experiences.

But they are coming up with interesting things and I'm pleased they seem to feel comfortable voicing these stereotypes. When Ebony says "lower class" she seems to mean not only that blacks are perceived as low income, but also that they are thought to exhibit unrespectable behaviors, possibly ones associated with low-income blacks. Anna's example is something like the flip side of Ebony's. "Preppy" describes a certain dress style—name-brand clothing with neat, straight lines, and a collar shirt. But it also implies being economically privileged. The economic background issue is important to white students in the high school, some of whom are upper middle class, but many are "middle middle" or working class. Anna doesn't want to be confused with the upper middle, and Ebony doesn't want to be confused with lower-class blacks.

I'm struck that Marissa calls herself "black and white." She is choosing to reveal something about herself that would not necessarily be apparent to the other students. But more striking is that Marissa chooses to identify with the white part of her ancestry when she comes up with stereotypes, even though most people would be likely to assume she is black. Leila's comment is the most charged, the most stigmatizing, stereotype of any offered so far. It's a stereotype that was used to rationalize Europeans' colonization of Africa in the nineteenth and twentieth centuries, and it is still out there and very hurtful. Many of our current media images of Africa—wars, ethnic strife, AIDS, famine, political instability, and corruption—can resonate with this "uncivilized" image. I can't tell if Leila experiences all this and feels that people think maybe she herself isn't really civilized, or if she is just reporting a stereotype she knows about her group.

Jacques also mentions Africa in his stereotype. But he does not seem overly upset that some people think he is African, so the negative associations may not be operating for him. He just wants his distinctive Haitian ethnicity to be acknowledged.

The comment I am most concerned about is Esteban's. I know that Dominicans often use the word *black* with a very negative connotation.[3] It is often used to refer to, and to put down, Haitians, with whom Dominicans have a history of fraught relations. The two countries share the island of Hispaniola, and many Haitians, who are on average poorer than Dominicans, come to the Dominican Republic to work; this has been one source of tension. Partly for this reason, but also because throughout Latin America and the Spanish-speaking Caribbean dark skin color is generally (if in no way officially) seen as undesirable, "black" expresses a negative value judgment for many Dominicans, both at home and in the United States. Later in the course I will teach the students about differences in the way race and skin color are regarded in the Caribbean, Latin

America, and the United States. That will be a good time to bring up this skin color issue, which is important to students of color and perhaps especially to blacks and Latinos. For now, I let the comment stand.

Yet, in retrospect I wonder if I should have replied to Esteban. Could I have said something like, "Esteban, I just want to clarify. You're not saying there is anything wrong with having dark skin, are you? You're just saying people assume Dominicans all have dark skin, and that isn't true, right?" The point would not have been to have Esteban answer those questions but rather to signal to the class that the teacher thinks it is wrong to stigmatize dark skin. This is just the sort of clarification that I was reluctant to ask for so early in the course for fear of discouraging students' sense that they can speak freely; but it can be hard to balance that goal against the potential for racial hurt, especially for darker-skinned black students. We teachers have to be on our toes in presenting this material. We need to know enough about the racial terrain to be aware of what might be hurtful or damaging to some, and be prepared to say something to block that hurt—while maintaining a spirit of openness in the class.

The students come up with more stereotypes:

> *Lovelle*: Pema is from Tibet and says people think all Asians are Chinese.
> *Anna*: Antonine is Haitian. She says people think Haitians all just got off the boat and that they smell.
> *Pema*: Lovelle is African American and says people think all black people have the same ethnicity.

Very different kinds of stereotypes are coming up here. You might think that all stereotyping is bad for the same reason. But the students' comments show that assumption is wrong. We can see two distinctly different things bothering the students. One is that their ethnic group is not being acknowledged within their larger racial group. So Pema's being Tibetan (her ethnic group) is not recognized because people think all Asians (her racial group) are Chinese. Jacques is concerned that his Haitian ethnicity is unseen when people view him as African. And Lovelle experiences people not recognizing different ethnicities within the black population. These students are putting their finger on what is wrong with some kinds of stereotypes. They involve not recognizing a group you are part of that is important to you. Let's call this "lack of recognition."

But some of the other examples involve something different—seeing your group as having a characteristic you find objectionable. The comments by Antonine (Haitians just got off the boat and they smell), Ebony (blacks are lower class), Marissa (white people smell like wet dogs), and Leila (Africans are uncivilized) are examples of this "objectionable attribution."

Anna's (whites are preppy) and Esteban's (Dominicans are dark-skinned) stereotypes can be either objectionable attribution or lack of recognition. Anna may think being thought preppy is objectionable and not like the stereotype for that reason. However, she may not think anything is wrong with being preppy, but just feel that she does not fall within the "preppy" group, and wants her less-well-off group of whites to be recognized. Esteban might simply not like that his lighter-skinned Dominican identity is not recognized because people think all Dominicans are dark-skinned. But he may also think there is something bad about being dark-skinned and not like the stereotype for that reason.

The two kinds of badness in stereotypes are quite different. Lack of recognition does not necessarily involve objecting to what someone is saying about your group. When Pema objects to people thinking all or most Asians are Chinese, it is not because she necessarily thinks they are seeing Asians or Chinese or Tibetans in a negative light. And objectionable attribution does not necessarily involve thinking that the stereotyper does not recognize your ethnic group within the larger racial group, that is, lack of recognition.

Let's look at "objectionable attribution" a bit more closely. Some stereotypes attribute much more objectionable qualities than do others, and they are more hurtful to the groups being stereotyped. Contrast Anna's saying that whites are (stereotyped as) preppy with Leila's saying that Africans are (stereotyped as) uncivilized. Just looking at the literal meaning of these two stereotypes, it is obviously more damaging and hurtful to be stereotyped as uncivilized than preppy. Antonine's example about Haitians "just off the boat" seems in between. It implies that Haitians are all new immigrants, with the implication that they are kind of "out of it" in this country and don't understand what they need to. By itself, this can be mildly hurtful and insulting, but does not attribute as deep a deficiency as being lower class (Ebony) or, worse, uncivilized (Leila). But it is perhaps more negative than "preppy."

What this shows us is that not all stereotypes of the objectionable attribution form are equally bad. There are moral *gradations* of badness of negative stereotypes, just as there are different *kinds* of badness (lack of recognition, objectionable attribution). Stereotypes aren't just one single, unitary bad thing.

One more twist: to know how hurtful an objectionable attribution is, the literal meaning is not the only relevant thing. We also have to look at the stereotype's cultural meaning, which is to say, the associations that tend to go along with the stereotype, even though they are not explicitly stated. Jacques's case of throwing darts is a good example. Taken by itself, being good at throwing darts is a positive skill. I'd like to be good at throwing darts. But when it's Haitians throwing darts, a different, negative set of associations comes in—Haitians as a backward people, with an allegedly superstitious religion (vodou, or as it is often spelled in English, "voodoo"). It seems clear that Jacques is aware of these associations, and this is part of what he is objecting to when he mentions throwing darts.

Another familiar example (not mentioned by the students) of a positive stereotype with negative cultural associations is that students of Asian descent are smart, especially in math and science. The manifest content or literal meaning of this stereotype is very positive. It is good to be smart and to be thought of as smart. However, in the case of Asians, "smart" gets associated with "nerdy" or socially out of it and a bit boring, not fun to be with.

The cultural associations of a stereotype can make something that seems positive into a negative, or at least a combination of positive and negative. These cultural associations are often specific to a particular group. If a black person is good at math and science, he is less likely than an Asian American to be seen as nerdy and boring, though he may not fully escape the stereotype.

Thus, if we are teaching about stereotypes, we have to know something about sociology and history so we can recognize the unexpressed associations that might go along with a particular stereotype. It isn't enough just to say that stereotyping is harmful. We have to know how particular groups are hurt by particular stereotypes, given each group's specific history and the characteristics associated with that group. This opening discussion was the first of many reminders that to teach about race in a responsible way, history has to come into the picture.

—⚌—

The stereotype discussion gives me a chance to survey the class. There seem to be eleven black students (one of whom is mixed), four whites, three Latinos, and two Asian Americans. I'm excited to get to know all of them and thrilled at the ethnic and racial diversity I'm seeing.

I actually had met three of the students before. Mirvole, a Haitian American, had been a student at the same elementary school as my children. Her mother had participated in the parent race group I mentioned in the introduction. Cristina, a Latina whose father is from El Salvador and whose mother is a white American, had been in an afterschool program with my daughter Laura during elementary school.

My most interesting acquaintance with a student prior to the class was with Jacques, and our meeting would raise issues important to the course. Laura and I had met Jacques at the end of the summer, at a play about the racial achievement gap that a group of students from the high school put on as part of an innovative summer theater program. Jacques was one of the players. After the play, Jacques, Laura, and a couple of other kids from the play or the audience ended up standing in the middle of Central Square, an area in Cambridge with a lot of street life, talking about the issues the play had raised. Jacques is a tall young black man. In the course of the conversation, Jacques complained that people often assume he is a basketball player; he hates this, he said. We got on to a more general conversation about stereotyping.

People were walking by, and a black man, perhaps in his forties, stopped and started chatting with us. Wouldn't you know, the first thing he said to Jacques was, "You must be a basketball player." I scrambled to think of some way to acknowledge Jacques's feelings—should I say, "Hey, you don't know that he's a basketball player!" or make the racial thing more explicit, "Are you assuming he's a basketball player because he's black and tall?"—but I couldn't figure out a response and just tried to ease the man out of the conversation; he stayed on and on. I was supposed to be an expert on race and thought I should be able to do something to stand up for this sensitive young man.

It was an awkward encounter but Jacques did seem very interested in racial issues, so after the man finally left, I told him about the racism class and asked him if wanted to sign up. He did. That's how I knew that in addition to not liking the stereotype that Haitians throw darts, and that people with dark skin are from Africa, Jacques *really* didn't like the stereotype that tall young black men are basketball players.

—⁂—

Back in the class, the period is almost over. I say, "I am very excited about working with you in this class. People in this country don't talk to each other about race very well, especially with people of different races; and a lot of people are, well, pretty ignorant when it comes to racial matters.

We've gotten off to a good start in talking about racial stereotypes, and we'll be building on that. We'll be talking more about what exactly is wrong with these stereotypes, and stereotypes in general.

"We also have a great range of experiences to draw on in this high school, and in this class in particular. You will learn a lot about race, and I want you to feel comfortable saying what is on your mind. I will keep the atmosphere in the class from getting out of hand and, with Justine's help, do my best to make sure that it feels safe for you. We'll have to talk explicitly about how you can feel free to speak what is on your mind, but at the same time learn to be sensitive to each other's feelings. But today's discussion of stereotypes got us off to a good start."

2 Comfort and Suspicion
The Historical Construction of Race

I began the course with the scientific criticism of the concept of race. I wanted the students to question the idea of race from the get-go. For most of them, your race is just something you are, or have, like having brown eyes, being from Cambridge, or having grandparents from Haiti. The course aimed to shift that understanding toward the notion that race is an *idea* or way of thinking about human biological diversity—a way of thinking that is false and also historically and socially destructive. It is also an idea that developed over many centuries during which it was foisted on humanity. That historical development—the "historical construction of race"—formed the heart of the course. But the history would work best, I thought, if the students questioned the idea of race from the very beginning. So that's why I began with the current scientific understanding and critique of race. (It was not news to all the students. One student wrote on her information sheet the first day, "I'm black but science has shown that there aren't any races.")

I found some intellectually challenging but not inaccessible popular scientific writings on the topic. Unfortunately, our main textbook, by Audrey Smedley (which I discuss in more detail later in this chapter), does not lay out the scientific critique in a focused way. However, the American Anthropological Association has written an official statement for the general public on race, criticizing it—and Smedley was the main author of this statement.[1] And Jared Diamond, the author of the best seller *Guns, Germs, and Steel*, which provides an explanation—one that does not assume the inherent superiority of the Europeans and Asians—of why Eurasian civilizations gained political and technological dominance over other parts of the world, has written a comprehensible article on race.[2]

In addition to having doubts regarding the intellectual difficulty of the scientific critique, I had also been concerned that the students would find it hard to wrap their minds around the idea that something that seems so central to their sense of self—their racial identity—is in a fundamental way false. And I was worried that this would prove most difficult for the black students, since (for historical reasons that we would study in the course) blackness was a particularly personally and socially salient identity. Indeed, some white students did not think their "whiteness" had any significance, and sometimes said they did not identify with it. (I discuss this issue in chapter 12.) And some whites have used the scientific critique of race to deny its historical reality. I was worried that some of the black students might experience the attack on race as a kind of attack on them, or at least find the intellectual and emotional challenge of distancing themselves from their blackness in order to examine it scientifically a difficult one.

As it turned out, this almost never happened over the years I taught the course. Most of the students in all racial groups were fascinated by the scientific critique, and many black students felt it provided a liberation from false ideas that hurt them or their ancestors. Diamond argues that we think of race as a classification according to some genetically based characteristic, such as skin color or eye shape. But he says that on this definition, we could use many different genetically based characteristics as ways to classify people. None of them is any less or more valid than any other. I made a chart to illustrate Diamond's point. One column has a skin color grouping, with Italians and Swedes to illustrate "whites," and Australian aboriginals, Xhosa (a South African ethnic group), and Fulani (a West African group) to illustrate "blacks." Another column sorts the groups by whether they possess a gene that protects the carrier against malaria. The antimalarial group includes Italians, Fulani, and most Africans; the non-antimalarial group includes Swedes and Xhosa. A third column sorts groups by whether they possess lactase, an enzyme that allows processing of milk sugar. (Since the students were aware of the issue of lactose intolerance, this was a good example.) Again, there were "whites" and "blacks" in *both* groups in these two gene-based schemas. The overall point is that classifying races by skin color is only one of many possible ways to use genetics to classify people. Since, as Diamond argues, the possession of different sets of genes is not "concordant"— that is, just because some group has gene A does not mean the group is likely to have gene B—no classification system can claim to define what everyone should take race to be. The students really related to this argument as well as the chart that illustrated it.

A second argument I gave, now very familiar in the literature on science and race, is that human beings are genetically almost identical—99.9 percent according to the results of the Human Genome Project. Of the 0.1 percent in which we differ genetically, almost all of that diversity can be found *within* the groups we think of as "races" (blacks, Asians, whites, etc). There is only a tiny average genetic difference *between* these racial groups (3–10 percent of the 0.1 percent).[3] So the idea that "races" differ greatly in genetically significant ways, which is implied in the way we think about race (at least until this scientific critique penetrates our thought and we come up with different ways of thinking about it), is false.[4]

There was more to the scientific critique that I gave the students, but this gives you a sense of the main ideas they were exposed to. And they had to write an essay explaining three distinct criticisms of the idea of race from the reading—no easy task![5]

After dealing with the scientific critique, I began a new unit, introducing it in this way:

Me: We've seen that scientists are critical of the idea of race. They have shown that the popular, familiar idea of race as a basic division of the human species—where people of each race are fundamentally different from those of other races in important characteristics such as intelligence, moral character, and responsibility; are fundamentally the same as the others in their racial group; differ in outward physical characteristics that reflect the inner differences; and can be ranked as superior and inferior—all that is wrong. You have now started to read Smedley, who agrees with this criticism of race, but also approaches it in a different way. Smedley wants us to think about where the idea of "race" came from. Is it just a natural idea, reflecting the way the world is? Or did human beings invent it? That is the big question of the book. In the section you read last night, Smedley discusses a part of that question: Do we naturally feel suspicious of people who look different from us, in the way that people of different races look different, or who are culturally different? Is this suspicion just part of human nature? Do you remember what Smedley calls the view that fear or suspicion of difference is part of human nature?

Behar: Primordialism.

Me: Yes, that's right, Behar. So before we discuss what Smedley says about primordialism, I want to know what you guys think. Is it natural to be suspicious of people who are physically or culturally different from you?

I don't try to clarify what "natural" means in this question because I want to see where the students take it.

> *Lovelle*: Personally, I'm not afraid or suspicious of people who are different from me.
> *Me*: Do you mean physically or culturally different?
> *Lovelle*: Both.

This brief exchange brings to the fore how talking about race in the class was almost always morally charged—not only when we were talking about explicitly moral issues like slavery. Lovelle may have been answering the intellectual question I asked, in saying that if she herself did not feel these suspicions, then they couldn't be "natural." But she might have been doing something else—declaring that she didn't have race-based suspicions, which she could have regarded as morally questionable or thought that her classmates, or I, might have so regarded them.

There were two immediate lessons here for me in teaching about race. One was that you can't always get students to immediately focus on a particular intellectual question you put to them. They may take your question as offering an opportunity, or a challenge, to let you (or their classmates) know that they aren't prejudiced.

A second lesson was that, whatever else it is, race is fundamentally a moral issue, and I had to remind myself not to lose sight of this—to stay in touch with my students' moral responses and use them to further our collective understanding, moral and intellectual, of race.

> *Tenzina*: If you see your parents turn away from certain kinds of people, you kind of learn to be suspicious without knowing it.
> *Antonine*: Yeah, you learn, like, not to trust certain people when you're really young, and you don't even know it, or know why.

It sounds like both girls are drawing on their own specific family experience, although they don't say so. The class setting allows the students to examine their families' and friends' attitudes without having to commit to the possible embarrassment or shame of saying they are doing so. Sometimes they will want to name their family's views explicitly, and a teacher should help them feel comfortable doing so, as this might help the student tie an understanding of something in the class to a growing understanding of their own world. But it would be stepping over the line of respect if we pushed them to do so. Plus it gives them more space to explore if we do not.

> *Adam*: I think there are survival instincts that make us suspicious in a society like, um, like ours, because racism is so, like, embedded. Based on the way history has worked out, if you see someone in a business suit, like a white guy in a business suit, and then a black guy in a hoodie, you think, "yeah, of course," because you are used to the stereotypes of blacks and whites. And so, of course you are going to be suspicious of the black guy in the hoodie.

Adam, a white student who is involved with a high school group that deals with racial and other social justice issues, introduces a new and insightful idea. He says suspicions of others are not natural but you don't get them from parents (or not only from parents). They are based on stereotypes, and the stereotypes are so deep in our society that we react instinctively to other people based on them. So it isn't natural, he is saying, but it feels natural ("yeah, of course"). His answer shows how difficult it is to test what Smedley is saying. If racial ways of thinking and experiencing people are so familiar that they become part of "common sense," then it is difficult to know whether a particular feeling like suspicion, fear, or comfort with physical difference is really a basic human tendency or only a product of this "common sense" that has really been historically produced.

[handwritten margin note: sinecdogue]

I am also glad that Adam makes his point concrete by introducing a familiar stereotype—the young black male in a hooded sweatshirt, face partly hidden, a target of widespread suspicion and sometimes fear. I want the students to connect the academic material to their lives, and to problems in their society. But I wonder how this example will play out with the large number of black students in the class. How will they feel about a white student introducing it?

Two black students reply quickly. Mirvole comes to the course having given a lot of thought to racial issues in general.

> *Mirvole*: I think it's natural to be suspicious of people you don't know or who look or act differently from you.
> *Norris*: If I were walking down the street at night in a dark hoodie, people would probably be afraid of me, because I'm black, you know, a black male, so . . . they'd probably fear me or be suspicious or whatever.

Like Adam, Mirvole directly addresses the question I originally posed—are suspicions of cultural or physical difference natural? And she comes down on the side of the "primordialist." But she does not pick up specifically on Adam's "black guy in a hoodie." Norris, however, and understandably, personalizes Adam's point—*he* is the young black male walking down the street. So the conversation now isn't just about a familiar stereotype and the fears and suspicions attached to it, but also about a particular kid in the class. It makes more vivid for the other students what it means to be on the receiving end of the "suspicion" and thus deepens their understanding of what "suspicion" feels like.

Norris states his point in an interesting way. What he says is not that people *are* suspicious of him, but that they "would probably be." I am struck by this. Is Norris not sure whether he has actually been the target of suspicion on the streets of Cambridge, or Boston? I have heard some white people say that black people are too quick to claim that they have been "victims." I don't see this much in my own students. Perhaps Norris does not want to admit to the class that he has been seen as fearsome? It can also be shaming to be seen as a public threat, a suspicious character, even if you know you have done nothing at all to justify the suspicion. Or maybe something different is going on—that this early in the semester, Norris does not want to put such an emotionally charged item out to the class so starkly, forcing them to stop and take notice of him.

I wonder about all this, but I don't think teachers should press students in such a situation, and so I don't. We have to leave it to them to develop their own sense of trust and comfort with the class, and to decide when or if to be personally revealing or vulnerable.

The students are very engaged in the conversation. I'm sure the personal dimension Norris introduces piques their interest. But they are also really tuning into the intellectual question Smedley posed. They are building on each other's contributions and pushing the conversation forward.

Hannah: I don't think it's natural to be suspicious of someone who is physically different from you. But maybe you are more likely to be afraid of someone in a different culture. I think it is the culture you are fearful of, but if you live in the same neighborhood as someone who is different physically, you aren't afraid of that person. I think it's the culture.

Hannah differentiates physical appearance and culture as base for suspicion. If you grow up near—in the same neighborhood as—people physically different from you, you are not suspicious or fearful of them. You know them, you can see beyond the superficial appearance. Culture is different. Hannah seems to be saying that cultural differences are a reason to feel suspicious. I am not completely sure what she means by "culture" here, although it is the word Smedley uses. Could Hannah be saying that if people of a different race than you act differently from you, this is because of their different culture, and it can be a reason to be suspicious?

Sometimes white people (and others too) use "culture" as a presumably more acceptable way to talk about "race." It seems more morally acceptable to say you are, or that it is all right to be, uncomfortable with people of a different culture than of a different race. But, though I am just getting to know her, Hannah does not strike me as someone who would say the more acceptable thing rather than what she actually thinks, nor do I think she means that she is afraid of people of other races. She has had many friends from other racial groups, especially blacks, since junior high. So what she may be saying is that people in the same neighborhood share a culture, even if they are of different races.

Sherilyn sits immediately to my right, and is always very thoughtful and engaged. Sometimes she talks very softly, almost as if she were talking only to me. I try to get her to project more, to speak to the whole class.

> *Sherilyn*: Common sense tells us that it is wrong to be suspicious, but if
> you have learned to be fearful, it's hard to ignore those ideas.

Sherilyn brings out a moral dimension to the discussion that has been there, but only implicitly. The class had been examining whether people *are* suspicious of those who are different. Sherilyn says that is *wrong* to be suspicious, a quite different matter. She says that "common sense" says that it is wrong. As the course went on, Sherilyn showed that she was quite often concerned about right and wrong, and what is right and wrong about race. Here, she seems clear that she thinks it is wrong to be suspicious, but she is also aware of why people have these suspicions; building on Antonine's and Tenzina's earlier comments about parents' influence on children, Sherilyn says that if you have learned to have these suspicions, it is hard to get rid of them just because you know they are wrong.

Jacques, the black young man whom I met at the end of the summer, is interested in the intellectual question Smedley poses about what is "natural." At the same time, there is a moral and political passion behind his intellectual engagement.

> *Jacques*: I don't think it's natural. I think you need to have a reason to fear someone or something. I think we are naturally curious.

Jacques opens up a whole new direction here, casting a wider net about which human impulses are natural, and more directly challenging the focus on suspicion as our response to difference. His remark becomes one of those wonderful classroom moments when you see one student opening up a new line of thought and then other students go down paths they might not have gotten to on their own.

> *Adam*: I think we are naturally cautious but not naturally fearful. Something has to happen to make us fear someone.

So Adam agrees with Jacques that we not naturally fearful, but he suggests a different natural impulse than curiosity—cautiousness, something less positive than curiosity (Jacques's suggestion) but less negative than fear (the primordialist view). (As the semester proceeds, Jacques's own natural curiosity becomes increasingly obvious. No wonder he sees curiosity as natural!)

Mirvole, responsive to her classmates, gives a personal example.

> *Mirvole*: Yeah, like I was watching this "native show" on TV this summer and they were, like, the people had no clothes on and stuff, and they were just so different and I was like, I started judging them in my own mind. You know? For no reason other than they were different.

Mirvole is the first student in the conversation to be explicitly and forthrightly morally self-critical. She admits that while watching a TV show with "natives," presumably in some traditional attire that looked to her like "no clothes on," she started judging them negatively. Reflecting on that reaction, Mirvole now thinks that the mere fact that they were "different" was wrongly influencing her to disapprove.

Students often say that "difference" is what makes one group fear, be suspicious of, or put down another group. This seems to me a kind of common sense among students. But I think it is misleading. It leaves out the way that certain kinds of differences have a whole history that causes us to see them as negative differences. This is a central point I am wanting to make about race in the course. Sometimes this backstory is taken for granted by those who just talk about "difference." Other times the students don't actually know the backstory; they have picked up that a specific difference is particularly negatively charged, but they don't know why. I am not sure which of these is true of Mirvole. In the first class, Leila had talked about the stereotype of Africans as uncivilized. Mirvole's response to the "natives" resonates with that.

I am also not sure how directly Mirvole thinks she is relating to what Jacques or Adam said. Her reaction doesn't really seem like either fear or caution to me. But her willingness to engage in self-criticism so early in the term is striking and heartening. I admire her courage and honesty. She is admitting to something other students could well have regarded as racism—looking down on a vulnerable or marginal group like the unspecified "natives." Often in discussions about race students understandably want to show how above reproach they are (as Lovelle did earlier), and here is a seventeen-year-old girl admitting to, and explicitly naming, immoral sentiments. I'm impressed.

I wonder if Mirvole is not as vulnerable to the charge of racism as nonblacks, and especially whites, would be if they said the same thing. Another time I taught the course, some black students had said that blacks cannot be racist, since they are a disadvantaged or powerless group. I disagreed. I said that if you express a racially prejudiced attitude, that is racist, in my opinion, whether you are Native American or African American or Muslim or whatever. Whether you have the power to use that prejudiced attitude to hurt the other person—like by denying them a job or excluding them from a social group—well, that is an important issue. I agreed with the black students about that. But it is not the same as whether you can be racist. In my view as a moral philosopher, racist attitudes are an equal opportunity scourge; anyone can have them, no matter what your group.[6]

Still, if Mirvole knew that a lot of kids thought that blacks could not be racist—and as one of the more racially aware students, she probably did—she might have felt less vulnerable to being thought racist in admitting to her ignorant response to "natives" than a white student might have. But regardless, clearly Mirvole sees herself as having engaged in a morally wrong kind of "judging," whether you call that "racism" or not. So Mirvole has publicly criticized her own reactions in a morally charged area. It is a good sign about her and about the class that she feels comfortable and trusting enough to make this admission.

The conversation so far has been deepening the students' understanding of race as a "natural" idea. They move on from the issue of suspicion to another element of a racial way of thinking—to whom are you drawn? Who are you comfortable with? If the answer is "people who look like me," that seems to support the idea that racial distinctions based on physical appearance are indeed "natural"—just as natural suspicion of physical difference supports that idea. Smedley raises this issue only briefly, but I think it is relevant, and let the conversation take its course.

Pema, a Tibetan student, is the first to head down this path.

> *Pema*: I would naturally choose my own kind in a room of all different people.
>
> *Hannah*: I heard somewhere that you are drawn to people who look like your parents.

On the "primordialist" view, people are drawn to, or comfortable with, people who look like them and are suspicious of those who don't. Since most people's parents are of the same race as they are, Hannah's view about parents could just be another way of agreeing with primordialism. But students at CRLS in the early 2000s were aware that some kids have parents of different races. So one or both their parents might not look the same as their offspring, and being drawn to people who look like your parents is not exactly the same as being drawn to people of the same race. Mirvole chimes in and makes that point explicit.

> *Mirvole*: So what do kids do who have parents who are different?

The question does not reflect Mirvole's own situation. Both she and her parents are dark-skinned Haitians, and later in the course Mirvole will write some thoughtful and powerful journals about skin color prejudice in Haiti and the United States. Still, she is clearly aware of "mixed-race" people, both in the school and probably in Haiti as well.

Marissa is the biracial/black-and-white girl who on the first day objected to white people's being stereotyped as smelling like wet dogs.

> *Marissa*: My father is white and my mother is black, and I have spent most of my life with white people, but my skin is black, so . . .
>
> *Antonine*: I know what you're saying, girl. I got you.

At first I am surprised that a (nonmixed) black girl would so force-fully ally herself with a mixed girl, expressing a strong sense of solidar-ity and support. I know of tensions that sometimes exist among African Americans over skin color (an issue we take up later in the course). Still, I shouldn't have had that expectation of any particular students, and I now know better. This was a situation where a teacher has no reason to invoke a generalization, whether accurate or stereotypical, but has only to deal with individuals. And I was pleased by the sisterly encourage-ment Antonine showed to Marissa, encouraging her into territory that Antonine certainly knew was sensitive.

Thus supported by her classmate, Marissa continues:

> *Marissa*: I don't really look at it [whom you feel comfortable with] as a race thing. I think it is a personality issue, what you feel internally. The people you feel comfortable with when you are young are the ones you feel comfortable with when you're older.

If Marissa thought the people you feel comfortable with when you're young are those you also feel comfortable with when you're older, you might expect her to say she is comfortable with both blacks and whites, given that her parents are of those two races. But she doesn't say this. She says she is comfortable with black people. This doesn't square with what she said at first, that she has spent most of her life with white peo-ple. Clearly Marissa has a very racially complicated personal situation. She has not spoken much in class up to now, and I am glad she feels the classroom space is comfortable enough for her to begin this exploration.

Sherilyn jumps into the opening Marissa's personal reflections on mixed backgrounds has created. She refers to her own complicated back-ground, as a way of making a point about the comfort issue.

> *Sherilyn*: My guardian is white, but if you were talking to her on the phone, you wouldn't think she is white. She ventured out of her own experience. She wasn't raised with blacks. My aunt is the same way; she had a child with a black man.

Sherilyn is saying her white guardian lives in a black environment and she "talks black" because that is how the people around her talk. Sherilyn uses her guardian's story against both Hannah's and Marissa's suggestion that you are comfortable primarily with people whose race is the same as your parents', or with the people you grew up around—her guardian grew up around whites and had white parents, but she is more comfortable with blacks. And this is also true of Sherilyn's aunt—presumably her guardian's sister—who had a child with a black man.

Sherilyn seems implicitly to be saying more than that you are not always most comfortable with the racial group of your parents. I think she is saying that it is *good* to go beyond the racial confines of your upbringing. She seems to be admiring her guardian and her aunt for "venturing out of their own experience," not just reporting their doing so. I am glad she is pushing beyond the confines of race in her own thinking. She is making a good use of her background in doing so, and by putting her view out to the class, she is also helping to create space for others to question whether their own racial group should define the boundaries of their friendships and even families. She is also bringing a moral element into the conversation that had been flitting around the edges.

As the end of the period approaches, Hannah plunges into new territory. She turns to Marissa and poses a question directly to her. Marissa does not bat an eyelash before answering.

> *Hannah*: If you walked into a room of people you didn't know and they
>   were all naked, who would you sit next to?
> *Marissa*: Black people.

This is a fascinating little exchange in all kinds of ways. Hannah addresses her question to another student precisely as a member of a particular group, mixed persons. No student has done this in the conversation so far. They have spoken increasingly personally. They have responded to each other. They have brought their own racial identities into the public classroom space. But none has addressed another student as someone with a particular racial identity.

As a white person, Hannah is crossing a particularly charged racial divide in doing this. White students are almost always more vulnerable to charges of racism, or racial misstatements or misconduct more generally, than any other group. This is partly for good reason—that historically most racism has been white people's doing. But this reason should not inhibit a white student from asking the particular kind of question that Hannah has on her mind. I am sure students sometimes wonder what members of another racial or ethnic group think about something, but feel reluctant to ask. I am pleased that Hannah feels comfortable enough to break through that barrier. At the same time, it is possible that she feels more entitled to do so precisely because she *is* white. As the teacher,

I would hope that the Asian, Latina, and black kids in the class would feel equally empowered if they had a comparable personal question on their mind about another student.

It is great that so many students from different groups are speaking *without* directly making a point of each other's race; in teaching a class like this, you don't want students to be hyperconscious about their own and each other's racial identity. Yet if you are teaching about race, you also need students to feel comfortable sometimes bringing another student's racial identity (or identities) to the fore.

But Hannah's actual question to Marissa startles me. Here again, my high school students' uninhibitedness catches me up short. I wonder if I'm blushing. Why does Hannah ask Marissa a question about people being *naked*? Is she imagining Marissa herself being naked, in the scenario? I shrink from thinking about this. It may be Hannah's way of getting at whether it is *culture* or *physical/racial characteristics* that trigger suspicion and comfort. In any case, unlike me, Marissa takes the question completely in stride. She does not seem the least bit rattled by the image of naked people in a room together with her. Without a minute's hesitation, she answers Hannah's question—she would go with black people. Perhaps after thinking the issue through in light of the class exchange, she is making clear that her primary identification and comfort group is blacks. This would be particularly interesting, in view of her earlier hesitant answer to the question about whom she felt more comfortable with given her mixed background, and her seeming identification with whites in the earlier conversation about stereotypes.

I try summing up: "This has been a good conversation. We have been looking at Smedley's view that 'race' is a human invention, given that scientists have rejected it as unscientific or arbitrary. It is a start on the way to thinking about whether 'race' is a natural category—whether it grew out of comforts and suspicions that are natural to human beings in the face of human biological diversity. And some of you were suggesting that it is not part of human nature to be suspicious of and comfortable with such differences. We'll keep looking at how Smedley describes the origins of these racial ways of thinking."

3 "Smedley Is a Woman?!"

Students Grapple with Challenging Texts

A few weeks later, I open the class with a discussion of the Spanish and English colonizing in the Americas and its relationship to the development of race.

Me: We've been reading Smedley for the last couple of weeks. The book has been showing us where the idea of race came from historically. Smedley emphasizes that both the Spanish and the English explored beyond Europe. They conquered people they found in territories they wanted, in what we call "the Americas"—North, Central, and South America, including the Caribbean. The Spanish and English also imported, traded, and used slaves from Africa. This bringing together of peoples from Europe, the Americas, and Africa set the stage for the idea of race; before that period, there were no races, you might say. No one thought in terms of races as we now understand that word. There were people with different phenotypes—that is, different physical features—and there were people with different cultures. But these physical and cultural differences were not thought of as "racial" differences. Europeans were not thought of as a single group, nor were Africans. And their skin color was not seen as indicating some inner psychological characteristic that made them superior or inferior to another group. You might say that the Europeans were not yet "white people" and the Africans were not yet "black people." That didn't happen until later.

The racial way of thinking that Smedley describes did not arise right when the Europeans first met the Taino, the Mayans, the Wampanoags, and other people who were indigenous to the Americas. Do you know what *indigenous* means?

Clara: It means they lived there, in those places in the Americas.

Me: Yes, it's a word we use to refer to people who lived in places that Europeans later came to, generally to conquer. We'll also see a bit later that the idea of race did not arise just because Africans came into the picture as slaves. It was more complicated, Smedley says.

It took about two hundred–plus more years before the idea of race was fully developed and became a part of the "common sense" of the descendants of people of European origins who came to the Americas. But Smedley also makes the point that before the encounter with the indigenous people and the Africans, the English were much more isolated than the Spanish from people who looked different and were culturally different from them. Can any of you remember the reason for this difference?

Marie: Was it that the Spanish lived much closer to Africa than the English and they were on a trade route so they encountered Arabs and other people from Asia?

Pema: Yeah, but also Spain was conquered by Muslims so there was even more diversity inside Spain.

Adam: And Portugal too.

Me: Yes, all of you are right about that difference. Smedley generally talks about the Portuguese and the Spanish together as "Iberians"— both nations are on what is called the Iberian peninsula—since they both set up colonies in what we now call South America, and had similar histories, although the Portuguese got into the African slave trade before the Spanish or any other European country. Smedley thinks that because the Iberians were more used to seeing and interacting with people who were physically and culturally different from them than the English were, this affected how these two groups treated the indigenous people they came into contact with in the Americas, and also how they dealt with slavery. We will be studying those differences in the next few weeks. I know Smedley's book is hard reading and you sometimes get a little discouraged. But I just want to tell you something about Smedley herself so you'll know something about the person behind this book.

Antonine: Herself! You mean Smedley *is a woman*?! [Other students murmur similar amazement.]

Me: Why are you surprised? Why did you assume the author was a man? The name "Smedley" is just her last name, and last names don't have a gender.

Antonine: Well, you always just talked about "Smedley" like that was her first name and you didn't give a last name.

Hmm. This is one of many moments when I suddenly realize I'm making college professor assumptions. As an academic, I almost always refer to books by the last names of their authors. But high school students don't normally think of books that way. They think of it as "the text-book," or by the book's title. But I also wonder if Antonine and other students who are also surprised that Smedley is a woman are making an assumption that a woman would not write this kind of academic book. I don't say that though. (Maybe I should have.)

Me: Well, yes, she is a woman.

I continued.

> Smedley's book is really fantastic. It is the first book I ever came across that worked out the history of the idea of race, or the "racial worldview," as she calls it. It is partly because of this book that I started to get seriously interested in race and racism. The first edition came out in 1993, and you are reading the second edition, which came out in 1999.[1]
>
> I love this book and I admire it so much and was so influenced by it that I wanted to meet the author. When you teach in college, sometimes another college invites you to speak about something you know about. One time I was invited to speak at the University of Richmond, in Virginia. I knew that Smedley—I hope it's OK if I keep calling her "Smedley"—taught at another college in Richmond, called Virginia Commonwealth University. [I like to mention real colleges and universities when I can to try to get the students to see higher education as a normal part of the world they live in.] If you look at the back of your copy, almost at the bottom, it says that she teaches at that university. I got in touch with her and arranged to see her when I got down to Richmond. I visited her in her office at her university. She had a large office with huge stacks of papers and hundreds of books on her shelves. It was kind of a mess, like my office, only with more stuff. Smedley is a black woman and she seemed to be a few years older than me . . .
>
> *Jean-Paul* [interrupting]: She's *black*??!!

Again, some other students murmur similar amazement. I should have asked them why they were so amazed about this. I was sure many of the students had read black women writers, at least in literature courses. But I'm afraid I missed the teachable moment.

> Yes, she is. She is an anthropologist, and she has done work in Nigeria. In the early 1970s she started to investigate the history of the idea of race. At that time, there was very little attention to this topic

in American universities. Professor Smedley was one of the first people to study it during that period. There were also very few black
women professors outside of historically black colleges and universities at that time. So Smedley is a real pioneer, in several different ways. In the 1990s the American Anthropological Association,
which is the professional organization of people who teach anthro-
pology in colleges and universities, published an official statement
about how the historical idea of race is scientifically invalid. We read
a part of that statement at the beginning of the course when we were
studying science and race. The anthropologists were trying to get the
public to understand this. Smedley was the main author of this statement, as I told you when we read it. Historically in the U.S., anthro-
pology was the first academic subject, or "discipline" as people who
teach in college usually call it, to challenge the idea of race. You read
a section from Smedley's book where she sharply distinguishes race
from culture, and we have talked about that a little in class. The idea
that people of the same race can have very different cultures, and
that people with the same culture can be of different races, was emphasized by Franz Boas, an important anthropologist from the 1920s
and 1930s; and he worked with teachers to help them recognize that
race was a false idea, and to teach this to their students. Smedley is
following in Boas's tradition.

In the beginning of her book, Smedley says she is trying to write
the book so that ordinary educated people can read it, not only anthropologists. But she was amazed when I told her I was using it in
a high school class. She thought it would probably be too hard for
high school students. But she was also really pleased that you were
reading it, and I told her about how I had prepared reading questions for each section to help you. So when you are reading the
book, you should think about how Smedley is glad you are.

The students were quite enthralled by these revelations about the author, but they also acknowledged how difficult the book was for them.
In a journal from around that period, Ebony wrote: "I think the text we
read of Smedley is the best I ever read. Although it's complicated, it is
still so informative that I learn a lot from it. And sometimes I read more
than I should because I get so into it and what I'm learning." Lovelle,
who often commented on how hard or easy the coursework was for
her—though always within a context in which she reaffirmed her commitment to doing it—said, "The reading [*Race as a Worldview*] is a little

confusing and sometimes difficult to understand, because some of the vocabulary isn't recognizable."

The exchange about Smedley stayed with some students. When I interviewed Mirvole months after the course was over, she brought it up, "We were so amazed that Smedley was a black woman. But why were we?"

Me: Yes, why was it shocking?

Mirvole: I guess it's not expected for a black woman to know those things or to write that way.

Me: Was it more about the way she wrote, or what she wrote about?

Mirvole: Probably more the way she wrote.

Me: How do you expect black women to write? Can you say more about that?

Mirvole: Like Maya Angelou.

So Mirvole confirmed my suspicion that the students had been exposed to black women writing their personal stories, like Angelou, where their voice as black women is central to the writing. But *Race in North America* is written in a neutral, academic voice in which the racial and gender identity of the author is not seen as relevant to the book's content.

I hoped that my personalizing of Smedley would help motivate the students to rise to the challenge of her book. Maybe it did. But it didn't entirely stop the complaints in the class. Once, when we had started reading chapters from *How Race Is Lived in America*, a collection of articles originally published in the *New York Times* that were much more contemporary, personal, and engaging, Antonine said, "Smedley's boring. Why don't we read more from that other book?"

I answered in this way: "There's something you get from Smedley that you don't get from any other book or article we read in the course. And that is the big picture. Only Smedley puts the whole history together so you see where race came from, how it intertwined with the history of slavery and conquest, how false and bad scientific ideas fed into it, how it changed over time, and why it is false. It's a false idea and yet it has had a big impact on American history, meaning North and South America and the Caribbean. It still affects you guys and all of us.

"I bet none of you have learned about all of this in your other classes, and I bet very few of your friends know about this, or even your parents. You are learning something very special by reading Smedley. You guys should feel honored to read this book. And when you are reading it and you think 'Ugh, this is too hard,' just remember how much wisdom is in it."

I wanted them to see the power of an academic argument that embraces a broad sweep of history. I hoped the message at least partly got through. But Antonine's complaint also raised an important issue about how I was structuring the class. The students' levels of preparation and current academic skills were all over the map, as I mentioned in the first chapter. I needed to find a way to challenge all the students intellectually, to try to bring the ones with weaker skills along, stretching them beyond what they had been exposed to before, while making them feel that they could accomplish that goal; and at the same time provide the kind of academic enrichment that the most advanced students would be accustomed to expecting from an honors class.

One of the ways I tried to do that was to diversify the readings, varying the particular kinds of intellectual interest and challenge that different ones provided. Smedley was the most sophisticated of the intellectually demanding texts, but I used other very challenging college-level works also. For example, I had the students read several selections from Ira Berlin's *Many Thousands Gone: The First Two Centuries of Slavery in North America*. (Berlin is one of the foremost historians of American slavery.) Berlin deals with the situation of slaves and other Africans in the English colonies in the 1600s. He fills out Smedley's argument that the status and situation of slaves and other non-slave Africans (and their descendants) was better in the 1600s than it ever was after that. For example, Berlin discusses the way that slaves were sometimes given plots of land to work on for their own benefit, had some legal rights against their owners, and could sometimes use the courts to protect those rights. All of these features disappeared in the 1700s as slavery became more entrenched. Berlin describes in detail one particular African, Anthony Johnson, who became a respected landowner in the Chesapeake area, and had a slave of his own. The students were fascinated by this, and none of them had known about it before.

The Berlin reading was intellectually complex for the students in that Berlin shows that slavery changed over the centuries, and that the "plantation" image that most of the students had of slavery applied only to a certain time period and to certain regions within the slave states and not others. And he shows that slavery differed in different states and regions in the South. Like Smedley, Berlin recognizes that ideas about people of African origins (who came ultimately to be thought of as "blacks") changed over time along with the historical changes in their circumstances and in the character of slavery. Essentially, the image of African-ancestried people became increasingly degraded, as the idea of "race" was created to rationalize their status as slaves with no rights. (Smedley captures this process nicely in the title of one of her chapters—"The Arrival of Africans and the Descent into Slavery.")

This Smedley-Berlin framework is quite intellectually sophisticated. At the most basic level it challenges the "progress" narrative that most students (and indeed most Americans) have about American history—that everything is always getting better. It requires a difficult and encompassing mental shift to see that this narrative did not apply to slavery. A related though somewhat separate point is that slavery was an ever-changing institution, and most students (who had had some brief exposure to slavery in their American history classes) had a kind of frozen image of the field slave, the house slave, and the plantation.

Over time most students were able to grasp these points. But the Smedley-Berlin framework involved an even more sophisticated dimension—how the changes in the character of *slavery* were bound up with developments in the idea of *race* (and of the status and character of indigenous people and, especially, people of African origin). Understanding this connection requires three intellectual feats: (1) recognizing that "race" is an idea, a way of looking at human diversity (discussed in chapter 2); (2) seeing that this idea changed and developed over time, over several centuries; and (3) recognizing that changes in the character of slavery affected changes in the idea of race.

It would have been unrealistic in such an academically diverse class to expect all students to fully take in all three of these points. What I hoped and aimed for was that all could understand them to some degree, and that the class would continue to stretch in those directions. At the same time, I also provided more accessible readings (and sometimes video material) that, while no less compelling, were less intellectually sophisticated. For example, I had the students read two slave narratives, one by Olaudah Equiano (briefly discussed in chapter 6), the other by Mary Prince. Prince was a slave in several English colonies in the Caribbean, and she writes of her horrible treatment at the hands of various masters over time, and her later sojourn in England, where she eventually became free and connected with the antislavery movement there in the early 1830s. Students who found the Smedley-type readings difficult could generally keep up with the more sophisticated students with respect to the slave narratives. At the same time, on their paper about Mary Prince, I did not ask the students merely to describe Prince's experience but pushed them to think on a more abstract level. Here was the assignment: "Describe Mary Prince's developing consciousness about slavery.

Does she always think slavery is wrong? When and how does she come to think it is wrong? How do her ideas about slavery develop over time? Describe any ambivalence or confusion that you can see in her view of the morality of slavery. Cite specific passages to back up your interpretation."

The two types of readings about slavery illuminated each other. The slave narratives deepened the students' understanding of the character and experience of slavery, while the historical readings helped to place the narratives in a larger historical context of the nature of and changes in slavery, and in the idea of race.

In the engaging and more accessible category I also used some contemporary readings, ones that illuminated the larger historical issues concerning race and racism. For example, from the book that Antonine liked, we read a poignant account of two Cuban friends—one light-skinned and one dark-skinned—who came to the United States, and how that difference, which had not meant much to them in Cuba, assumed a large importance in this country and drove a wedge between the two friends. It is a powerful portrayal of the way racial ways of thinking and experiencing operate in the United States.

This reading also illustrated another overarching theme of the course—the differences between the United States, the Caribbean, and Latin America in the way race and skin color have been understood, growing out of the different experiences of slavery and colonization in those regions. (These in turn were related to the differences between England and Spain/Portugal mentioned at the beginning of this chapter.)

Like the Mary Prince narrative, the reading about the Cuban friends was easily accessible to all, yet raised complex intellectual issues that allowed different students to get different things from it in relation to the overarching themes of the course.

The range of readings allowed all students, with their very different academic readiness, to forge some relationship with all of the readings, to enter into conversations about them from which all students benefited, and to grow intellectually within the scope of the course. By the end of the course the particular range of grades did not reflect their starting points. Some of the students who first appeared to struggle with the more abstract readings had made real progress on that score by the end. We cannot always tell where a student will end up based on where she or he starts, and we have to stretch all of our students.

4 Intervention in Racial Incidents
The Question of Moral Symmetry

From early in the course, I wanted to encourage the students to start thinking about race-related wrongs as situations in which they could intervene, not just something to notice or criticize. It was part of the moral and civic education I was looking to promote in the class—that they should take responsibility for racism that goes on around them, and eventually in the society at large. The students of color, especially, confront such situations all the time but seldom are given an opportunity to think them through in a systematic way in an academic setting and a facilitated group discussion. Although the bulk of the course was a serious academic study of race and its history, I wanted to establish early on that this study was supposed to illuminate their lives and experience.

To further this exercise in moral responsibility, I used a "racial incident" assignment. I asked the students to write a description of a racial incident they had witnessed or been involved in. I retyped them to distribute to the class, changing the names to disguise the authors, and allowed the students to choose one or two incidents to discuss in class. Here is the one they picked: "In elementary school I (a Latino) went to a Latino-themed dance.[1] A white couple was there dancing and some Latino kids made fun of them for their 'stiff white hips.' Other Latino kids laughed at this statement."

I ask the students what they think they *would* have done in this situation, and then what they think they *should* do. At first only black students speak.

> *Norris*: If I was in that situation, I would laugh at the white couple too, and everyone else would laugh at them too.
> *Jean-Paul*: If I were black, I'd laugh; if I were Latino, I'd laugh. But if I were white, I wouldn't know how to dance, so . . .

Norris: I'm not trying to offend them [the white couple], but I would still think that white people are too stiff to dance well.
Ebony: Who are you to say they are stiff or not?
Antonine: But they are!

Norris is honest about what he thinks his reaction would be. Jean-Paul is also honest in saying that he too would laugh. But he brings in a new element—different points of view. He imagines himself in different racial groups at the dance—black (which he in fact is), then Latino. In both cases, he says he would laugh. Then he imagines himself as white. He sees that the situation looks different to the whites. This is already an advance in moral understanding, although Jean-Paul does not go from adopting the white couple's point of view to criticizing laughing at them—possibly because he buys into the stereotype that they can't dance, as two of his classmates do also.

But Jean-Paul's saying he would laugh at the couple prompts other students to reflect in a way they might not have if they had been the first to answer. Norris now begins to think about the white couple's point of view, and he backtracks from his original reaction and says it might be wrong to offend them. He still says whites don't dance well, but now he distinguishes between *saying* this—which would definitely offend—and merely *thinking* it.

Ebony is the first student to object to laughing at the white couple. She doesn't quite say it is wrong, but rather challenges her classmates' (and by implication, those at the dance) authority to judge the couple's dancing as "stiff." Maybe she thinks that different groups have different styles of dancing, so no one should criticize others. Or maybe she thinks that *individuals* have different styles, and this rules out criticism.

The brief discussion has already turned a relatively unthinking and no doubt common reaction of laughing at peers toward the moral question whether this is right or not. It shows the power of the classroom to prompt moral reflection and insight. Once the students reflect on what they would do, they are led (with my prompting question) to ponder whether what they think they would do is right or wrong.

The students are starting to feel that what you say on this moral question needs defending. I am pleased at their willingness to reflect, to change their minds (at least a bit), and not to just dig in their heels and stay with their first stated views.

I encourage other students to give their opinions:

Jacques: It reminds me of *Comic View* [a TV show that apparently makes use of the stereotype of white dancers as "stiff-hipped"]. I don't think it's necessarily racist or something that people should be offended by.

Antonine: The stereotype is already in the air.

Cristina: If they have stiff hips, that's one thing, but when they say stiff *white* hips, it means they are insulting all white people.

Jacques seems to say that if a well-known comedy show on TV (on BET) makes use of a stereotype, that stereotype is outside the realm of the offensive. Because everyone knows that these shows insult all groups, there is nothing to get upset about, no moral worry. Antonine, still not seeing anything wrong, builds on Jacques's point. If someone is just repeating a racial stereotype that everyone is aware of, she says, it can't really hurt anyone. You can just shrug it off because it's so familiar.

Jean-Paul had previously mentioned race as a source of how different groups might look at the situation. But Cristina is the first student to say that the racial dimension of the put-down bears on whether and why it is wrong. It is one thing to insult someone for being unable to dance, but if you link that inability to their race, then you are insulting the whole group. It isn't the insult to the particular white people at the dance that Cristina sees as the main problem, but the implied insult to a whole group.

Hannah: It's OK on *Comic View* to make fun of whites, but what if a white person was on *Comic View* making fun of blacks?

General response from several kids: But that's OK, they did that last night. So what?

Hannah, the first white student to speak, takes the racial dimension of possible wrongness that Cristina and Jean-Paul introduced to a new level. If it is OK to insult whites, as many of the other students are saying, is it also OK to insult blacks? She evidently thinks her classmates will not find this acceptable. She appears poised to make the case that if it is wrong for whites to make fun of blacks, it is equally wrong for blacks (or Latinos) to make fun of whites. She is bringing up the important issue of "racial symmetry," which I will discuss later. But the other students don't accept Hannah's premises. I don't have a record of their words here, just the sentiment. They agree with Jacques that the TV context makes a moral difference and means you shouldn't get upset about a show making fun of racial groups, especially whites.

> *Sherilyn*: We are thinking of this incident as petty; everyone gets teased—we all do. But if I were a bystander, I wouldn't say anything [i.e., wouldn't tease].
>
> *Mirvole:* I wouldn't either.
>
> *Norris*: I won't just make fun of somebody, but if he hits a bad note [i.e., on an instrument], I don't care who it is, I'll just say it.

Sherilyn is saying she hears her fellow students judging the incident to be fairly trivial—as the discussion of *Comic View* seems to imply. But she doesn't agree, so, she now thinks (somewhat implying that she is changing her view), she would not participate in the teasing. She is the first student to state unequivocally that she herself wouldn't engage in the teasing. Then Mirvole agrees with her. It is interesting where Norris now goes, having heard arguments against the original insult. He seems to feel the force of the moral objection, and so backtracks—but only somewhat. He defends insulting, but only if there is a good reason for it, like playing an instrument badly. He doesn't say it, but his statement implies that insulting someone because of dancing a certain way may not be right.

I think something important about moral education is going on here. Students may understandably not totally abandon a view that they have taken publicly when they hear viewpoints on the other side. It isn't easy to do so, and one saves face a bit by essentially saying, "I agree with part of what you say, but I am not taking back all of what I said." But that does not mean the student is locked into the position where he ends up in class. I'm sure that often when the student is outside the classroom and has the mental space to think more about an issue without worrying about saving face, it is easier for him to go further along the path he started down in class. I think we all do this to some degree, not only students, and it should be factored in when examining individual moral change.

> *Ebony*: Listening to this discussion, I guess I am changing my mind. I guess if I saw it, I would laugh, but I wouldn't say all white people

in general. But I want to comment on what Antonine said about stereotypes [presumably, about them being "in the air" and therefore all right to use] . . . I don't agree.

As we've seen, Ebony is not the first student to change her mind in the conversation. But she is the first to say that she is. She engages in some honest personal scrutiny here, and she comes up with a quite complicated moral position. She decides or admits that she would indeed laugh at the white couple. But she holds to her guns that racial stereotyping is wrong, so she would not insult the couple's whiteness. Ebony doesn't seem to change her opinion in order to go along with the reigning view of the moment; it feels like this is what she has really come to think. But she does listen to her classmates very attentively and she responds to what she hears. It is not easy to admit being wrong about racial matters. I admire Ebony's unusual ability to admit that she is doing this, relatively early in the course. It is good that she is not only feeling free to speak her mind in class—something she reported in an early journal she wrote—but also listening and responding to others. These kids are showing adults how it should be done. We find it very difficult to admit we are wrong in a racial situation, especially to people of different races. The students are doing it.

> *Antonine*: I am not saying it makes it right, but it's already in the air. It's not new material; but no, it's not right.

Antonine is also explicitly reacting to her classmates. She had said that if a stereotype is already out in the world, no harm is done by someone else using it. But now she says that it is wrong to use it. Perhaps Ebony's changing moral direction makes it easier for others to do so too. Something more general seems to be going on in the class dynamic—that the thoughtfulness and honesty of some students' contributions encourages other students to realize they don't have to hold on to an opinion they have expressed. Some real moral growth seems to be going on here, both in the students' more complex moral thinking as well as in the way they interact with one another.

> *Cristina*: If I were in that situation, I wouldn't say anything, but I would probably go and dance with the person and, like, show the person how to dance.
> *Esteban*: I would take the opportunity to meet them and teach them.

This is a really fascinating turn in the conversation. Cristina takes the discussion in an especially civic direction—not just whether something is wrong, but how do you intervene when it is, especially when the harm is connected to race in some way.

Cristina's solution is very sensitive and appropriate. Instead of trying to get the other students at the dance to stop making fun of the white couple, she finds a way to help them dance and be accepted as part of the party scene. This solution allows Cristina to express solidarity with the couple. By dancing with them, she includes them in the community of people who have to be treated with respect. She both helps protect them against the sting of the other students' ridicule, and also conveys to the other students that she thinks they should not be making fun of the couple. I'm not sure if Cristina is aware of all this, but I think it is implicit in her proposed intervention.

No doubt going up to the couple would actually be a more effective way of stopping the other students from making fun than telling them to stop. If she had suggested chiding the other partiers publicly, they might have become defensive and perhaps hostile. I don't want to teach my students that they should never challenge others in public spaces. But Cristina has intuitively hit on what is likely to be a more effective form of challenge, one that displays real moral insight.

Esteban, another Latino student, immediately gets into the spirit of Cristina's solution, connecting with the white couple and teaching them to dance. Perhaps he sees himself having some agency in this situation because he is also Latino. Esteban's suggestion also joins Cristina's earlier one that challenges the racial overtones of the expression "stiff white hips"—implying that stiff hips are just part of whiteness, and there is nothing white people can do about it. That implication is wrong, he suggests, because if you could *teach* the white couple to dance, as the students now seem to be assuming, then the stiffness is a matter of culture and learning, not racial limitations.

—∽—

Cristina's response also raises a new and important question that echoes Jean-Paul's initial reaction. When she sees herself going up to the white couple, is she thinking of herself as acting *as a Latina*, or just as a kid at the dance no matter what race? Being Latina herself might make it easier to imagine herself being proactive in this way than it would be for the other students. Perhaps this is true of Esteban as well. The black students who had spoken said what they would have done if they had been there;

and in his first remarks Jean-Paul explicitly imagined himself as a Latino in that setting. But apart from Jean-Paul, you can't be sure how they were imagining themselves being present. The black students still could have been imagining themselves as present at the dance *as black*; after all, there was a white couple there, so there may have been blacks.

I don't mean to say that whenever a student thinks about a moral situation that involves race in some way, she inevitably imagines herself as having a specific racial identity. A student of any race could well think she would have done a certain thing in the situation, or that she should have, without explicitly taking on a particular racial identity. And, from the point of view of moral education, we as educators don't want the students to be limited by their racial identities. This is a place I think we should want symmetry—that no matter what your racial identity and that of other parties to the situation, you can think about what is right and wrong and what should be done about it. In this spirit, I was glad all the students felt they could discuss the situation. None of the blacks, whites, or Asians said, "Well, it was a Latino dance, so it isn't up to me to say what is right or wrong." None of the students saw moral responsibility in that way. Just because one group controlled the social space of the dance does not mean only members of that group had the right and responsibility to respond to it morally.

But at the same time, the racial identity of the participants can make a certain type of moral difference. I remembered a conversation in a previous offering of the class, where we were discussing a black student's racially insulting an Asian student in the school hallway. All the students agreed that this was wrong, but they differed about the responsibility they felt to deal with the situation. Some thought that if you weren't black or Asian, it wasn't your "issue" and you shouldn't get involved. Others disagreed. But some of the students who agreed about the responsibility thought that if you weren't black or Asian, you couldn't be *effective* in intervening; no one would pay attention to you. Certainly there is a difference between moral responsibility and effectiveness—whether you do the effective thing is different from whether you do the right thing. But they are not entirely unrelated either, and I think some of the students appreciated this. If your intervention is likely to be counterproductive or even just ineffective, your intervention might not help the situation. You might say your responsibility extends to being helpful, and if the students were right that your racial identity affects whether you can be helpful, maybe your racial identity does have something to do with your moral responsibilities.

There were further complications about racial identity and taking action that emerged in that same discussion. Some black students thought that if you were black and you challenged the black kid who was insulting the Asian kid, you might be letting yourself in for even more trouble, because you wouldn't be supporting a fellow member of your racial group, and maybe because you could be seen as embarrassing a fellow black student in public. But other black students thought you had *more* of a responsibility to intervene if you were black. And some black students fell into both categories—they thought blacks had more responsibility but they would be more inhibited because of fears of black racial disloyalty. I think they got the moral responsibility right, and hopefully recognizing the source of inhibition will help them get past it if a similar situation presents itself.

There is an important difference between this hallway situation and the one at the Latino dance. Because *several* of the partiers laughed at the white couple, an individual "perpetrator" was not so readily identifiable. It was also less of a confrontation than the hallway insult, where the single insulter was known to the bystanders. The diffuse responsibility in the party situation muted the risk in intervening.

What we see in these two situations is that racial identity may not be relevant to who can assess the situation as right or wrong, but it may be relevant to who should intervene, and how. It is entirely appropriate for teachers to discuss this complicated matter with their students. And I think it can be appropriate to note students' particular racial identities in such discussions. For example, in the discussion of the hallway incident, I asked students of a particular race how they thought their race affected whether they should and whether they would intervene: "Dana, as a black student, do you think you should try to stop the black student from insulting the Asian student? I want to make clear that I am not assuming you will have the same view on this question as other black students."

Generally, a teacher should not ask a student to speak for her racial group, especially for a minority racial group. It makes the student "hypervisible," generally making them uncomfortable, and can also imply that the teacher believes that all members of the group have the same opinion.[2] But it is a different matter to ask a student to think and respond as an individual member of a racial group, where you make clear that you are not treating her as a spokesperson for her group. Since in this particular class discussion we were talking explicitly about how the students' racial identity impacts their moral responsibilities, I had to ask the students to respond explicitly to that issue, while making it clear that I didn't expect all students from a given racial group to have the same opinion. I found that the students appreciated the relevance of their racial identity to the issues at hand and to my way of acknowledging their identities.

—∿—

The class period is almost over, but Jacques chimes in with a whole new perspective. "I can see where the Latinos [those who were making fun of the white couple] are coming from," he says. "These whites are intruding on this scene. So if Latino people are having a good time, why did white people impose?"

Several black students strongly object to this and seriously get on Jacques's case: "What do you mean, 'impose'?! I don't agree with Jacques." And Mirvole asks: "If *I* went in to dance [i.e., as a black person], would I be imposing?"

This exchange is really fascinating. It's remarkable that so many students who were at first willing to make fun of the white couple in a racial way now affirm the white students' right to go to a Latin-oriented dance in the first place. We saw that the discussion led several students to reject the view that it was all right to make fun of the white couple, so Jacques's even more exclusionary suggestion that the whites shouldn't even be allowed to come to the dance seems to the other students even *more* wrong, by this later point in the conversation. In any case, the black students' strong reaction to Jacques's remark suggests they believe it is wrong for one racial group to keep another out of their dance space. Mirvole, somewhat outraged, makes this explicit and personal. Is Jacques saying that she, a black student, shouldn't go to a Latino dance?

Although the students strongly disagree with Jacques, they do not present their criticism in a shaming or stigmatizing way. Their remarks don't have the feel of "Ooh, you said something racist" but are respectful and civil. I don't know if the conversation would have been different if a white student had said what Jacques did. The black students might have felt comfortable jumping on Jacques precisely because he also is black. Still, I am pleased that they are willing to criticize another black student in a mixed class. I am glad they feel enough trust in their fellow students not to worry that this criticizing will somehow be used against them by the other students. Overall, I feel my students have managed to carry on a conversation on a racial topic that was civil in tone, morally complex in the insights generated, and open minded in the way the students responded to each other.

The period ends with this mild chaos, without resolution. (How often that happens!) After class Jacques comes up to me. He wants to explain the remark his classmates jumped on, though he has only a moment before going to his next class. Jacques says that minority groups have to be protective of their own cultural territory. There is always a danger whites will come in and take it from them. Perhaps he has in mind the fact that suburban white kids have become the major consumers of hip-hop, or the way white artists like Justin Timberlake, then of 'N Sync, a popular but minimally talented white pop group, move in on the hip-hop world (sometimes under the tutelage of a black producer) and become more commercially successful than more talented black artists. Jacques is not expressing any general hostility to white people in the way he makes his point. He is just analyzing a dynamic he sees around him.

This worry about protecting a minority group's space from majority group incursion is a new angle on the Latino dance controversy, one that reintroduces the symmetry issue that Hannah had raised without getting any uptake. I would describe that issue this way: moral symmetry says that whether any act or practice that involves race is morally right or wrong is independent of the racial identities of the kids involved. If a black kid excludes or makes fun of a white kid, that is no more or less wrong than if a white kid excludes or makes fun of a black kid—the point of view Hannah seemed to be taking. Moral *asymmetry* says that the wrongness or rightness, or at least the degree of it, does depend on those racial identities. This is the point of view Jacques is taking here. It isn't easy to figure out when we have a case of symmetry and when asymmetry. It's hard to generalize (and some situations can be both). But the issue comes up again and again. The students were often coming to grips with the symmetry question and I was always looking for ways to engage and clarify the issue.

Jacques is saying there is a difference—an asymmetry—where Hannah had implied that there wasn't. It is wrong of white people to take over or intrude upon a minority event, he says, but it would not necessarily be wrong for Latinos, say, to "crash" a white dance.[3]

Jacques sees a political and asymmetrical dimension to this situation that the others missed, or at least didn't bring up. Historically, white performers have taken over cultural forms originating in minority communities. White cultural brokers often determine whether these cultural products will be changed to fit white sensibilities. So I think Jacques is onto something very important when he points to this element in the racial dynamic in the dance incident.

Jacques isn't saying it is fine for the Latinos at the dance to make fun of the white couple, especially in a racial way. He isn't engaging with that issue directly. Making fun of them might be symmetrical, at least in the sense that it is wrong for any racial group to make fun of another one. But Jacques is pointing to an asymmetry in the wider world of cultural exchange and appropriation.

—⚉—

In a way, this whole conversation concerns a relatively minor racial incident and a relatively harmless racial stereotype—that white people are stiff and can't dance. Certainly this is not as harmful as the stereotype that young black males are dangerous, which came up in chapter 2. But stereotypes that might be considered harmful just by themselves can have more serious implications in a broader context, as we discussed in that chapter. The stereotype that Latinos and blacks are good dancers—the flip side to the idea that whites are not—is historically linked to the notion that both groups are closer to nature, more uninhibited, more physical, possibly less civilized, and whites are more intellectual. These stereotypes have historically been used to rationalize slavery and colonization and to treat blacks and Latinos in demeaning ways.

But minor as the stereotype is, the incident was a good way to show that being insulted racially is hurtful to anyone, even whites. Students of color are certainly more likely to see a problem with stereotypes than are white students, who often see "hypersensitivity" where there is actual hurt (although none of my white students voiced this view out loud). So they might tend to object to stereotypes in general more than do white students. As I mentioned in chapter 3, one view I had heard at the high school (and elsewhere) is that whites could not be a target of racism since they are the dominant group. I am not so much concerned about the word *racism*, which is used in several different and often conflicting ways in general conversation. But I am concerned if students of color think it all right for their peers, or even themselves, to make white students the target of a racial insult, stereotype, or exclusion. The class discussion of the dance incident suggests this is not a serious problem in my own class. My students of color had mostly come around to the view that it was wrong to insult the white dancers. Some of them, such as Jean-Paul, Sherilyn, Mirvole, and Cristina, and perhaps others, had shown real empathy for the white couple.

In fact, in the years that I had these "racial incident" discussions, as a general rule the black and Latino students showed more outrage and concern than white students when kids of any group were mistreated. As Richard Weissbourd points out, African American kids are often not given adequate credit for these sorts of moral strengths.[4]

Part of what I think anyone teaching about race to young people would want to get across is that students should see, and feel, the harm of *any* group-based insults, stereotypes, and exclusions, even toward relatively less vulnerable groups, like whites. Whites may be the dominant group in our society as a whole, but they are not so in every particular setting. Vulnerability matters in the racial arena, and whites often don't appreciate how race discrimination against blacks and Latinos is, everything else equal, worse and of more moral concern than discrimination against whites. But in some situations, like the Latino dance, the vulnerability factor works against whites where they are the minority.

It would not be good for students of color to see themselves as the only possible sufferers of race-related harms. They need to see that all kids are vulnerable to exclusions, insults, and stereotyping based on their race or ethnicity, as the white couple was at the dance. This is an important racial symmetry, and its recognition is part of the moral development we have to strive for in teaching about race. The Latino dance conversation suggests that discussing racial issues in a focused and comfortable setting can lead students to see for themselves that empathy has to be directed toward all groups.

Still, it's too bad the point Jacques made after class did not get discussed. It showed an insight into a particular asymmetry between whites and people of color that was not articulated by any student in the discussion. However, the class had started to engage with issues of racial symmetry and asymmetry in a fruitful way that later conversations would deepen. They also had started thinking about racial incidents as something they should confront, and were debating how to do so in a constructive way. It was a good start to a civic direction in the course, and carried further the moral engagement and learning that was almost always present.

5 Reflections on Immigration and Race

Complicating the Discussion of Racism

As teachers dealing with the ever-changing demographic of America and of our schools and classes, we face some complicated race-related issues. One of these is the increasing number of nonwhite immigrant students and children of immigrants. All are "students of color." But immigrants and their offspring are in important ways different from the long-term native-born—African Americans and Latinos who have been in the United States for many generations. Perhaps the most confusing development in relation to race is the increasing number of black immigrants from Africa and the Caribbean (and occasionally from European countries). These groups will form an increasing percentage of our students. How do we think about the similarities and differences between these groups and African Americans?

A related question is how we think about racism and racial prejudice in this changing panorama. We know how damaging racism can be to our students, and we want to be alert to it in our own responses to students and in interactions between students. Painful as it is to confront our own racism, we, especially white teachers, know we must do so to give our best to our students. But we generally think about racism as directed toward whole racial groups. What happens when we are confronted with a daunting array of ethnic groups *within* the larger racial groups? Can racism in relation to blacks somehow take different forms depending on whether the blacks are from Haiti, Nigeria, or the United States?

These two issues—the increasing number of immigrant students of color (especially blacks) and how we should think about race and racism in light of this diversity—were especially relevant in my class. I had recent immigrant students, "one-and-a-half-generation" (students born elsewhere but immigrating at a young enough age not to speak with a "non-American" accent), and second-generation immigrants (a standard although somewhat misleading term for the American-born children of immigrants), including non–African American blacks, as well as African Americans.

Partly to help me prepare for the class, and partly out of concern about tensions or prejudices between the native-born and immigrants, I consulted some recent scholarship I think is particularly important for educators to be aware of (although it is really useful for all Americans to know about). In this chapter I focus largely on that scholarship, although I also make use of some snippets of class discussions and conversations with students, all which can guide us through this complex terrain. The chapter provides some background information and a conceptual framework to help teachers think about the complex and fraught territory of race and immigration in an educational context.

Let me start with a class discussion. I assigned a newspaper article about whether African immigrants and Caribbean-born blacks in the United States should be called "African American."[1] In the article, an Ethiopian immigrant, twenty years in the United States, is baffled and somewhat hurt that American-born blacks whose ancestors were U.S. slaves do not all embrace him within the "African American" label and community. As the article probes a bit deeper, it suggests that immigrant blacks differ in important ways from African Americans. So African Americans are not merely being exclusionary or narrow-minded in caring about that difference.

I asked the students what differences the article pointed to between immigrant blacks and African Americans.

> *Sherilyn*: The article says African Americans are more stigmatized than immigrants, even though both are black; the stigma of blackness hurts them more, and this affects how well they are doing. This is part of why African Americans are not doing as well as black immigrants.
>
> *Pema* [somewhat heatedly]: Immigrants come to the U.S. with a determination to succeed that native populations do not have. This is why the immigrants are doing better. Racism doesn't have anything to do with it.

Pema's reaction shows how charged this territory is. That immigrants have a strong work ethic compared to natives is conventional wisdom. I had worried that this idea could arise in a divisive way in the class, as Pema's remarks could have. The scholarly work in history and sociology I had read before the class helped prepare me to respond if that proved necessary.

My students with immigrant backgrounds were part of the post-1965 immigrant wave, when racial barriers were finally lifted on immigration.[2] But to understand these newer immigrants, we have to go back to the earlier wave of southern and eastern European immigrants from 1880 to 1920. Those earlier immigrants and their descendants figure prominently in popular understandings that draw implicit contrasts to African Americans, such as Pema expresses. Those immigrants faced barriers of prejudice and strong anti-immigrant sentiment that ultimately led to a virtual shutdown of immigration to the United States from outside the Western hemisphere in 1924, lasting until 1965. It is familiar American conventional wisdom that if these Europeans were able to overcome these barriers and become successful, African Americans (by which I mean native-born blacks with ancestry in the United States in the slavery era) should have been able to overcome racial barriers. If they haven't, it's their fault. I think as teachers we have to understand this view and why it is wrong.

Although European immigrants did face anti-immigrant sentiment, African Americans faced much more severe obstacles. Immigrants gained access to industrial jobs—such as clothing and textile manufacturing, mining, meat processing trades, plumbing, electrical work, paper hanging—largely closed to African Americans. Eventually these jobs became unionized. In the South, where most blacks lived, at least prior to the Second World War, blacks endured discrimination in education, occupations, and political participation rooted in a legal structure of segregation until the 1960s that the European immigrants did not. In the North there was de facto if not de jure discrimination in housing and jobs, at least until the 1960s, not faced by European immigrants. For example, federal housing policy in the 1930s and '40s facilitated the movement of white city residents to homes in the suburbs, but not of blacks. Restrictive covenants prevented whites from selling to blacks. Later these covenants became illegal but by then the inequalities in home ownership, housing access, and home value had already been put firmly in place, and anyway there were ways around the legal restrictions. For these and other reasons, blacks had a much lower rate of home ownership than whites (including the descendants of the European immigrants), and home ownership was an important foundation of personal assets and financial security.[3] And the homes blacks did own were never worth as much as white homes of similar character.[4]

The GI Bill after WWII was a tremendous government program that provided various benefits to veterans, including access to a college education, enabling much greater mobility by people of modest means than would have been possible otherwise. In their formulation, the various programs—home loans, job training, higher education—were blind to race; and indeed they aided many black veterans. But in its administration, the GI Bill was racially discriminatory, as its programs were administered on the local and state level, an arrangement that was required to secure political support from Southern white Democrats, who wanted to ensure that the bill's programs did not challenge white supremacy in their region. Ira Katznelson summarizes his account of the GI Bill and the way it worked in practice: "On balance, despite the assistance that black soldiers received, there was no greater instrument for widening an already huge racial gap in postwar America than the GI Bill."[5]

These are just some of the ways that white immigrants, despite the earlier discrimination against them and their descendants, had access to resources not equally available to blacks. They passed those advantages to their descendants, and they are the historical foundation of the disparities in home ownership, education, occupation, and asset accumulation between whites and African Americans today.

Indeed, the presence of American blacks made it easier for the European immigrants and their descendants to become fully accepted "white Americans," a status they were not automatically granted by white American natives upon first arrival. Distancing themselves from blacks was a way they could be more accepted as white.[6] So while European immigrants did face barriers, and many did work hard, blacks had nothing approaching a level playing field. The advantages white immigrants enjoyed were built into the racial order of those decades. While understood as race-based advantages at the time, they have fallen by the wayside in the "heroic immigrant" narrative in subsequent generations. As teachers we are in a position to cast a critical eye on that narrative and not let it confuse us about the real obstacles faced by African Americans historically, with consequences for today.

—∾—

The immigrants among my students, or those with immigrant parents in the post-1965 generations, inherit a history that differs from the earlier period of European immigration, but shares some important continuities with it. Students in my class, or their parents, came from the Caribbean, Africa, Southeast Asia, and Central and South America—all groups not seen as "white."[7] Thus all these groups face barriers the European immigrants did not.

At the same time, those racial barriers have been greatly diminished compared to earlier eras by the efforts of black Americans in the civil rights movements of the 1940s, '50s, and '60s. The results of their actions were to establish protections against racial discrimination for all nonwhite groups in major life domains—housing, education, jobs. The protections did not stamp out the discrimination, but they reduced it. Those efforts also helped to change social attitudes so that it became much less acceptable to voice a prejudice or to discriminate, especially overtly, against people based on their (nonwhite) race. Of course, this process is far from complete, and there is still a great deal of racial prejudice that operates in less overt and public ways. But the opportunity landscape for immigrants of color of the past forty-five years is much more favorable than it would have been without these admittedly imperfect protections and cultural shifts.[8]

Since African Americans did so much to make these changes happen, it is ironic that contemporary immigrant groups—even including black immigrant groups, who benefit from these advances—often also benefit from being seen as *not* African American (similar to the earlier European immigrants who distanced themselves from African Americans), and many do not recognize the historical struggles of African Americans that contribute to their own successes. The sociologist Mary Waters has studied English-speaking Caribbean ("West Indian") immigrants to New York City and their relations with African Americans. She finds that employers often favor immigrants over native blacks.[9] The immigrants generally recognize that whites usually view them more positively than they do African Americans—the point that Sherilyn took from our reading. Some of them respond by trying to make sure that white Americans recognize them to be Afro-Caribbean or West Indian—that is, *not* African American.

So we might say that in American history it has always been an advantage to be white, and to be seen as white. But it has also been an advantage not to be black, even if you are not white. And within the black group, it has been an advantage not to be African American. It's a complex picture, important for teachers to understand and convey to students.[10]

My one-and-a-half-generation and second-generation Haitian immigrant students struggled to negotiate and make sense of this complex terrain, as we can see in exchanges that two of them had with their parents (reported to me in conversations we had the summer after they graduated).

> *Jean-Paul*: My mom would say—this was before I graduated—"You know you're black, right, and it will be harder for you going to college?" I'd say, "Why do you say that?" and she'd say, "Well, we don't have any money and they don't really expect black kids to go to college." I'd be like, "Oh, really??!!" So I studied and did my homework and I got into college and I was like, "See, I got into college."
>
> My dad would say, "Black people are always loud, they're arrogant, blah blah blah." And I would say, "It's not black people that are always loud, everybody's loud." My mom used to say that "only black people do this and only black people do that, like drop out of school or disrespect their moms . . ." Yeah, they're tough on blacks.

I asked Jean-Paul whether when his parents referred to "blacks" they were differentiating African Americans from Haitians, and he said they didn't, that they had these negative views of black people in general, including Haitians.

> *Jacques*: One message that was very clear was that it would benefit you to have a clean image and doing that meant, you know, having a really clean house and, um, not dressing like a quote-unquote thug . . . I mean I always got the impression that it was important to look good in the eyes of white people . . . There was already the stigma of black people being really violent and, um, the court system not in our favor. My mother didn't want us [Jacques and his siblings] to wind up in trouble; because, you know, we were in a new situation in a new country and she really didn't want there to be problems.
>
> *Me*: Did you get the message that it was African Americans' behavior that you're supposed to be different from?
>
> *Jacques*: Yeah, the whole thug thing was associated with being African American, instead of Haitian. She'd say, "African Americans get in trouble all the time and you don't want to be in that situation."

I asked Jacques whether his mother thought there was something wrong with African Americans themselves or whether they were just treated worse than other groups.

Jacques: I think my mom was figuring it out for herself . . . Because they're discriminated against, she doesn't want to be seen as one of them . . . But later, because a lot of our [Jacques and his siblings] friends were African American and my mom's coworkers [in a nursing home] were African Americans, she started to realize that they were in the same situation as she was. So, like, it wasn't really feasible to say that they were bad people or to be prejudiced against them.

Both Jean-Paul and Jacques present their parents as holding negative views of African Americans, though in Jean-Paul's case, this view encompasses all black people, including his parents' own group, Haitians. Whether the parents brought these attitudes from Haiti or acquired them in the United States isn't clear.

Both young men's parents also worry about disadvantages to their children of being black or being associated with African Americans.[11] This is quite different from thinking there is something wrong with African Americans themselves, the question I asked Jacques to clarify, although it is perfectly possible to have both views, as both young men's parents seem to (at least for some period of time). Jean-Paul pushes back against his parents' negative generalizations about black people. He somewhat disputes his parents' stereotypes. Mainly, he wants them to see that he himself does not conform to them. He does his homework and he ends up going to college, things his mother says black people don't do.

Jacques reports that his mother's views changed over time. As she gets to know her children's African American friends and her own largely African American coworkers, that knowledge challenges her negative views of African Americans and leads her to abandon them. She also seems to abandon trying to distance Jacques from African Americans.

These young men are coming to terms with the general racial terrain I described earlier. Immigrants have found it advantageous to distance themselves from blacks, or specifically African Americans. Black immigrants have even more reason to do this because it is much more likely that distinction won't be recognized in their case. Research shows that many black (though by no means all) immigrant parents try to pass those distancing attitudes onto their children, but it is often difficult to do this. The children do not have accents that mark them as immigrants. They may socialize more closely with African Americans in school and in their neighborhoods and feel more akin to them. Both Jean-Paul and Jacques do so and do something else, too: they actively dispute their parents' negative views of black people or of African Americans. They don't think those views are right so they do not bring them to their own social relationships.

So neither Jean-Paul nor Jacques experiences an important divide between themselves and African Americans. They are happy to accept a "black" identity that does not make that distinction. This does not mean that these young men don't see themselves as Haitian Americans. They do; but they don't define that identity *against* African Americans.[12]

—⁓—

This discussion of immigration history and racial dynamics speaks to the point on which Pema disagreed with Sherilyn—whether African Americans are not doing very well because "immigrants come to the U.S. with a determination to succeed that native populations do not have," as Pema says, or because of racism, as Sherilyn gets from the article we read about the African immigrant and African Americans. The history I have laid out here, and that the article alludes to, shows that African Americans have certain historical, structural disadvantages not suffered by pre-1965 waves of (white) immigrants. And these disadvantages—in housing, jobs, education, and assets—remain today. In fact, these disadvantages have become partly compounded by discrimination in favor of more recent immigrants of color over African Americans. But this analysis does not really speak directly to the conventional wisdom that Pema articulates, about the motivational deficiencies of native blacks compared to immigrants.

Recent research reveals some important advantages and disadvantages that immigrants have compared to the native-born that speak to this question. Immigrants as a group, on average, are in some ways disadvantaged in their ability to negotiate and succeed in American society. Many have weak knowledge of English. Their level of education is lower than that of the general population; in one major study, a third lacked a high school degree, compared to 20 percent of the general native population. All these things also make it more difficult for them as parents to help their native-born or one-and-a-half-generation children with and in school. They have fewer financial resources than the general population, by a good deal; the same study had a $54,000 mean income for immigrants and $74,000 for natives (of all races).[13] They face hostility from many Americans.

Of course, immigrant groups differ greatly. Some immigrants of color come from English-speaking nations, or nations in which the educated speak English—Ghana, India, Jamaica, Nigeria—so they do not have the language barrier (though they might face "accent prejudice"). Since 1965, some aspects of immigrant policy have favored immigrants with special skills and training; this has sometimes resulted in favoring certain national origin groups, such as Indians. For example, in the 1990 census, 71 percent of Indian immigrants had college or postgraduate degrees (compared to 60 percent for non-Hispanic whites).[14]

However, we can look at immigrants in an overall way to see some advantages they have as a group compared to the native-born, especially those of their same racial group. By comparing immigrants to those of the same nation of origin who do not immigrate, we can see something of the resources immigrants do bring that turn into advantages in the receiving country (that is, the United States). For example, the sociologist Cynthia Feliciano compares the education levels of immigrants to nonemigrating members of the societies from which the immigrants come. Looking at different sending countries, she finds Jamaican and Haitian immigrants to be the twenty-sixth and thirtieth highest—out of thirty-two—in the education ranking; Haiti is right below India, for example.[15] (For the record, Mexico, Portugal, and Italy are the least-educated immigrant groups among those surveyed; but they are still more educated than the average member of their nation who does not immigrate.) Feliciano finds that immigrants to the United States from virtually every country are more educated than those that do not immigrate. So immigrants are more educated than those they leave behind. This means the immigrants are a self-selected group with various human capital advantages. In addition, while their average education level may be lower than the average American's, it is higher than that of the average African American (and Puerto Rican).[16] And among immigrants, blacks (from different sending nations) are among the most comparatively educated of all groups, and this is especially true of Africans.[17]

These advantages are evident and measurable, as Feliciano documents. But immigrants also bring some less measurable advantages that are often overlooked in comparing immigrants to the native-born. The sociologist Philip Kasinitz and his coauthors, in an extensive and important study of immigrants and their offspring in New York, summarize these advantages:

> Immigrants are a highly selected group. Even when they have relatively modest educations and few financial resources, they have shown that they have the drive, ambition, courage, and strength to move from one nation to another . . . At first glance, a Dominican father

who does not speak English and has only a second grade education may appear to have characteristics similar to those of the least well-off New York–born Puerto Rican father, and even fewer resources. Yet as an immigrant parent he has other qualities that separate him from most uneducated Dominican men who stayed at home on the island, qualities that contributed to his success in migrating to New York. His lack of education may not have a significant effect on his ability to instill a desire for education in his son or daughter.[18]

Another important motivational difference between immigrants and natives is that when immigrants think about how well they are doing in their adopted country, their reference point tends to be what their or their children's situation or prospects would have been in their country of origin—rather than how attractive a given job is considered to be in this country. So an immigrant in a low-wage job in the United States may see this as a step up from unsteady employment in her home country.[19] Or, even if it is a step down, she may feel that her children's prospects are much better in the United States than they would have been at home. But a native-born American might appropriately see that job as demeaning or at least unsatisfactory compared to what she wants for herself. The native-born are not to be faulted for being dissatisfied with working low-wage jobs at long hours. And, for the record, research has shown that low-skilled native blacks do not reject low-paying jobs; they just resent them more than immigrants do—entirely appropriately, it seems to me.[20] The native cannot simply choose to adopt the viewpoint of the immigrant, because he or she does not have the "home country" as a reference point for a current job or prospects. You cannot adopt an immigrant mentality without having the experience and situation of an immigrant.

For all these reasons, Pema's statement of the conventional wisdom that immigrants have a "drive to succeed" is not far from the mark. But the mistake in this view is to think that this observation tells us anything important about why African Americans (and Puerto Ricans, according to Kasinitz's study) have the lowest socioeconomic status of any racial minority group. The comparative resource and motivational advantages that immigrants on average bring with them do indeed help them succeed, but they do not reveal any "cultural" deficiency in African Americans. It is not possible for a group that is entirely native to the United States for many generations to adopt the motivational psychology of an immigrant group, and it is not reasonable to expect them to do so. Immigrant success explains nothing about why African Americans continue to do worse, on average, than whites on measures of health, education, income, wealth, and occupation.

We should indeed admire the pluck and determination of immigrants who brave many hardships to get a better life for themselves or their children. And when we see some second-generation immigrant children succeeding in school partly through the push these parents give them, they too deserve our admiration. At the end of every school year the *Boston Globe* publishes pictures of the valedictorians of every public school in the Boston public school system, with their nation of origin. In 2011, as I am writing this, sixteen of the forty-one valedictorians are foreign-born, and the article says that a not insignificant number of the others are second generation.[21]

The educational success of these foreign-born valedictorians is amazing, and it doesn't take anything away from their accomplishment to recognize the immigrant dynamic I have been talking about in this chapter, which makes their success seem less surprising. But our response to these students, and to immigrants more generally, should not occupy the same mental space as our thinking about African American students. "Why can't they just act more like the immigrant students?" is not the right way to think about the barriers to African American success in school (and society more generally). Immigrants do indeed have advantages, everything else being equal, over natives; but these have nothing to do with deficiencies in the cultures of native groups. These advantages do not require us, for example, to buy into the idea that blacks contribute to sabotaging themselves through adopting racial identities that oppose being successful in school.[22] And indeed, it adds insult to injury when employers prefer immigrants to native blacks, then blame African Americans for not being more like immigrants. And teachers should not add to that insult by looking down on African American students for not being more like immigrant and second-generation students.

Remember that Pema disagreed with Sherilyn about whether racism is to blame for African Americans' disadvantages. Pema agreed with the conventional wisdom that what holds American blacks back is their own failure to adopt the kind of commitment and determination that immigrants and their children have. I have tried to show that this is not the right way to look at it. But this still leaves us with the question of how we (especially teachers) should understand racism and its different forms, as we increasingly deal with multiracial populations. As the class conversation proceeds, two students take up that issue. Anna responds to Sherilyn's earlier point from the article that native blacks were more stigmatized than immigrant blacks.

> *Anna*: That can't be true. A prejudiced person would not make that kind of distinction between two kinds of blacks. Being prejudiced is being ignorant about the groups you are prejudiced against, and lumping groups together.
>
> *Sherilyn*: I agree. Racism is color-blind.
>
> *Me*: Can you explain what you mean by that?
>
> *Sherilyn*: Racism means you don't make distinctions about people's ancestry or culture, just their physical characteristics. A racist doesn't care if you're from the U.S. or Africa; they only care if you're black.

Sherilyn here seems to abandon the view she (accurately) reported earlier from the article the class read, and which I had assumed she agreed with—that African Americans are more stigmatized than black immigrants and are hurt by the stigma. The view both young women articulate here is, by contrast, certainly a familiar one about racism or racial prejudice—that it is equally directed toward any member of the target group, and that it involves ignorance of or overlooking of important differences within the group, including ethnic differences. Saying that racism is "color-blind" is a striking way of expressing this opinion; but it does not really capture her point. The view Sherilyn states is not blind to color but to culture or ethnicity.

I think the two young women have hit upon a familiar view of racism—that it involves ignoring differences within a group. Their view is akin to what some of the students on the first day objected to about stereotyping—that you don't feel recognized for who you are if you are stereotyped. Similarly, if you are just "homogenized" into the "black" racial category, your distinctive ethnicity as Haitian American or African American is not recognized. There is an important lesson here, because with the ever-increasing plurality within the "black" group—paralleled by a similar development within "Asians" and "Latinos"—we have to be alert to these ethnic differences in our students. We shouldn't say something that implies that we think Mexicans and Dominicans are somehow interchangeable.

But notice that racism-as-homogenization is something quite distinct from what Sherilyn herself said in the beginning of the conversation—that racism involves *stigmatizing*, that is, having a devalued identity in society. She had in mind the way African Americans are often seen as stupid or criminally inclined or lazy. This is not the same as not having your ethnicity recognized. Perhaps both are kinds of racism. But they are not the same, and indeed being stigmatized seems a more harmful form of racism than homogenization. So, as Sherilyn took from the article, if African Americans are seen in a more negative light than are African immigrants—that is, if they are more stigmatized—this is a more serious racial harm, and one that can fall upon different groups of blacks (or any other race) differently.

—∽—

It seems, then, that we need to get clearer on how racism works so we can clarify its differential impact on different ethnic groups within a larger racial group. One way to think about a "racist" is as someone who has hostility toward, or disrespects, all racial groups other than his own. Some racists are like this. Certainly historically, such attitudes were pervasive among the white population in the United States and Europe. All nonwhite peoples were seen as inferior in important respects. This is classic white supremacy and ideology.[23]

But someone can be a racist without disrespecting all racial groups other than her own equally. Someone can be hostile to Hispanics without being hostile to Asians, or vice versa. There is a specific history to racist views and treatment toward each distinct group, bound up with the history of that group's relation to other groups, and especially to the dominant groups in society. On a more basic level, groups are different, and can trigger differing prejudices in others. Prejudice against blacks has a distinct place in U.S. history—as we were studying in the course—so it is no surprise if someone thinks badly of blacks or is hostile to them, but does not feel that way toward other groups. We sometimes speak of "anti-black racism" or "anti-Asian racism" to express how racism can be targeted specifically to one particular group. Let's call this *specific-group racism*. And we can call racism targeted equally to all groups *all-group racism*.[24]

This important difference is not always recognized. Abigail and Stephan Thernstrom, influential writers on racial topics and especially race and education, confuse all-group racism with specific-group racism. They note that Asian students do much better in school than blacks and Latinos, and comment, "How can that be the case in an allegedly racist society?"[25] Their rhetorical question assumes that there cannot be prejudicial or discriminatory attitudes or behavior directed toward blacks and Latinos that is not also directed toward Asians. But obviously there can be and often is. The Thernstroms belittle a scholar who says,

"Although Asian-Americans experience racism, they do not usually get stereotyped as less intelligent than whites, so they internalize and transfer messages about themselves that are different from those of blacks, Latinos, and Native Americans." Yet this scholar seems to me to be right on target, capturing the way that "racism" targets different groups in different ways. The Thernstroms make this comment on the quote: "It is of course a neat trick to 'experience racism' and yet escape being stereotyped as inferior; the two usually go hand in hand." Maybe, but they don't *always* go hand in hand. Asians can be the target of racist hostility and resentments without also being regarded as inferior. Although in the nineteenth and early twentieth centuries Asians tended to be seen as inferior, the form of racism toward Asians has changed, especially in the post-1965 period. As several writers have pointed out, the idea that Asian Americans are a "model minority" can generate a good deal of racial hostility, in addition to wrongly homogenizing the experience and cultures of the great variety of Asian Americans. But the divisiveness is connected to seeing Asian Americans as *superior* in certain respects rather than *inferior.*[26]

Just as racial prejudices can have different characteristics when targeted toward racial groups, they can also differentiate *within* racial groups. This is very familiar. There are different prejudices against black males than black females; black males are much more likely to be stereotyped as dangerous or threatening than are black females. Perhaps older black people are looked upon more benignly than young blacks by many nonblacks. Asian women are sexualized as exotic more than are Asian men. Hispanic young women are often belittled as being pregnant all the time (a stereotype I heard at the high school); obviously this gendered racial stereotype cannot apply to Hispanic males. And so on. Racial prejudices can differentially target subgroups within a given racial group because they involve different stereotypes, and different degrees or types of hostility or stigmatizing, of those subgroups.

This differentiation can run along ethnic as well as age, class, and gender lines. Why not? Some black ethnic groups can be seen more negatively than others, or have particular stereotypes attached to them that do not attach to others. Another time that I offered the course, a Haitian student in the class complained about the stereotype that Haitians smell. This stereotype of Haitians is in fact common among the people of non-Haitian Caribbean ancestry in New York whom Mary Waters studied.[27] This same stereotype is not necessarily applied to other black ethnic groups.

This subgroup differentiation is exactly what Sherilyn originally reported the article as saying: "African Americans are more stigmatized than immigrants, even though both are black." It is a form of specific-group racism that is entirely analogous to age, gender, and class-related differentiations within racial prejudice.

—◊—

"Wait a minute," you might say. "If someone's prejudice is directed to something other than the person's race—like their class, gender, skin color, or ethnicity—then why is this *racial* prejudice at all? If this person sees black immigrants in a positive light, she can't be racist, even if she sees African Americans in a negative light. Her prejudice is *ethnic* but not *racial*." This objection presents an important issue, since being seen as racially prejudiced is something everyone wants to avoid, but ethnic prejudice is not so socially stigmatized.

But the specific-group prejudice—prejudice toward subgroups of the larger racial group—still seems to me racial in character. The prejudice against poor black people is not simply a prejudice against poor people in general, of any race. That could be part of it, but something more is going on. Poor black people have a distinctly negative reputation in the American imagination that has something to do with their being black, not *only* their being poor.

What is the psychological structure of specific-group prejudice? In some cases it may simply be two distinct prejudices coming together—one against poor people, and one against black people. But it is probably more often something more complicated. For example, American white, or nonblack, hostility to young black males is not likely to be a simple combination of a generalized antimale prejudice, an antiyouth prejudice, and a generalized antiblack prejudice—although those prejudices may also be present. Differentiated, specific-group prejudice works in a more holistic way. For the (subgroup) prejudiced person, that specific group—say, young black males—triggers certain fears, hostilities, or negative associations. It is still a *racial* prejudice, because the particular race has to be part of the mix in order to elicit the prejudice. The response of a store security officer to young Asian males would probably be different. The racial factor is why, when Norris was walking around in a hoodie at night, he felt that he generated suspicious looks and avoidance behavior. The blackness is a necessary part of the prejudice, making it racial in character.

Once we see that racism is not always of a "whole-group" form we can see that people can be prejudiced against "blackness" without necessarily having negative feelings or thoughts toward all blacks. A familiar example of this is when a nonblack person says to a black person, "I don't see you as black." We understand this as meaning, "I recognize that according to the way we classify people into racial groups in this country, you are 'black'; but I like you and respect you and you do not seem to me to possess the negative characteristics that I associate with black people." The person who makes this remark does not recognize that this is what she means; she thinks she is saying something complimentary, but she is actually being insulting. "Making exceptions" for some members of the group in question turns out to be another example of group prejudice.

This differentiated antiblack prejudice can also be seen in the view that some subgroups of blacks are "more black" than others, and are therefore more stigmatized. You might say that it is blackness itself that is stigmatized, and some subgroups of blacks are seen as having more of it than others. President Obama does not seem "as black" as Jesse Jackson or Jay-Z, for example, because he has a white parent. Some white voters clearly felt less hostility toward Obama because he was not seen as "fully black." But the "degrees of blackness" idea can work in the opposite way. Some black voters might have felt that Obama was not "black enough"; that was something one heard when he first started running for the Democratic presidential nomination. But this does not make the two attitudes exactly symmetrical. Whites who would have found someone they thought of as "more black" unacceptable for that reason were prejudiced against blacks, or blackness. Whereas blacks who might have thought Obama "not black enough" were not, or at least not necessarily, prejudiced against whites. They just wanted a black candidate to be more culturally black, or to have two black parents, or to make them feel more confident that he would advocate for black interests.

This whole way of talking only makes sense because "black" has two different meanings, which have sometimes been called "thin" and "thick" blackness. Thin blackness is a classification based purely on phenotype and ancestry. You are black in the thin sense if you have certain physical characteristics associated with people of African ancestry, or if you have that ancestry yourself even if you don't have the physical characteristics. On the thin meaning of blackness, Africans and African Americans are equally black. Barack Obama is as black as Jesse Jackson and Jay-Z. But on the "thick" meaning, "black" has a richer set of associations, which can be negative, neutral, or positive; but for the racist they are negative. A black person who primarily likes classical music can be seen as less black (in the "thick" sense) than one who is primarily into jazz or hip-hop.[28]

In this "thick" sense, African Americans can be viewed more negatively, and seen as "more black," than Haitians, in the mind of the subgroup racist. The racist does not make the same negative associations with Haitians that she does with African Americans. Because they are immigrants, the Haitians may be seen as having positive characteristics associated with immigrants, such as being hard-working and having strong family ties.[29]

So subgroup prejudice is possible and familiar. We can see, then, that the stigmatizing of African Americans more than black immigrants is still a form of racism, rather than a merely ethnic prejudice, even though it differentiates among ethnic subgroups in its degree of stigma.

This brings us back to the question on which Pema and Sherilyn originally disagreed—whether racism, or something else, is the reason African Americans are not doing better. If we accept subgroup racism, and give up the idea that all racism has to be "whole group," much less "all group," in form, then we have to admit the point that Sherilyn drew from the article—that African Americans can suffer from a greater stigma than black immigrants and this can hurt them. This acknowledgment hardly gives us a full answer to the question of what has hindered and still holds African Americans back, an undertaking that would take us far beyond the scope of this book.

—m—

"Why can't African Americans act like immigrants, who come here with nothing, work hard, and succeed, or at least make sure their kids succeed?" That's the familiar refrain. The answer is that a group that is not an immigrant group cannot adopt the mentality, the "culture," of an immigrant group. In this chapter I have tried to show why this whole way of looking at African Americans in relation to immigrants is wrong. The story of African Americans and the story of (black) immigrants are two different stories. And immigrant success does not in any way diminish the responsibility American society as a whole has to rectify the historical legacy of injustice from which African Americans still suffer.[30]

6 The African Role in Slavery
Morality, History, and Economics

I continued our long unit on slavery, begun two weeks before. We had looked at the beginnings of slavery in the Americas, a result of the slave trade that imported Africans to the Iberian and English colonies. We had discussed Smedley's assertion that without African slavery, the idea of race itself would probably not have developed. But now I wanted to move to a less familiar aspect of slavery.

Me: Today I want to focus on a different aspect of the slave trade—the role of Africans themselves. We've learned that after the very first years of the slave trade, in the 1400s, European slave traders did not go into the interior of Africa to get slaves. How did the Europeans get those future slaves?

Marie: Africans sold slaves to the Europeans.

Me: That's right. But who were these slaves that were sold to the Europeans? This question does not have a simple answer. In the early years of the slave trade across the Atlantic, the Africans who were sold to the Europeans were often already slaves in African societies. Many were captives of war, but they could also be people who had committed a crime or could not pay a debt. As the slave trade progressed, especially at its height in the 1700s, Africans began to raid neighboring tribes or societies for the sole purpose of getting captives to sell to the Europeans. We read something about this last week. Do you remember what that was?

Cristina: It was Equiano. He described how he and his siblings always had to be on the lookout for raiders, when their parents were away from their house working. And one day when he and his younger sister were the only ones around, raiders climbed over a fence and captured them. Then he was taken to a lot of different places and masters, but he ended up being sold to English traders who took him to Barbados and soon after that to Virginia.

Me: Yes, that's good, Cristina. Equiano, who you remember wrote the first slave narrative in English, published in 1789, was only ten when he was first captured. He was a member of the Igbo tribe, which still exists in present-day Nigeria. The way Equiano tells it, he was moved—he doesn't say whether he was sold—to several different masters, some of them speaking his language and some not. So he had already become a slave by time he was taken to the West Coast of Africa to be sold to Europeans.[1]

We've already talked a little bit about the morality of slave owning at the American end of the slave trade. But today I want you to think about the role of the African slave traders. Let's start by focusing on the traders who sold people who were already slaves, as Equiano was, to the Europeans, knowing that the Europeans were going to ship them across the sea to sell as slaves. This is the question I want you to answer: Was it morally wrong for Africans to sell people who were already slaves in their own societies to the European slave traders?

Here is some of the students' discussion:

Norris: I think it was wrong, like really not moral, because it was betraying their own people. Like, how could they just do that to their own people? And taking someone out of their own society, like selling them to another country, is just wrong.

Mirvole: The Africans, the African traders, knew what was going on on those boats. They knew how bad those conditions were and they still sold their own people there. It was totally wrong.

Norris and Mirvole raise an issue related to race that I am sure is on some other students' minds also: How can Africans do this to other Africans—"their own people"? It is an understandable way to think. The students are taking an identity that is important in their world—"black," "African"—and projecting it back into history. I suggest that the perspective back then was different.

Me: Norris and Mirvole are wondering how one African could sell another African into slavery. They see how Europeans could do it to Africans, but not how Africans could do it to each other because of being fellow Africans. Maybe they are also thinking that because the captor and the captive are both black, this should make the captor think it was wrong. But think back to the 1600s and 1700s, when all this was taking place. Did members of the Igbo tribe look at members of the Wolof tribe and think, "We are all Africans" or "We are all blacks"?

Tenzina: I don't think so. They just thought of themselves as members of that tribe.

Me: That's right. They didn't identify with the continent of Africa. They didn't think they had something in common with a person just because they were both from Africa. And they didn't think of themselves as "black people" either. As we saw, that only occurred once they were in the Americas as slaves, and even then it took a while for that to fully happen. We'll look more closely at that process later. At first the slaves still thought of themselves just as members of a tribe or ethnic group, as Tenzina said.

The students then come back to the moral issue:

Norris: Yeah, so, he's already a slave but now you're taking him away from everything he knows, and he will still be a slave. So his life could not possibly be better in another country.

Mirvole: Well, that wasn't the idea; I mean I don't think the slave traders cared whether the slaves would have a better life in a new country. It was just wrong for them to do that, period.

Marie: It was wrong because slavery is wrong. Slavery was wrong in Africa because they were using another person. So, selling someone who is already a slave is still wrong because it is wrong to begin with.

I am not sure about this, but Norris seems to be exploring the idea that part of what is wrong with what the African slave traders do is taking the captive from a known context to an unfamiliar one; and on top of that, the captive remains a slave, which means he can't be better off in the new society. Mirvole attempts to get past the issue Norris raises by saying that the slave traders did not care whether the slave would have a better life in the new country. It isn't clear that this is relevant to the moral question, whether what they are doing is wrong, but I think this is how Mirvole works her way from a response to a fellow student to a clearer recognition of what she herself thinks (at this point), which is that what the African slave traders were doing was just plain wrong.

Then Marie affirms Mirvole's view, but builds on it to say more fully *why* it was wrong—it involves using another person.

> *Adam*: Slavery is immoral. To enslave someone to work for you is fundamentally immoral. Even though we have been doing it for centuries, that doesn't make it OK. Only people who were moral finally realized that slavery was wrong.
>
> *Clara*: Even though I agree with you [Adam], I think you are being idealistic. While it would be nice, I don't think it works that way, especially when money is involved.
>
> *Anna*: I disagree [with Clara]. No, it's not too idealistic, because we don't have slavery any more.

Adam echoes Marie's view—slavery is simply wrong, so any involvement with it is wrong—but adds a historical and social dimension to the moral question. He says that just because slavery has taken place for centuries (and he uses the present tense, so I am assuming that he knows that slavery is still practiced today), this does not lend any moral legitimacy to it. Moral people are able to see that slavery is wrong.

Clara brings in a new angle. Adam is being "idealistic." I am not sure if she means that people at the time of slavery (not counting slaves themselves) could not have been expected to know that slave trading was wrong since at the time they just saw it as a business proposition. Or perhaps she means that even if they did know it was wrong, they would do it anyway since there was gain in it for them. I appreciate her injecting a note of realism into the moral conversation. We have to be able to examine morality in relation to the historical facts. Clara is certainly right to note that slavery wasn't just a practice driven by immoral impulses but one based on economics. I had emphasized this aspect especially in our study of the early years of the slave system, before the concept of race was solidly in place to rationalize it.

But Anna counters Clara with a point that takes Adam's a bit further—if slavery doesn't exist any more, someone who lived at a time when slavery was an accepted business practice must have known it was wrong. Morality is capable of trumping economics.

I thought afterwards that Anna's view is actually consistent with Clara's, even though they seem to pull in contrary directions. You can think that slavery is an economic transaction but still believe it is morally wrong. Some people may think that market transactions are immune from morality and moral criticism. But just because something is "standard business practice" doesn't make it right or acceptable.

I shift the ground a bit: "We've been discussing whether slavery, or a practice involved in slavery like capturing and selling people to slave traders, was wrong. But I now want you to think yourselves back to the time of the slave trade in Africa. Do you think African slave traders thought they were doing something wrong?" The students had approached this question, but I wanted to hit it head on. In a way it was a shift from a moral question to an historical one, albeit one involving morality. I was asking them to get inside the heads of a historical actor—an African slave trader—and see what that person thought about a practice he was engaged in. I was in a way using morality in the service of history. By figuring out how the African slave traders thought about the morality of slave trading, we would gain a better understanding of what that practice meant in its historical setting. But at the same time, the question also should spur moral understanding itself. Understanding how people of different eras thought morally about their world can challenge us to wonder whether something we have taken for granted as wrong or right needs to be given more thought.

> *Lovelle*: I think yes, slavery is morally wrong, even though these people were already slaves. But if slavery was already in Africa, then I guess they might have thought there was nothing wrong with selling slaves to other countries.
>
> *Jacques*: Yes, they did know it was wrong, to an extent. Europeans used the idea of race to justify what they were doing. Africans used the idea of lineage to justify slavery. Anyone outside a certain lineage could be a slave. So, just by using this justification, they must have known it was wrong.
>
> *Adam*: With the moral instinct we have as humans, deeply ingrained in us, how could these people *not* know that what they were doing was morally wrong?
>
> *Clara*: I disagree. I think they [owners/traders] thought of it as a business, and if had been going on for years, why would they question it?
>
> *Anna*: People can make themselves believe anything, especially if they don't want to know if what they are doing is morally wrong.

This is a fascinating exchange. Lovelle poses the historical challenge I mentioned—if slave trading and owning was accepted in their own

society, the traders might very well have thought it was all right to con-
duct the same business with the Europeans. Jacques brings together
several different threads from our studies so far. As we will see again
later, Jacques is particularly good at using previous knowledge from the
course to illuminate what is going on in the present context. Here he
picks Smedley's strong emphasis that the whole idea of race was developed and popularized as a way for Europeans to rationalize (racial) slavery. By saying that blacks were inherently inferior, slave owners could
rationalize that it was all right to enslave them. Then Jacques puts this
together with something he has learned about African slavery in the
class (although we did not go into this point in nearly the same depth),
that when Africans from one group raided a neighboring group, they
would think that this was all right if the group was of a different ethnicity or lineage.

Then Jacques puts his own twist on the idea of providing a justification or rationalization for slavery—that you wouldn't provide the rationalization if you really thought slavery was morally all right. You provide
the rationalization only if you know it *isn't* morally right.

Adam seems to be working within the spirit of Jacques's moral position. But he is also deepening his earlier assertion of the wrongness
of slavery. Now he ventures a bit of an explanation of how we know
this—through a moral instinct that all humans have, one that is deeply
ingrained. If so, these traders and owners must have known slave trading
was wrong.

In line with her earlier remarks, Clara is having none of the view that
traders and slave owners knew they were doing something wrong. She
adds a slight historical dimension to her view that they just saw it as acceptable because it was a business—that it had been going on, and seen
as acceptable, for a long time.

Anna ponders her classmates' views and seems to come up with something in between. "People can make themselves believe anything" implies that maybe the slave traders didn't actually believe slavery is wrong
(as Clara said), but they *sort of* knew that if they thought about it, they
would realize it was wrong (as Jacques and Adam said).

The discussion seems to have enhanced the students' critical thinking about both morality and history. They are recognizing that moral
issues look different in different historical eras—practices that seem ab-
horrent to us may have seemed acceptable to the majority in an earlier
time. Yet they are also seeing that it is not a simple matter to discern
whether the practice was seen as acceptable. And finally, they are also

recognizing that historical variability in moral judgment does not tell us whether the practice *was* actually right or wrong at the time. They still have to think that question through for themselves. The students are responding to each other, learning from one another, and building on each other's thinking.

I am struck by something else in this entire exchange. None of the students, blacks or nonblacks, tries to justify African slavery by saying that it was not really so bad, compared to New World slavery. When I taught the course another time, an East African student took that view. This student knew more about African slavery than most American students do, and, although my own knowledge of the character of African slavery is not very extensive, I know that slaves performed a wide range of tasks and functions in different African societies. In general there was a preference for female slaves, who were used as domestic workers, concubines, bearers of children, and agricultural workers.[2] By contrast, the Europeans preferred male slaves, for hard labor. Although slaves performed a variety of functions in both the African and the American contexts, it is probably fair to say that on the whole, the slave status in Africa was less degraded than it was at the peak of U.S. slavery. It was worse than my East African student claimed; it was not a "benign" system. But slavery in the plantation systems of the Americas was worse.

In a later class, looking back on our slavery units as a whole, some students reflected on the African role in slavery and the slave trade.

> *Pema*: I did not know that there was slavery in other countries in the old days. I also understand now that slavery was also started with African people in Africa giving away slaves. It helped me understand about race better, because I was never taught that way in other history classes.
>
> *Leila*: Studying slavery affects the way I think about American history because I learn more deeply about what went on in the past and the struggles some racial groups faced. Before I studied slavery, I did not care about the past much, and I never thought slavery was as bad as it sounded like. Also, I learned a lot more, like how the slaves were captured, and it made me realize that slavery was not only white people's fault but it was also some Africans' fault for capturing other Africans as slaves and bringing them to the Europeans.

It is interesting that Leila connected not caring about the past with not seeing that slavery was as bad as it was—as if perhaps she needn't be too concerned about history because nothing back then really required her to know about it, or perhaps because nothing in the present required her knowledge of the past. I hoped that taking slavery so seriously as an object of study, and having the students achieve a deeper understanding of it than they had received in other history courses, would help the black students feel that their own history was being acknowledged.[3] At the same time, I was glad that these two students recognized some of the moral complexity in the fact that Africans were involved in their own form of slavery as well as in the Atlantic slave trade. But I want to make clear that I wasn't presenting slavery in this way because I was afraid of sparking black hostility in the class toward whites if I presented only the fully racialized system of slavery that eventually developed in the U.S. colonies. I was teaching what I took to be the truth of slavery in the Americas and in the U.S. and the British pre-U.S. colonies. I did not soft-pedal the horrors of slavery or the fact that for most of U.S. history, slavery was an oppressive structure of whites over blacks. I continually emphasized that the racial history of the United States cannot be understood without taking this racial slavery seriously.[4]

One student, Jean-Paul, picked up on the broader context of slavery in a good way.

> *Jean-Paul*: I just think about how people could be so cruel. But we have to remember the fact that slavery didn't begin here. It was just the racial fact [about U.S. slavery] that made it so HEAVY [his emphasis].

Jean-Paul is onto something I set up the course to try to convey. Americans did not invent the cruelty of slavery, but its racial justification and thus its eventual racial character added a whole extra layer of horror to it. This is different from African slavery.

—⚹—

In an interview several months after the class was over, Tenzina drew an interesting connection between the historical development of slavery and our current views on race. I asked her, "Was there a particular idea that you learned in our class that stuck with you?"

> *Tenzina*: The only thing I can remember now is the history part of it, like the fact that slavery existed a long time ago before it came to the U.S., and that it was a different kind of slavery than we had here in the U.S. Then you would see slavery in the U.S. and there was

always this distinction that I could never quite grasp. I was, like, "Why don't people make such a big deal about this other kind of slavery but only the U.S. kind?" But now that I took your class it's like, "Oh, because it's race-based and the earlier kind wasn't."

I asked her to elaborate.

Well, when I was little I would watch Bible movies and you see how the Pharaoh in Egypt, the Egyptians, enslaved the Israelites a long time ago. Then you hear about slavery in the U.S. and it was like, "Yeah, that was wrong, but why is everyone still talking about it? They both happened such a long time ago." My parents didn't teach me about racism and I didn't know that it existed. But in school I started learning about black leaders like Martin Luther King and Harriet Tubman, and then in your class I learned that slavery in the U.S. was based on race, that they took advantage of race and used it as a reason to enslave people. And they used it for so long that it still almost exists now, it keeps going through the generations.

So what Tenzina was struck by in the class was that she had always sort of known that slavery in the United States, and earlier slavery, such as in biblical times, were different in some important way. But she had never really understood until my course what that difference was—that our form of slavery was based on race, and the earlier forms were not. And so what Tenzina saw as the connection between U.S. slavery and the present was that slavery created the idea of race, and that race is still on the scene and still matters, affecting the situations of different racial groups in the present.

Looking back on the course, I do wish I had given more attention to this question: Does the fact that Africans were involved in slavery and the slave trade let Europeans off the hook morally, or seriously diminish their moral responsibility as slave traders and slave owners? Leila seemed to head in that direction, and two other students said something like this in some later written work. The issue was given high-profile treatment in an op-ed piece by Henry Louis Gates Jr. in the *New York Times* in 2010.[5] The piece was misleadingly titled, "Ending the Slavery Blame-Game." In it Gates describes new research showing the importance of African slave trading to the overall Atlantic slave system, and how some contemporary African leaders are acknowledging the African role and seeking forgiveness from African Americans. But Gates is expanding the subjects of blame, rather than ending talk of blame. If someone commits murder, we don't think he is exonerated, or even that his guilt is in any way diminished, if we discover that he had an accomplice. We just think the accomplice is also to blame. Just because the African slave providers were an integral part of the slave system does not render Europeans less blameworthy for their role. I wish I had discussed with the students how the African role in slavery should affect our thinking about the moral culpability of American slave owners, or those whites who benefited from slavery explicitly.

Returning to my current class, I don't know if my students knew more about the character of African slavery than the very brief account we read in Equiano's autobiography. But in any case I did not ask those students whether what the African slave traders or holders were doing was *worse* than what the European slave traders or holders did; whether African slave traders were worse than European ones; or (the question just discussed), whether African participation diminished European moral blame. I asked only if slave trading was wrong, and whether the African slave traders knew it was wrong. I think it is interesting that none of the students seemed attracted to the idea that "it might be wrong for us, but it was all right for them, because they accepted it." While some of them thought the slave traders might have truly believed slave capture and trading were morally OK, none of them took the further step of saying that they were acceptable then *because* the Africans thought they were. That straightforwardly relativist position did not surface. Not that it did not deserve to. Relativism is a familiar moral position with a long historical and intellectual pedigree. Ultimately I do not think it can be defended. There are some human activities and practices that are just wrong, even if they were once accepted, and even if they are still accepted somewhere. Slavery is an obvious example of this. But here I am just noting its perhaps surprising absence in the class discussion.

In addition, none of the black students seemed to be looking for a way to defend the Africans as fellow black people. The East African student from the other class does not quite count here, since he was actually African, while my present black students were not (Leila excepted, and she did not weigh in on this conversation). It may be that Equiano's anguished account of his and his sister's capture helped to personalize the practice of slave capture and trading, and so made it easier to regard the African "perpetrators" as fully responsible for doing wrong, just like the European slave traders and American slaveholders, whom the students rightly regarded as choosing to perpetrate a moral abomination. Although we saw that initially both Norris and Mirvole thought there would be a natural connection among all Africans, this doesn't necessarily mean American blacks (including those of Caribbean ancestry) would have that connection with Africans. The continent-based connection may be of a different character than a race-based one. It may be that my black students, Africans excepted, did not identify, either contemporaneously or historically, with African blacks.

It is also possible that something more general was going on here—that this younger generation of black students is less "identitarian" in its moral reactions and thinking. These students may simply be less inclined to "defend the race" than earlier generations. If this is happening, it would have one very good consequence for moral development—it would permit a more open and responsive moral sensibility to develop. That is, students would be more open to recognizing when someone of their own racial group has acted badly, and would not cut a "fellow race member" undeserved moral slack.

But that is not to say that such a moral sensibility would be entirely color-blind. As I have argued often in this book, racial identity does and should make a moral difference in some contexts—for example, in the obligation to intervene in bad racial situations, as discussed in chapter 4, or in the degree of your personal identification with a historical figure or event (discussed in the next chapter). But it should not make a difference in one's judgment as to whether someone acted wrongly.

7 Banneker, Walker, and Jefferson

Challenging the Notion of Black Inferiority

Teaching the history of race in America means contending at some point with the idea that black people are inherently inferior to white people. Black inferiority is at the historical heart of the American idea of race, and it is intimately tied to American slavery. Without slavery we would not have developed our particular idea of race. And without race and black inferiority, the philosophical underpinnings of slavery would have been much weaker than they were. "For no other group has there been such a persistent, well-articulated, and unabated ideology about their mental incompetence," says Theresa Perry, an educational theorist.[1]

But how should I teach the perilous subject of alleged black inferiority? I could not assume that the students thought the idea of black inferiority was safely behind us, merely a dead idea from the past. Claude Steele's recent research on "stereotype threat" demonstrates that current black students labor under a worry that others will judge them as intellectual inferiors. This anxiety interferes with their school performance, and many black students don't perform up to their potential.[2] So in teaching about the history of the American race idea, with black incapability as its center, I had to be aware that I was dealing with powerful and hurtful ideas. I wanted to use the words and views of black thinkers to help counter those (hurtful) messages. How should I approach the issue in the context of my racially mixed and black-majority class?

The class was prepared in a historical sense for this sensitive topic. They had learned that blacks were not the only group the English colonists had utilized for agricultural labor and personal service, and that African slavery was by no means inevitable. The students were surprised to learn of "the descent into slavery" (in Smedley's phrase)— that, compared to other sectors of the population, Africans' status got worse, not better (at different rates in different colonies) as the 1700s wore on, and particularly as the plantation system established itself in the South. With this background, the students could more easily accept that the idea of black inferiority itself had not always been a part of the conventional wisdom even of white people in the period before slavery ended—and that, like the idea of race itself, it had changed and morphed over time.

With this framework as a backdrop, I wanted to help students understand "black intellectual inferiority" *as an idea*—an evil idea, but an idea nevertheless. That means that this lesson lent itself particularly well to the focus on higher-order thinking—critical thinking—that I emphasized as part of the college-level character of the course, but which is no less important in high school. I would have the students use and develop their critical skills and abilities by applying them to the pernicious idea of black intellectual inferiority. But this approach also raised another concern—that learning how whites had created and invested in the idea of black intellectual inferiority to justify slavery would create hostility in the black students toward the whites, defensiveness in the white students, and perhaps some version of either in the Asian and Hispanic students. Theresa Perry says that black schools in the segregation-era South routinely affirmed black students' intellectual capability in the face of a racist ideology.[3] But how can teachers manage this in schools with white, Asian, and Hispanic students too?

I decided to wade into this pedagogically and morally challenging terrain by focusing intensively on the post–Revolutionary War period, into the 1830s. Slavery became more deeply entrenched in the American South in this period, and the Northern economy became more dependent on Southern slavery, even though slavery itself had ended in the North. At the same time, the idea of race, with its central component of black inferiority, was developed and articulated more fully and with wider circulation than ever before in American history. But—and this was a point I wanted to emphasize with my students—both slavery and racist ideas about black inferiority began to be challenged publicly by a small number of blacks and whites.

Thomas Jefferson is a good starting point for these historical developments. Most of my students knew he was the author of the Declaration of Independence, with its stirring paean to human equality, and that he was also a slave owner. They were less likely to know that in his many years as a leader of the new nation—as secretary of state, vice president, then president—he did nothing to advance the end of slavery and that he supported its extension westward to the Louisiana Purchase.

A journal entry from Behar, a student who had recently immigrated from southeastern Europe, expressed an interesting take on Jefferson's ambivalent legacy. The entry was written before we plunged into our unit.

> In this journal I want to focus on Thomas Jefferson. What I learned about him in [my home country] is very different from what I'm learning here about him . . . It is true that he is one of the founding fathers and one of the most prominent Americans. It is also true that he inspired the American revolution and developed the country by serving as Secretary of State and as President. I discovered that although he wrote in the Declaration of Independence that all men are created equal, he never acted like that. According to Jefferson all men were created equal, but black men were not even humans. He never thought that black men were created equal. Or maybe he thought of that, but instead of acting in a fair way Jefferson was led by his economic interests and didn't consider black men to be created equal. What I learned at CRLS about him has created in me great confusion about this character and I really don't know if it right to say that Jefferson was one of the most prominent Americans. Someone who owned slaves and used them in different shameful ways does not deserve to be called a prominent American.

Behar reports the very laudatory view of Jefferson that he received in his home country. I had the impression that as a recent immigrant he had a distinct investment in Jefferson's positive accomplishments, perhaps more so than many native students. Some immigrants embrace American national mythology more than natives. But Behar is troubled when he comes to the United States and learns about Jefferson's dark side. Behar has a strong sense of social justice and he expresses pain but also outrage at Jefferson's stated view that blacks are not the equals of whites. Behar seems personally disappointed in Jefferson in a way that none of the other students express (although I did not ask their view of Jefferson explicitly). Perhaps other students, especially the black students, are already too cynical from what they have learned in their families and communities about the Founding Fathers to be disappointed. But this is speculation. I don't know what the other students think. I am just struck by Behar's struggles to assimilate what he has learned about Jefferson. I do not want my students to sink into cynicism about our nation's leaders. I want them to expect these leaders to do the right thing, and to be disappointed or outraged if they don't, as Behar is.

Presenting Jefferson to the class, I say: "In your textbook, Smedley emphasizes that Jefferson was one of the first prominent Americans to offer something in the form of a scientific account of the innate capacities of different races, and to argue for the inferiority of the black race. In doing this, Jefferson contributed in a major way to popularizing the idea that blacks were inherently inferior to whites, and also that this inferiority was a matter of scientific truth.

"Jefferson sets out his ideas in chapter 14 of his 1787 work, *Notes on the State of Virginia,* which was widely read at the time. There Jefferson mentions some proposed changes in Virginia laws that had not yet been adopted. One of these proposals is to free all slaves born after the passage of the law (if it were to pass) and to send them outside the United States, an idea that some whites and a very small number of blacks favored, and which was called 'colonization.'

"Jefferson then brings up an objection that had been made to this emancipation and colonization plan: 'It will probably be asked, why not retain and incorporate the blacks into the state, and thus save the expense of supplying, by importation of white settlers, the vacancies they will leave.'[4] Jefferson spends several pages replying to the view that after emancipation blacks should be incorporated into U.S. society. His answer is that he does not think that blacks and whites can ever live together in a shared society. He does not change his mind about this over the course of his life. Jefferson spells out his views on blacks' inherent nature, as well as their historical situation. Jefferson says that compared to whites, blacks are inferior in the 'faculty of reason'; in their capacity for loving attachments to family members; and in physical appearance. To put it crudely, Jefferson is saying that blacks are stupid, ugly, and don't care about their families, compared to whites. Later in the passage, Jefferson pulls back a bit from these harsh views and says these claims about blacks and whites 'must be hazarded with great diffidence.' So maybe he isn't 100 percent sure about black inferiority, but he does not say anything specific against that idea."

But Jefferson's views about blacks were criticized in his historical period, and I decided to focus on two black Americans who explicitly challenged Jefferson's ideas about slavery or black inferiority—Benjamin Banneker and David Walker.

I told the students a little about Banneker: "Benjamin Banneker was born free in 1731, in Maryland. He was able to receive some education and he achieved some stature as an astronomer and surveyor, even playing a small role in surveying the area that would become the District of Columbia (that is, Washington, D.C.). Starting in 1791, and until 1797, he created a yearly almanac, a book with useful information, that contained his painstaking observations and largely accurate predictions of the positions of the sun, moon, and planets, as well as political observations concerning peace, religion, and education.

"In 1791 Banneker wrote a letter to Jefferson, who was then secretary of state under George Washington. Along with the letter, he sent Jefferson a copy of his first almanac, somewhat implying, though without stating this explicitly, that his producing this almanac was evidence that blacks are the intellectual equals of whites.

"Banneker begins his letter in this way, as you read in your homework:"

I am fully sensible of the greatness of that freedom which I take with you on the present occasion; a liberty which seemed to me scarcely allowable, when I reflected on that distinguished, and dignified station in which you stand; and the almost general prejudice and prepossession which is so prevalent in the world against those of my complexion . . . We are a race of beings [who] have long been considered rather as brutish than human, and scarcely capable of mental endowments.[5]

"Banneker goes on to question Jefferson's failure to challenge slavery when he had written so powerfully of the natural right of all men to liberty. Banneker says that he hopes Jefferson is 'willing and ready to lend your aid and assistance to our relief from those many distresses and numerous calamities to which we are reduced,' and urges Jefferson to use his power and influence to the relief of any people suffering under oppression."

I asked the students, in their reading questions, why Banneker used such a respectful and even deferential tone in his challenge to Jefferson, and we then discussed this issue in class.

Clara: I couldn't quite tell if he really respected Jefferson or if he was being a little sarcastic. Also I think he wanted to show how a black person could write at the same level as a white, but he may also respect Jefferson a bit for showing even some support for slaves.
Mirvole: I would characterize the tone of voice with which Banneker approaches Jefferson as very calm, collected, and articulate. Although the reader senses some tension in Banneker's voice, it is collected

and he comes about it in the right way. Instead of cursing or insulting Jefferson, Banneker states the facts along with his opinion. I do
not believe Banneker admires Jefferson. I believe he just wants Jefferson to keep his word.

I like the way Mirvole and Clara recognize that Banneker's deferential tone to Jefferson, highlighting Jefferson's elevated standing in society,
does not necessarily mean that he admires Jefferson. I wonder if Mirvole's
perception of "tension" in Banneker's tone, or Clara's that he was a bit
"sarcastic," refers to Banneker's contrasting Jefferson's high standing
with the way blacks are seen as an inferior, and barely human group—
possibly a subtle implication that Jefferson should recognize that this
view of blacks is unjust.

Still, Banneker may have actually admired Jefferson, at least to some
extent. Banneker refers in his letter to "a report which hath reached me,
that you are a man far less inflexible in sentiments of this nature than
many others." It might be difficult for contemporary students to think
that it would be possible for a black person to admire someone who
supported black subordination and held slaves.[6] But one of the values
of studying history is recognizing a historical figure's reference group.
Banneker lived at a time in which virtually no prominent white people,
and hardly any white people at all, really thought of blacks as equals.
The Quakers who helped educate Banneker were a rare exception. In the
1790s Jefferson may well have seemed to Banneker more enlightened
than his peers, and thus possibly worthy of admiration.

On the other hand, Mirvole might be entirely right that Banneker's
tone was essentially a strategy to encourage Jefferson to live up to his
stated ideals about the inherent right to freedom of all human beings.

Philippe, who took the course a different year, said something similar in a journal entry, but with an interesting gender slant: "The letter
Benjamin Banneker wrote to Thomas Jefferson broke assumptions of a
black man. He wrote respectfully and was clear in what he had to say. I
felt he challenged Jefferson's ideas of black people and made him think."

I think Philippe is saying something both historical and contemporary—that he does not think black men currently are expected to write
respectfully and to be clear in what they say. They are not expected to
be intellectual and articulate. Interestingly, Philippe is himself a student
who often gropes for the words to express his thoughts, and more than
most students defers to others as saying what he wanted to say. At the
same time, I think he also underestimates himself, and is in fact quite

well-spoken, insightful, and even eloquent. Philippe admires these qualities in Banneker. And he also admires Banneker's having tried to make Jefferson reconsider his ideas about black people.[7]

—⚏—

I introduced the fascinating and still too little known figure of David Walker: "A later important black thinker who challenged Jefferson's ideas after his death was David Walker. Walker lived in Boston in the late 1820s, and he was involved in the abolitionist movement. That was a movement of black and some white people who called for slavery to end and tried to make that happen. We will study this movement in more depth soon. We have run across Walker before in the course. Do any of you remember when?"

A few students said, "When we visited the Black Heritage Trail on our field trip." That visit had occurred about six weeks earlier. I scheduled it such a long time before the unit on Walker and the abolitionists because I was concerned about it being too cold in December for the students to pay attention as they walked around the part of Boston—Beacon Hill— where the African American community of free blacks lived in the early to mid-nineteenth century. (The cold had been a problem on a previous field trip.) The students learned about several prominent Boston-area African Americans and community landmarks on the tour. Many of the students were particularly taken with several examples of the black community sheltering runaway slaves, or storming a facility in which slaves were being held for deportation back to their master (in the period when the Fugitive Slave Law of 1850 was in force). They were enthralled by the dramatic and successful escape by train and boat of a slave couple, Ellen and William Craft, in which the light-skinned Ellen pretended to be a white man and William pretended to be her servant. They learned about the abolitionist presence in Boston, among both blacks and whites, though one of the students, Sherilyn, objected that the tour guide seemed to be downplaying the economic dependence of the North on Southern slavery, and also to be implying that there was greater support among white Bostonians for the abolitionist cause. I was glad that the students remembered Walker's name from this earlier field trip.

I provided a little background. "Walker was born in Wilmington, North Carolina, around 1796. He was free because his mother was free; even though his father was a slave, the laws of North Carolina gave the child the same status as the mother rather than the father. (The overall purpose of this law was to make sure that the children of slave women would be slaves, no matter whether the father was free or not). Walker traveled through the South and developed a very strong hatred of slavery based on what he saw. He thought American racial slavery was the worst form of inhumanity any one group of people had ever perpetrated on another group.

"There was also a slave rebellion planned in 1800 not far away from Wilmington, in Richmond, Virginia, organized by a slave named Gabriel Prosser. We will study that rebellion later. Walker was probably influenced by it. Walker spent some time in Charleston, South Carolina, and may have had a small role in another attempted rebellion there in 1822. Unfortunately, not much is known about David Walker's life before he moved to Boston in 1825, so we can't be sure about his role in the 1822 rebellion, or other facts of his early life.

"One thing that influenced this spirit of rebellion among slaves, and also greatly influenced David Walker, had to do with religion. Slaves in the Wilmington area had founded a Methodist church there. Methodism was a branch of Protestant Christianity that emphasized direct religious experience, and believed in the spiritual equality of all God's children, black as well as white. Methodism had come over to America from England in the 1770s. It was part of the evangelical movement that swept both North and South in that period, and that included Baptists as well. The movement welcomed slaves as well as whites.

"In their early years here, Methodists took a strong stand against slavery, and some congregations even said that white Methodists had to free their slaves. Methodist congregations in the South included slaves, free blacks, and whites. However, almost immediately pro-slavery Southern whites pushed back, and over time white Methodists began to feel the pressure to accommodate to slavery. The Methodist opposition to slavery softened.

"Nevertheless, David Walker remained a devout Methodist his whole life. He eventually affiliated with the new African Methodist Episcopal, or AME, denomination founded by Richard Allen in Philadelphia in 1816. Richard Allen was one of the most important African American religious leaders in American history. Unlike most other Christian congregations, the one Allen founded was for blacks only. At first the blacks in Philadelphia were reluctant to go along with a black-only denomination. But in a famous incident around 1792, the white leaders of St. George's, a Methodist church that had allowed black parishioners, demanded that blacks sit apart in the back of the church, and then in a separate balcony that had been built for that purpose. This led to a walkout from the church, and eventually to Allen's founding of the AME denomination, and blacks all over the Northeast began to form their own black-only churches.[8] As most of you know, the AME church is still a very important institution in the African American community. Do any of you go to one of the AME churches in Cambridge?"

Two students raised their hands.

"Walker was a great admirer of Richard Allen. In Walker's *Appeal*, which you read a part of for today's class, he said that he thought Allen was the greatest religious leader of black people who had ever lived.[9] Walker, like Allen, saw both Christianity in its Methodist form and African American church institutions as foundations for black liberation and equality."

> *Hannah*: "Why would slaves and blacks be interested in Christianity or see any value in it, when we saw that slave owners used Christianity to justify slavery [as we had discussed in earlier classes]? Christianity was such a powerful part of the system that oppressed them.
> *Sherilyn*: Jesus too was oppressed, as blacks were, and God was on the side of oppressed people, who would eventually triumph over their oppression with God's help. This is Walker's view."
> *Jacques*: Maybe the slaves saw something different in Christianity, something that the slave owners missed.

It is good that the students can have an intelligent, probing, and critical discussion of religion like this. Hannah (whose religious affiliation I do not know, but one of her parents is Jewish and one not) raises a very important historical question, and it is one that could make some Christian students, like Sherilyn, defensive. But Sherilyn isn't defensive. Making use of Walker, she explains why slaves might have seen Christianity as a powerful supportive religion for them. And Jacques (whose religious views I do not know, but who was brought up Catholic) specifically addresses the historical issue of slave versus slave-owner understandings of the same religion. On a more general level, it is good that the students see that different groups can get different messages from the same religion. That is an important insight about religion in relation to social groupings in society, and is very much part of the way religion is deeply interwoven with race in American history. Both race and religion are enormously sensitive areas, yet without teaching about them, students are deprived of vital understandings and opportunities for mutual enlightenment.

It is also important that students be able to think critically about both their own religion and other faiths. The latter involves adopting in imagination the point of view of a group to which you do not belong and then thinking from that vantage point, a crucial higher-order thinking ability. In a country like the United States, with its dazzling plurality of religions and faiths, this aspect of critical thinking is vital for students to learn. I felt the students in my class were taking important steps down that road.

I continued with my lecture on Walker. "By 1825, Walker had made his way to the free black community in Boston. He owned a used clothing store. On our field trip we saw a house where he gave antislavery speeches; I can't remember if it was the same as his store. He became the Boston agent for *Freedom's Journal*, the first black American newspaper, which was based in New York. The paper aimed to serve the entire free black population of the United States with its anti-slavery stance. Walker also joined a local black Methodist church, whose minister was the fiery antislavery preacher Samuel Snowden, an ally of the famous white Boston-based abolitionist William Lloyd Garrison. Walker quickly became an important figure in the well-organized black community, and especially in abolitionist circles. He helped to organize an annual parade in the Beacon Hill area of Boston—the area we walked around on our Black Heritage Trail field trip—home to the African American community (including himself) at the time. The parade celebrated Haitian independence (achieved in 1804) and the end of slavery in Massachusetts (in 1783)."

I hoped that Walker's connection to the abolitionist movement, and his and its connection to Boston, would spark some interest and pride in the students. I also hoped this pride would cut across the other differences in the class—of racial, socioeconomic, and immigrant status. I was inviting the students to think of themselves as "Bostonians," an identity most could share. And through that identity, they could think that they were inheritors of a tradition that took a strong stand against slavery and racism. Part of that tradition, which I emphasized in our later unit on the abolitionist movement, was the interracial nature of that movement. Given the more recent historical image of Boston as the site of protracted white resistance to busing for school integration in the 1970s, I was hoping to put in place a counternarrative about racial cooperation in resistance to racism that might challenge that one to some degree. (At the same time, I tried to heed the point Sherilyn made on the field trip—not to overstate general white support for abolitionism, which was far from extensive.)

I also was aware that in many traditional history textbooks, the abolitionist movement is portrayed as an overwhelmingly white movement. Garrison's name is well known, but not Walker's (or Snowden's). I wanted to make sure the students became well aware of Walker as an important abolitionist, although his influence was cut short by his premature death in 1830 of consumption (tuberculosis).[10] Walker himself was very aware of the importance of his being black in the struggle against slavery, and I brought this to the students' attention.

"In 1829, Walker published his famous work, the *Appeal to the Coloured Citizens of the World but in Particular, and Very Expressly, to Those of the United States of America*. Nothing like this vehement, outraged, and militant abolitionist manifesto had ever been published before, though blacks had begun to write against slavery. The *Appeal* challenges head-on the idea that blacks are inferior to whites, and attacks the arguments whites had used to back up this false idea. Walker also argues that the form of slavery endured by American blacks rendered them 'the most degraded, wretched, and abject set of beings that ever lived since the world began, and I pray God that none like us ever may live again until time shall be no more.'[11] Walker compares American slavery to that of the ancient Greeks. Part of what makes American slaves so degraded is that whites have tried to teach them that they are inferior beings who deserve nothing better; this ideology had no counterpart in the Greek slave system.

"Walker explicitly calls for slaves to overthrow the system of slavery by force. He uses Christianity to argue for the equality of blacks and whites. He strongly claims that the U.S. belongs to blacks as well as whites. He vehemently rejects the tendency among some African Americans (inside the abolitionist movement and out) to support white colonization schemes, such as Jefferson favored, that involved sending blacks to Africa or elsewhere outside the U.S.

"Walker's main intended audience for the book was black Americans, slave and free. He found ways to get his book into the hands of Southern blacks. Remember when our guide on the field trip told us about sailors sewing copies of his book into their clothes to deliver them to contacts in Southern ports? ['Yeah, that was dope,' Jean-Paul said.] Walker's success in distributing his book resulted in state laws quarantining all black sailors entering Georgia ports and punishing anyone bringing 'seditious literature' into the state. Also, partly because of the rebellious atmosphere among slaves throughout the coastal South during this period, Walker's *Appeal* prompted several states to strengthen their laws against slaves' learning to read, and to make it a crime to circulate what the ruling elites regarded as inflammatory literature. But the book did find its way into some slaves' hands or hearing."

—⁓—

In the *Appeal* Walker discusses Jefferson's remarks about blacks in *Notes on the State of Virginia*. I had the students read that section. (Jefferson had died in 1826, a few years before publication of the *Appeal*.) Walker accurately saw Jefferson as a central figure in making racist ideas about black inferiority intellectually respectable. Walker exhorts his readers to read Jefferson's book and to learn how to refute its arguments. He believed that black liberation required blacks themselves to produce arguments against Jefferson. I called this passage to the students' attention:

> We and the world wish to see the charges of Mr. Jefferson refuted by the blacks themselves, according to their chance [i.e., opportunity]; for we must remember that what the whites have written respecting this subject is other men's labors, and did not emanate from the blacks. I know well, that there are some talents and learning among the coloured people of this country, which we have not had a chance to develop, in consequence of our oppression; but our oppression ought not to hinder us from acquiring all we can.[12]

When I highlighted Walker's urging blacks to do this intellectual work, Jacques raised his hand. He said, "If slavery was anything like what Mary Prince described in her memoir about being a slave in the Caribbean—working from before dawn until dusk, always to the point of exhaustion—slaves would not have an extra second or energy to do any reading of Jefferson's book or the learning necessary to show what is wrong with what he says."

I admired this remark. It was characteristic of Jacques to situate something we were currently learning in relation to something we had learned earlier. This is a central goal of teaching, a pillar of the higher-order thinking that minority and low-income students often fail to be educated to master to nearly an adequate degree. Students do not generally make connections between different readings without a lot of help—without being explicitly encouraged to relate the author they are reading to a previous author. What was striking about Jacques was that he did so much of this internalizing on his own. He had already brought Mary Prince and her appalling experience of slavery in the Caribbean into his own mental scaffolding concerning what slavery is, so it was available to help him think about the new ideas he was getting from Walker.

I liked Walker's challenge to blacks to learn to understand and criticize ideas that were used to keep them down. He was testifying to the important civic role of intellectuality, of working with ideas. Ideas matter. They can help to keep a whole people in misery. What Walker was saying fit nicely into the trajectory and point of my course. Students had learned from our science unit that the traditional idea of race was false; and they had learned from the history of slavery where that idea came from and the unjust purposes to which it was put.

I thought it would be valuable and interesting for the students to see how black American thinkers took this idea of race seriously, and believed it important to attack and refute. Those blacks thought the struggle against racism, as we would call it, involved understanding the idea of race, showing how it was used to oppress black (and other nonwhite) people, and exposing its intellectual defects. In the weeks following this unit on Walker, the class would study slave escapes, slave rebellions, and more about the abolitionist movement. I knew many of the students were already somewhat familiar with these forms of resistance to slavery. But I wanted them to see that resistance to slavery needed to take many different forms, and that challenging racist ideas was one of them.

Studying Walker (and Banneker) helped me bring the critical thinking tools of my discipline of philosophy into the course. I wanted students to see that ideas could be examined, analyzed, broken down into parts, and further scrutinized—even when the ideas themselves were very emotionally charged. Even my college students sometimes react against a text because they see or sense that it insults a group or violates their own values in some other way. Yet when I ask them what exactly is false or wrong with the text, they cannot always pinpoint it. Perhaps they say "it's racist," but that very general and imprecise characterization doesn't identify exactly where and how the author goes wrong. I wanted my high school students to experience the power in the ability to take a heinous idea, examine it dispassionately, and be able to state clearly and convincingly what is wrong with it.

These skills are a particularly good example of the higher-order critical thinking that educators agree is essential to citizenship. Citizens need to be able to evaluate ideas, policies, and political ideals. They need to know how to assess the realities in which they live, or in which other people lived in the past, in light of those ideas. When students are assigned to classes according to some measure of prior achievement, those in the highest "level" are usually taught these critical thinking and civic skills, but those in lower tracks are generally not.[13] The gap in civic skills is an important part of the "achievement gap" among racial groups, and is detrimental to equality of informed participation in civic life.[14] The philosophical analysis of Banneker and Walker's ideas is one way a course like mine can enhance students' critical thinking and civic skills.

But analyzing arguments such as those by Jefferson, which say that blacks are inferior to whites, raises the worry I voiced at the beginning. To take that argument seriously might seem to be giving it some legitimacy. Even just to state the argument—although the whole point of the exercise is to show what is wrong with it—might seem to give it recognition it does not deserve. I was concerned that the recognition and the legitimacy might do psychic harm to the black students, and moral harm to the nonblack students by lending credence to this immoral belief.

At the start of this chapter I mentioned Steele's and others' research that seems to show that many black students suspect that many nonblacks regard them as intellectually inferior. I did not want to reinforce that suspicion. Steele does not say that the black students believe that stereotype about themselves. He just says that worrying about being judged by others in light of it undermines black students' ability to perform to their potential in academic settings. But if the stereotype is out there in the culture, as Steele assumes, I worried that at the very least many black students were unsure that it was not true, even if they did not believe it themselves. And in a study by the educational anthropologist John Ogbu, 82 percent of black students surveyed in Oakland, California, reported that some member of their family had said that blacks were not as smart as whites.[15] I did not want to reinforce the impression that the view that blacks are inferior might actually be true.

The problem would have been much worse if I had taken a "controversial issues" approach to the material. That approach involves taking a topic on which people disagree and having students become much more informed about it, becoming capable of recognizing and producing arguments on both sides. The approach is often used with issues like abortion, capital punishment, oil drilling, welfare, taxation, and affirmative action. The controversial issues framework is valuable for civic education and can serve several educational goals—helping students to be knowledgeable about issues facing their society on which people differ; encouraging civic engagement through involvement in particular issues; learning sensitivity and respect for people with whom you disagree; learning skills of deliberation and argument construction.

The controversial issues framework works for issues on which reasonable people disagree. It implicitly affirms that both sides of whatever issue is on the table are intellectually and morally viable. This is precisely why it is *not* a suitable framework for studying the view that blacks are inferior to whites. The harms I was worried about contributing to—creating or playing into black students' worries about being intellectually incapable, or being thought incapable by others, and creating or legitimating those same views in nonblack students—would be tremendously magnified if I presented that issue as one on which reasonable people could believe that blacks are actually intellectually inferior.

The framework I used did not provide any such legitimacy to that view. I presented Jefferson's view as one that we know to be false, just as we know that slavery is morally wrong even though in Jefferson's time many whites thought it was not. I said to the students that we wanted to see how the two black thinkers tried to prove Jefferson's views were wrong. But I wasn't sure this approach was sufficient to negate any whiff of credibility that this view might receive simply from being stated, or from being presented as something that needed to be criticized as Banneker and Walker did. What I hoped was that showing how Jefferson's views were taken apart by Banneker and Walker—within the general setting of the course, which from various angles critiqued the idea of race itself—and asking students to reproduce and analyze those arguments would have the cumulative effect of weakening the idea of black inferiority to a much greater extent than it might be affirmed merely by being seriously addressed in the class.

—⚉—

Banneker and Walker agree on the importance of producing reasoned arguments that challenge the ideology of black inferiority. The ways they present their arguments are completely different. We saw Banneker's calm and even deferential tone in writing to Jefferson. Walker's *Appeal*, very much in contrast, is in part a fiery sermon, mainly meant to rouse blacks to take action against their oppression, and (perhaps secondarily) to call whites to live rightly and according to the true principles of Christianity for the salvation of their souls.

The writing assignment I gave the class focused on one passage typical of Walker's outraged tone in his intellectual challenge to Jefferson:

> [W]hen that hour arrives [for gaining our freedom and natural right] and you move, be not afraid or dismayed; for be you assured that Jesus Christ the King of heaven and of earth who is the God of justice and of armies, will surely go before you. And those enemies who for hundreds of years have stolen our *rights*, and kept us ignorant of Him and His divine worship, he will remove. Millions of whom are, to this day, so ignorant and avaricious, that they cannot conceive how God can have an attribute of justice, and show mercy to us because it pleased Him to make us black—which color Mr. Jefferson calls unfortunate!!!!!! As though we are not as thankful to our God, for having made us as it pleased himself as they (the whites) are for having made them white. They think because they hold us in their infernal chains of slavery, that we wish to be white or of their color—but they are dreadfully deceived—we wish to be just as it pleased our Creator to have made us, and no avaricious and unmerciful wretches have any business to make slaves of, or hold us in slavery. How would they like for us to make slaves of or hold them in cruel slavery, and murder them as they do us?—But is Mr. Jefferson's assertion true? Viz. "that it is unfortunate for us that our creator has been pleased to make us *black*."[16]

Here is the writing assignment I gave on this passage: "Walker is critical of Jefferson's statement 'that it is unfortunate for us [blacks] that our Creator has been pleased to make us black.' And he is also critical of whites for thinking that blacks wish to be white in color. (a) Explain Walker's criticisms of Jefferson's statement, and (b) explain Walker's criticisms of the whites' view just stated."

Sherilyn answered in this way:

> What Walker is saying is that Jefferson believed that Blacks wanted to be more than free but that they wish they could be white. That even the black race wishes to be white. Now Walker's response to Jefferson is that this is not true. Just because whites have blacks enslaved does not mean that they wish to be white. They just wish for the same freedoms that their God gave to the whites, the freedom to live and not be locked under bondage. He is saying that the black race will come up and the white race should be ashamed for their treatment of blacks because they would not want to be treated the same. Walker argues

against Jefferson's view on not just the desire for freedom but Walker stands up for the color which he is.

Sherilyn grasps the basic logic of Walker's argument. Walker says that Jefferson seems to think that because blacks are so miserable in being enslaved by whites, they must wish to be white. But, Walker says, they do not wish to be white, but only to have the freedom "to live and not be locked under bondage." Although she could have stated it more clearly, Sherilyn sees that Walker is saying that Jefferson confuses whether blacks want to be free with whether they want to be white. She also recognizes Walker's appeal to a Kantian or golden rule–like argument that whites would not want to be treated as blacks are, and so they should not treat blacks in that way.

Marie answered in this way:

The whites' view is that blacks want to be whites. Blacks are not grateful for our color. Walker's response to the white view is that blacks don't want to be white, just because whites enchained blacks because of their color they think that blacks blame the creator for it. Walker said that how would whites feel if we enslave them and killed them because of the color of their skin? Blacks aren't mad at the creator, they're mad at the whites for enslaving them.

Marie gets off to a good start, stating the whites' view (that blacks want to be white) and Walker's rejection of this view. And she suggests a reason *why* whites might have thought that blacks wanted to be white, namely that blacks had been enslaved because of their color, so they might have wished not to be that color. This shows some imagination on Marie's part. However, it is not explicitly in Walker's argument. He does not say that blacks are enslaved and oppressed *because of* their skin color. In the passage we read, Walker does not say why blacks are enslaved, only what is bad about their being enslaved. But it is reasonable of Marie to infer that he is saying blacks are enslaved because of their race.

Marie does not distinguish quite as clearly as Sherilyn does when she is presenting Jefferson's argument, or the view of whites, and when she is presenting Walker's answers to these arguments. This is a very basic but crucial academic skill that takes practice to learn. Many of my college students have not mastered it before they take some philosophy courses. It requires recognizing that one author can state a view that he himself does not believe, but which is the view of a different author. And he can then go on to say what he thinks about what that second author has said. It is often tricky to see when this is going on in a passage of text, and to learn to distinguish the different authors' views. Walker weaves his own beliefs around views he attributes to whites, or to Jefferson, and it takes some work to clearly distinguish his views from theirs.

Both young women have yet to fully acquire and refine the skills of argument analysis, but they are well on their way, Sherilyn a bit more in this assignment. At the same time, both girls basically understand the passage and the fundamental logic of Walker's own argument—that even though the reason blacks are not free has something to do with their being black, blacks do not want to be white, but only to be free.

Marie also follows Sherilyn in focusing on the moral element that Walker discusses, but which I did not explicitly ask about in the assignment. Sherilyn says whites should be ashamed because they should see that they would not want to be treated by blacks the way they treat blacks. Marie poses the rhetorical question—"how would whites feel if we enslaved them"? In using "we," and earlier when she says "our color," Marie seems to be putting her own racial identity into her answer. (In the first instance she might be referring only to Walker's own invoking the blacks of his time; but the second does not allow for this ambiguity.)

Some other black students also brought in their own racial identity. Mirvole did so in this answer to a slightly different question: "Walker is basically making the point that the white man along with the system has reduced us to deplorable conditions and then insulted us even further by saying we are not part of the human family."

This personalizing of their answers did not mean these students showed a greater understanding of the issues than nonblack students, nor, on the other side, that their personalizing was getting in the way of their analyzing the argument objectively. I hoped it meant that these students were more definitely identifying with the criticisms that Walker was making of Jefferson—and thereby were assembling ammunition for undermining any hint of black inferiority in their own minds. It suggested to me that these students were seeing the importance of the issues, and not just doing an assignment. But this could be just as true for students who do not identify with any historical agents within a given assignment.

I wonder, however, if this kind of personalized answer might worry some educators, especially but not only white ones, that the study of slavery will inflame antiwhite emotions in black students. If black students identify with slaves, or blacks in the slave era, mightn't this encourage hostility toward whites, especially in less mature high school students? It's a complex issue, and we will look at it again in chapter 10. But one point is relevant here. The students who did place themselves back in time within their answers did not use that perspective to express any more hostility toward whites than did other black students; and indeed, none of them expressed any generalized antiwhite hostility at all. (Perhaps they would have responded somewhat differently had I been a black teacher.) They appropriately recognized the hostility Walker himself expressed, but that is a different matter. I wanted students to read Walker in part to see how it made perfect sense for a slave-era black person to feel hatred for large numbers of white people. Why shouldn't he? Walker's feelings about white people of his era are well-founded in his understanding of slavery, and of white people's use of Christianity both to defend it and to make it more onerous by demeaning the humanity of black people.

—⁓—

In a later class discussion about Walker, we focused more on his saying that whites keep blacks in bondage, and have done so for hundreds of years. Given the times in which Walker was writing, and his desire to rouse blacks to action against slavery, there is nothing problematic about this general statement about white people. Nevertheless, in the class I had tried to sensitize the students to the need to be careful when generalizing about racial groups. So, while reminding them of Walker's specific context, I ask whether they think it in some way unfair of Walker to talk about "whites" in this general way.

> *Ebony*: I don't think that he meant all white people when he said this.
> *Cristina*: Well, exactly which whites did he mean, then?
> *Sherilyn*: Maybe all the white people Walker had met were actually racist, so it would be reasonable for him to generalize that way.

I point out that since Walker was involved in the abolitionist movement in Boston, he was very aware of white people like Garrison, who devoted themselves to the abolitionist cause.

> *Clara*: Walker just meant *most* white people, which would make the statement true, since most white people in the U.S. did support slavery, even if only a minority had slaves themselves.

Jacques: In a way talking about white people in such a general way un-
dercuts what Walker was arguing because Walker is criticizing black
people being seen as a group and being seen as inferior as a group—
yet in a way he is saying that white people as a group are deficient.

The students are rising to the challenge of trying to situate what
Walker said in his historical context while grappling with the issue of
racial generalizations. They all see the issue that can be raised here, and
I think all are more sensitized to the need to be careful when you make
generalizations about large groups of people, and especially racial groups.

Jacques's insight is particularly noteworthy, coming from him. Jacques
is acutely sensitive to the ways that blacks were indeed oppressed as a
group, and still suffer from group-based discrimination. He is not rejecting talking about groups, nor does he want to pull back from Walker's
basic point that whites have oppressed blacks. But Jacques is seeing a
danger in not being more careful about how broad you want to make
your generalizations about groups. It matters whether you say *all*, or
most, of a group. It matters that you try to be more careful about saying
that some members of the group are *not* encompassed by your generalization. And he is seeing an analogy between black people as a group
being seen as inferior, and Walker's sometimes (but not always) seeing
whites as hopelessly and unchangeably greedy and cruel.

I think Jacques is being affected by the general critique of race that
is central to the class. That critique makes you suspicious of any racial
generalization, because you see how race has been the home to so many
false generalizations. This does not mean that you can never make generalizations about racial groups. If we understand racial groups as "racialized groups"—groups that have been seen as and treated as if they were
races—then these are real groups, and we can say something about them.
We can investigate, for example, the average income of one racialized
group compared (or not) to another. For example, in 2010 the median
white (non-Hispanic) household income was $54,620; black, $32,068;
Hispanic, $37,759; and Asian, $64,308.[17] And social scientists can take
surveys that reveal what percentage of whites or Asians or blacks (or ethnic subgroups, such as Italian-Americans or Jamaicans) hold a certain
racist view.

What the critique of race tells us about these generalizations is that if
they are true, it is not because of something inherent in the genetics or
biology of the group in question. It is just a sociological fact about them.

The critique of race should guide us to avoid any implication of "racial inherency" when we make generalizations. To put it briefly, we must recognize (1) any true racial generalization will be true only of *averages* or *means* of groups, not of every single member of the group; and (2) when they are true, they will be true for sociohistorical reasons, not for genetic reasons, as the case of income illustrates.[18]

Walker himself, for all his broad condemnation of whites, does not seem to be saying that the greed and cruelty he sees in their behavior are part of their racial nature. He thinks that whites can see the light, repent of their sins, and treat blacks justly. Unlike Jefferson, he believed blacks and whites were capable of sharing the American society. True, he did not think it was very likely that whites would transform themselves in this way. But as a Christian, he thought it was possible for whites to be morally transformed, that Christianity would have to be part of this process, and that it was worth striving for.

I received some confirmation that the way I was teaching students about Jefferson, Banneker, and Walker would help the black students feel more confident in rejecting a suspicion of their own racial inferiority. Justine, the class teaching assistant, who was also a student in the class herself several years earlier, wrote in a retrospective look at the class several years later when she was a student of mine at UMass: "I think for many of us who were Black it was a relief to learn that we were not inferior, and that the idea of race was built on false premises." Justine implies that she is speaking not only for herself when she expresses this relief, and virtually says that she and others either actually regarded themselves as racially inferior, or at best were far from sure they weren't. She implies that they were carrying this burden around with them, and the course provided some relief from it.

I was also pleased that Justine recognized the connection between the idea of black inferiority and the historical idea of race itself. In a passage from her paper immediately before the one I just quoted, she speaks of learning about "the evolution of the idea of race" in the course. I had tried with this evolution to show that the idea that the groups we think of as "races" or "racial groups" have significant group differences in intelligence, moral character, and other important human characteristics is entirely false. Justine did not single out our exercise on Banneker, Walker, and Jefferson, and in fact she was right that the critique of black inferiority was a central theme in the whole course—though nowhere was it so sharply focused as in this unit. Justine's reflections reinforced my feeling that doing head-on battle with Jefferson's ideas could actually help black students deal with their doubts about their own abilities, and about whether nature consigned their race to inferior capabilities.[19]

—⚬—

Let me close with some brief thoughts on Claude Steele's work, which has had an enormous impact on thinking about race, and group identities more generally, in education. Steele is not concerned with blacks who harbor internalized, race-based self-doubts. What he is interested in is the way that blacks who lack self-doubt can nevertheless be derailed in their schoolwork by a concern that *others* see them as inferior. He and his colleagues have carried out a large number of diverse experiments that seem to clinch the case that a concern about group-based stereotypes alleging inferiority can interfere with the best performance of black students, or members of any group.

With his focus on how others view them, rather than the subjects' own self-doubts, Steele looks for ways to create spaces free of stereotype threat where students can perform according to their own abilities, unencumbered by a diversion of their energy and focus caused by worrying how others in those spaces will view them.[20] For example, a test may be presented not as an assessment of the test-taker's ability, but as testing the test itself. Or an instructor may assure a student that she is confident he is capable of doing well on a difficult assignment.

What I was concerned with in my class is distinct from, and complementary to, Steele's diagnosis and recommendations. I was worried about black students who do have self-doubts. The self-doubts range on a spectrum from those who have fully bought into the stereotype that they are inferior (like the adults reported by the Oakland students in the study mentioned earlier in the chapter) to those who are not totally sure the stereotype is false, though they don't affirmatively believe it either. (Perhaps this is Justine's view.) These students need something different from the race-free, or stereotype-free, zone, since for them the problem is inside themselves. It is not just a worry about what others think of them (although it may be that also). I am suggesting that giving such students the intellectual tools to see that the idea that blacks are less intelligent than whites simply isn't true will help them psychically. They will not be certain they are out from under the stereotype until they are convinced through their own intellectual effort and understanding that this stereotype is entirely false. In a way, what I propose is a version of what David Walker was trying to rouse his fellow blacks to do—to face stated claims of black inferiority and to develop arguments to show that those claims are false.

Having the intellectual tools to see that a stereotype of your group is false has two distinct effects. One is that it helps relieve the individual student of the harmful repercussions of self-doubt about her abilities, which can range from simply not performing up to your abilities—the effect with which Steele is also concerned—to the extreme of giving up on academics entirely and disidentifying with that entire domain.[21] And it can depress the student's sense of self-worth and self-esteem as well. When Justine says she is relieved to learn that blacks are not inferior, presumably this helps her as an individual student to not be hindered by self-doubt.

But Justine is reporting a second effect when she says that "for many of us who were Black it was a relief to learn that we were not inferior." It helps her to regard her entire group in a more positive light—as being as capable as whites, a capability that racist ideology denies. So she changes her view both of herself and of her group when she is able to shed her worry that blacks are inferior.

The individual effect and the group effect are different. It is perfectly possible for a particular black student to feel sure the stereotype does not apply to her—and yet not to abandon the view that blacks as a group are intellectually inferior to whites. This may well have happened with many of Steele's high-achieving students. They may each think that they themselves are exceptions to the generalization that blacks are intellectually inferior—after all, they have performed well enough to be admitted to very selective colleges—but that the generalization is still true of blacks as a whole.

This individual distancing from a stereotype is a very familiar process, and we saw it on the first day's discussion of stereotypes, if only implicitly (see chapter 1). Some students complained about stereotypes because they did not think they themselves fit that description. But that does not mean they were complaining that the stereotype was false with regard to the whole group. Ebony could well have thought that most blacks were indeed "lower class" even if she herself wasn't. Anna could have thought the same of whites being "preppy," even if she herself was not. We can't tell whether the students thought this way or not; but they could have. Their main concern in that discussion was to deny that the stereotype applied to themselves, not so much to challenge the stereotype itself. This distinction between thinking that a stereotype is not true *of your group as a whole* and that, whether it is true or not, it *does not apply to you yourself* may not matter for the performance of the individual black students Steele is concerned with. I am in no way questioning that. But only a tiny minority of the black students in my class went to really selective colleges (the kind whose students Steele mainly studied). I wanted to help equip them to puncture the group stereotype itself, and thereby relieve their own race-based self-doubts. Of course I am not saying I fully achieved that goal, which could in any case not be accomplished in a single class, or even in school as a whole. But Steele's emphasis on getting individual members of the group into stereotype-free spaces would not have had the reach that I was hoping for from my approach. At the same time, I recognize that even someone who is fully convinced of the falseness of a stereotype of her group may still be subject to stereotype threat—the concern that others judge you in terms of the stereotype whether you believe it yourself or not. So I think we need both—tools to criticize stereotypes, recognizing that one might have internalized them, and initiatives to keep social stereotypes at bay in students' academic lives.

Returning to the class, of course the exercise of examining Walker's arguments against Jefferson was not only for the black students. Latino students would certainly have reason to think that many non-Latinos questioned the intelligence or capability of Latino students. We have seen that the "achievement gap" is between whites and Asians on one side and Latinos and blacks on the other. More generally, it is important for all students to learn the falsity of beliefs about innate intellectual differences between racial groups. It is damaging from both a moral and a civic standpoint to hold such beliefs because they make it much more difficult to treat those from other groups as equals. And it dulls your conscience about the need for all groups to be treated equally in society. So I thought it would help students from all groups to be able to recognize the arguments that challenge Jefferson's views about black inferiority as well as formulate their own critiques.

Like Theresa Perry, I worried earlier whether the message of black intellectual equality could be adequately conveyed outside of all-black educational settings, leaving aside for the moment the other personal, moral, and civic advantages of racially mixed schools and classes (discussed in the conclusion). Perhaps you cannot duplicate the full focus on black equality that is possible in an all-black school. But it seems to me that black students can pick up a message of equality taught to a mixed class. That message is not only to help black students achieve at their highest levels, nor is it the only variable relevant to their performance.

It is a message required by the legacy of our particular history in the United States, and thus a responsibility of schooling more generally. To build a society based on equality, all have to internalize the message that while race does mark *socioeconomic* inequalities, but it does not mark *inherent* inequalities or differences. Although blacks are most damaged by the failure to reject inherent black inequality, all students are morally, civically, and personally damaged by an inability to see those of all other groups as equals.

Any serious engagement with race and racism has to take on the ideology of black inferiority. I hoped that studying both the abolitionist David Walker's fierce challenge to Jefferson's views of black inferiority, and Banneker's respectful but pointed admonitions to Jefferson to follow his egalitarian philosophy consistently, would model black challenges to the ideology of black inferiority; and that examining the arguments of these two thinkers would help give all students tools to make their own critique.

8 Reflections on Expectations and Potential

Different Students, Different Needs

As I taught students from different backgrounds and saw them grappling with difficult material, I began to reflect on current debates about how to close the racial achievement gap—so called because Asian and white students are, on the average, more likely than blacks and Latinos to meet reasonable standards of academic achievement.[1] "Expectations" have become part of the conventional wisdom about how to close the achievement gap. It is often said that many teachers, especially in urban schools, have low expectations of their black and Latino students, and that this at least partly explains why those students do not perform better. All students respond to teacher expectations, and some research suggests that black students respond more than white students. For example, one study by Ronald Ferguson finds that black students say they do schoolwork to please their teacher, while whites to a much greater extent say they do it to please their parents.[2] If so, then presumably the black students are more affected by what the teacher expects of them.

Yet the constant mantra of "high expectations" in education circles also worries me. For starters, it can mean very different things. It can mean a teacher evaluates students' work according to a high standard, giving low grades to those who do not perform up to that standard. But the teacher could do this without really helping students get from where they are to the standard she is setting. That wouldn't really be different from being a "tough grader," and yet it is one way "high expectations" is sometimes understood that is not particularly constructive.

"High expectations" is also often taken to mean aiming to get students to perform well on standardized tests. But this is much too narrow a goal. The expectations that seem to me worth talking about are tied to rich and comprehensive educational aims and standards that include critical thinking, deep historical understanding, the ability to see things from different points of view, and other elements of higher-order thinking—as well as moral growth, civic capabilities, and personal enrichment.

Equally troubling is the "silver bullet" way of thinking about education, implying that some single change, like having high expectations of students, can "fix" our educational problems and close the achievement gap.

In this chapter I describe some of my interactions with five students to see what light they throw on the issue of expectations. Individual contact was a particularly challenging aspect of my teaching arrangement. I did not have a classroom of my own. I had to vacate my borrowed classroom right after my class was over. I had nowhere to hang around and work at the high school (and on many days had to get to the university right after class anyway). With some exceptions, I mostly got to know the students who seemed to need the most help from me.

NORRIS

In an educational autobiography he wrote at the beginning of the course, Norris presented himself as a "good student" but also one who "can tend to slack and act like a fair student." He said that his parents "make sure I always do my homework and help me stay focused" and that his friends help him with his schoolwork. Norris seemed very thoughtful about his attempt to take on the identity of a serious student, and honest about the struggles that had gone into this attempt. But by the third week of our course, Norris had not turned in any work besides the educational autobiography.

I arranged to meet with Norris one morning before first period, the only time I could generally have such meetings. Norris told me my course was his only academic course this semester. He was interested in the music business and wanted to attend a music college. When students find the course rough going, the one card I can usually play is that the work in my course is exactly what they can expect in college, so they may as well try to take it on now. This argument did not work with Norris, who was aiming for a college with a minimal academic program.

A few weeks later, he told Justine, my teaching assistant, that he was planning to drop the class. With the help of his guidance counselor, Mr. Neary, I persuaded him not to. Justine and I spent a good deal of time talking about Norris in our debriefing and planning meetings (two or three times a week). She worked at a community center not far from Norris's home, and she tried to get him to come in for tutoring. Over the semester he did that a few times, but not nearly as many as Justine arranged with him.

Throughout the first three quarters, Norris's engagement with the class had ups and downs, mostly the latter, although every once in a while he would turn in satisfactory work or say something interesting and insightful in class. Once he told Justine, "There are times that I'm not interested in what I'm doing, and right now I'm not interested in school." He wasn't being defiant, just reporting what he felt, or thought he felt. Justine eventually became frustrated, and she was not sure there was any point in putting so much energy into this one kid who was showing so little interest.

But in the fourth quarter something completely unexpected happened. Leila, the African student, forwarded to me an e-mail message from Norris saying that even though he had failed all three previous marking periods, he wanted to get back on track. Leila had helped him do some reading questions, and he turned them in soon after, proudly telling me that he had stayed up late to do them. Leila also said, "Norris and I are going to meet up and do our homework at least four times a week." She said that she has known Norris since elementary school, and that he is like a brother to her. "I'm not going to let him down," she said to me.

Leila's intervention seemed to help put Norris over the top. He started to do some work, made up some past work, and kept doing reading questions. In January he told Mr. Neary how proud he was of getting back on track. He completed the marking period with a C. The way his friendship with Leila became such a fantastic resource for him was really moving. It could not be typical among students to have a friend who will meet with you four times a week to help you do homework, and intercede with your teacher to arrange to make up for lost work. But perhaps we should be more attuned to ways to facilitate this.

ANTONINE

Antonine approached me to say that she did not know how to do the race and science assignment, which was really difficult, and would I help her. Knowing what you don't understand is a really vital ability that cannot be taken for granted. Many students think they understand when they don't. It may also take a certain degree of personal strength for a student to acknowledge that she doesn't understand. Shame may make her suppress that fact, not only from others but from herself. I was pleased that Antonine recognized her lack of understanding of the assignment, cared enough to do something about it, and was comfortable enough to ask me.

I arranged with Antonine a time before school to get together to discuss the race and science essay. But she didn't show up, and later gave only a feeble excuse. After class that same day, I was sitting on a bench in the hallway near the classroom, doing a postmortem of the class with Justine. Antonine happened by and I buttonholed her about what she was planning to do about the assignment. She reiterated that she didn't understand what I was asking on the paper, and I said, "OK, let's meet at 7:30 before the class."

Antonine replied, "I can't come that time. I have a yearbook meeting at 7:30. How about 7:15?" I said that wouldn't work; fifteen minutes was not enough time to discuss that difficult assignment. Further down the bench sat a security person, Elpidia, whom I had seen around but did not know. Elpidia, whom I had no idea was listening to this conversation, chimed in, saying to Antonine, "What's more important—going to one yearbook meeting or getting serious about your academics?" It was a great moment, and it did the trick. Elpidia had a kind of authority with Antonine that I did not, at least not yet; or maybe she just provided that little extra oomph. It shows that even a security person can play a role in creating a school culture that promotes academic seriousness.

With the help of that tutoring session, Antonine got over the hump with the race and science essay and rose to the intellectual challenge. She was reasonably conscientious about her work in the ensuing months, and did not need further special help from me or Justine.

EBONY

From the beginning Ebony expressed strong opinions on racial questions. She did not like it when someone in class echoed a generalization made in a documentary we watched that blacks were genetically superior as runners. She did not like racial generalizations, whether they were flattering or unflattering to blacks.[3] But she was not incapable of changing her mind, as we saw in the discussion of the Latino dance incident in chapter 4. Once, in an early journal in the course, she said, "I've found that this class makes me change my attitude, even the way I speak and act around people. I stop using the 'N' word as 'slang' because I now know that not only am I oppressing people who had to actually go through slavery, but I am oppressing myself as a black person." But she also sometimes missed the complexity of Smedley's argument.

At one point in class we had been discussing how over time Africans came to be the sole slave labor force in the English colonies, after a period in which other populations (pauperized Irish and English indentured servants, and Native Americans) had served a similar function of providing bound labor and personal service. The students weren't used to looking at slavery in this way—as an economic system whose existence and structure were driven not by racism but by the characteristics of different populations, such as their price and availability, the kind of work they performed before captivity, and a skin color that made it easier for the colonists to find escapees and thus to keep control over the population in question.[4]

To help reinforce this way of thinking about race and slavery, I put the following statement on the board: "Why did the English colonists choose to have Africans as their main labor force starting in the early 18th century, or late 17th?" I offered the class two alternatives, one being the explanation just mentioned. This was the other: "The colonists were racist. They wanted to oppress black people, and the best way to do that was to enslave them." I asked if students thought this second view was the reason for enslaving Africans. Several students said no almost immediately. They had understood and bought into Smedley's explanation. But Ebony wasn't sure. She said, "Well, if anybody thinks that way [the second view], black people do." I appreciated her honesty about this, since it was clear by then that this was not the answer reflecting the class's understanding of the material.

It seemed evident that Ebony was finding it hard to get out of a mind-set that blacks were always being persecuted by whites, who took every opportunity to do so. For example, she seemed to find it difficult to believe that whites and blacks could be allied in a shared cause. This came out again later in our unit on the abolitionist movement. She resisted the idea that blacks and whites worked together as partners in that movement.[5]

In her journals, Ebony gave me what I thought might be some clues to her thinking about race. In one entry, she described an incident in which she and her mother were disrespected by a salesperson, who overcharged them. Her mother protested to the manager and refused a consolation deal the manager offered. Ebony wasn't sure at the time that her mother should have done this, but by the time she wrote the journal, she had come to agree with her mother, and admired her mother's standing up to racial discrimination. I admired it too and expressed that in a comment on her journal entry. But I also wondered if Ebony was picking up a message at home (whether intentionally conveyed or not) that whites are generally not to be trusted, and that this might be part of what made it difficult for her to wrap her mind around certain historical material involving the interaction of blacks and whites.

JACQUES

Jacques got a D+ on the midterm exam. But in class he seemed to show a very good understanding of the material. He could see that race is a constructed and false idea that has been imposed on people, that it has an historical development, and that it did not always exist. He also made creative use of his understanding. For example, in class he asked whether, if the Irish had worked out as a slave-like labor force in the American colonies—if there had been enough of them and if the problems of keeping them under control had been solvable, so that mass African slavery was not necessary—would we have the idea of race that we do have now? That was a fascinating question to put to the material he studied.

I arranged an afterschool session for students who had done badly on the exam, and Jacques showed up. On the exam, many of Jacques's answers had been too short, leaving out crucial explanations of the ideas or connections between different ideas that he mentioned. I now asked Jacques about one of the questions on the test that he had not answered correctly: "What does Smedley mean by 'primordialism' and how does she argue against it?" He now gave me a good answer. He said that Smedley used the alliance in the late sixteenth century between Sir Francis Drake and the Cimarrons (a community of slaves escaped from the Spanish in Panama and living in their own communities) as an argument against it. But Jacques did not explain *how* that alliance was an argument against primordialism.[6] As Smedley sees it, it was an alliance between persons of European and of African lineage that did not seem to involve either party looking at the other in a racial way. So racial thinking was not always part of human society or human nature.

Our conversation showed that Jacques understood these connections, but he did not state them on the test. I didn't know at the time whether he just didn't have time to make these connections, didn't understand that he had to, or wasn't clear enough about them in his own mind to write them on the test.

Jacques also told me he had been thinking about the racial achievement gap. He was seeing a lot of white kids in his senior class getting help from their parents, especially in applying to college. The parents were educated and had many resources to help their kids, compared to himself and many of his friends. He mentioned that his mother, a Haitian immigrant, worked long hours in a nursing home; his father did not seem to be on the scene. Jacques wasn't blaming anyone for this inequality, or resenting it; he was just thinking it through and trying to understand—both the general disparity issue, which he was concerned about from a justice point of view, and his own situation.

I wanted to affirm Jacques's recognition of injustice, as I had with Ebony. Jacques was seeing one piece of the achievement gap right before his eyes. From a privileged family's point of view, it is only natural to help their children. But in the larger picture, it does not seem fair that just being born into such a family gives that child a serious advantage over Jacques and his working-class friends. The injustice is of a social class rather than a directly racial nature—an advantage attached to parents' education. But it is tied up with race also, since on average black parents have less education than white parents—itself a product of a history of inequality in schooling—and thus their children get the short end of this class inequity more than white children do.

But, you might think, isn't it dangerous to encourage a black student to feel that the cards are stacked against him in society, that he is the victim of an injustice? I don't think so. It was empowering for Jacques to recognize and name as an injustice an obstacle to his success in applying for college, just as Ebony learned an important lesson when her mother challenged the salesperson who had disrespected and tried to cheat her. It was not necessarily part of a downward spiral to discouragement and opposition. This knowledge could prevent Jacques from beating up on himself for not doing a better job. It might prod him to seek out help in the school—for example, from his guidance counselor, or some teachers. (The school does run one class for seniors in which a key assignment is to write your college essay. Jacques was in that class.)

I do think it is our responsibility as teachers to help our students turn their recognition of unfairness toward a problem-solving strategy, rather than simply sinking into discouragement. And we should also help students to recognize injustice in the first place. It is an important dimension of civic education.

As an important side note, I found out something very interesting about Jacques in this conversation—that he played on the school basketball team. He had not been keeping this information under wraps. But since our first conversation before the course started, when he had said how much he hates it when people assume that he plays basketball just because he is tall and black, I had naturally assumed that he *didn't* play basketball. Usually the reason younger people object to being stereotyped is that they feel the stereotype does not apply to them. What they object to is not being seen for who they are—not being recognized, we called it in chapter 1—because the stereotype gets in the way.

But Jacques's objection to being stereotyped did not have to do with not being seen for who he was, for, as it turned out, he actually *was* a basketball player. He just didn't like people to assume he was a basketball player based on a stereotype. Jacques showed a stronger appreciation for what is wrong with stereotyping *in general*, not only when it leads to false assumptions about himself. In the first chapter we identified two different things wrong with stereotypes—they deny recognition to the individual member of the group who is speaking, since the stereotype does not apply to that individual; and they stigmatize the group as a whole by characterizing it negatively. Jacques's objection to stereotyping may not fall into either of these categories. He did not seem to be saying that assuming tall black boys are basketball players stigmatizes them, though it is possible he meant this. And he was not saying that the stereotype fails to recognize him by not applying to him, since it does apply to him. Perhaps his objection was that all members of the group are denied their individuality simply by being stereotyped, no matter what, or how positive, the stereotype. So denying individuality would be a third harm of stereotyping.

But back to Jacques's career in the class. Despite the weak test grade, over time I came to see that Jacques was an exceptionally intellectually engaged student. In class, as we have seen, he often used ideas we had studied earlier to illuminate or question an idea we were studying in the moment. And we develop this capability by periodically asking students how something they are reading is like and unlike something they have read before. Jacques was always mulling over ideas from the course, from elsewhere, from things people said to him, from his own reading. These ideas are all present to him when he thinks about anything. He is really an intellectual. He loves ideas.

I wanted to nurture Jacques's love of ideas and help him to adopt that love as part of his identity—for example, by trying to get him to come with me to a lecture at a nearby university given by a distinguished historian whom we had read in the class. I thought it would be good for Jacques to see in the flesh someone who wrote the academic books he was reading, and to be in a space where ideas are valued for their own sake. Many very bright students do not walk around ruminating on ideas and loving new ideas, as Jacques does. But budding intellectuals who come from educated families generally have that identity supported within their families. Jacques's intellectuality was not so easily recognized and nurtured in his working-class, immigrant, single-parent family.

Yet some of Jacques's academic skills were definitely substandard. I did not fully understand the nature of Jacques's difficulty until a later test. This test was longer than previous ones, and I arranged for students who needed extra time to have it. Jacques took an extra period and a half to finish, longer than Adam, the one student who had let me know early in the semester that he had some learning difficulties. I learned that Jacques had difficulty translating his thinking into writing, and that he found it more challenging than most students to organize his time in order to get his tasks done. The open timing of the exam made it a good deal easier for Jacques, and he got a B.

In this particular situation, it benefited Jacques to be recognized as having a learning disability. But it is important for us to recognize that black male students at all grade levels are often overdiagnosed as learning disabled when their actual problems are behavioral or emotional rather than related to cognitive processing. So their actual learning problems can remain underdiagnosed.

MARISSA

Marissa was taking the class because my son Ben, who was teaching at the high school at the time, encouraged her to. She had taken his algebra class the year before. In my class she sat to my immediate left, the first student in the inner horseshoe around me. She was pleasant and warm-hearted, and well-liked by her fellow students. But from early on she did not seem comfortable in the class setting. She sometimes spaced out. On her information sheet, she wrote, "I really, really, really do not like to be called on when my hand is not raised." She did sometimes volunteer—we saw her sharing her thoughts on her mixed parentage in chapter 2—but not often.

In mid-October I gave the first exam, which Marissa and three others missed. I scheduled a make-up exam for them. I called Marissa at home to see if she had the materials necessary to do the make-up—handouts and study questions. The subject was the early years of slavery in the Western hemisphere and the early development of the idea of race. I was worried Marissa would not be able to study for it effectively without some help.

I asked Marissa how she was using the reading questions to study. She said she just pulled them out of her folder in random order and looked at them. I tried to give her the appropriate historical overview that put the specific questions in context and showed why it was important to read them in order.

Some days later I called Marissa again to follow up, but she was not home. I had a long talk with her half-sister Chanel, who is also her guardian and has been since Marissa was three. It was a very poignant conversation. Neither of the girls' parents was on the scene. Chanel said that Marissa did not like Chanel to look at her work, and she had failed history twice before. She said Ben was one of the few teachers who has managed to keep Marissa engaged. Chanel said she does everything she can for her sister because Marissa has had such a deprived childhood, but worries somewhat that her efforts may have hindered Marissa's developing as strong a sense of personal responsibility as she should have.

A few weeks later I gave a take-home exam. This time I had made an arrangement to tutor Marissa for this exam and met her one morning before school. It was difficult to get hold of her to make these individual appointments. But the few I did have with her made me wonder whether Marissa needed an intensive one-to-one relationship with a teacher to connect academically with difficult material. She showed some real engagement with the material I discussed with her; she asked good questions and seemed to make progress. It was almost as if the classroom setting was an obstacle to her ability to access her genuine interest. Obviously I could not become a private tutor for Marissa. But I wondered how to facilitate her path to intellectual understanding and self-confidence in light of how schools are organized, and of her academic vulnerability. As I mentioned earlier, some research says that black students are more responsive to personal relationships with teachers (of any race) than are white students.[7]

Even if Marissa was not entirely comfortable in classes with demanding material and with other students who showed they could master that material, she might still be gaining something from those classes. Perceiving that higher academic bar right in front of her might help her recognize that standard more acutely. Research demonstrates pretty clearly that students will aim for a higher level of work if they see that work happening around them.[8] This is the educationally sound reason for making classes "heterogeneous," on top of the civic and personal enrichment that this diversity brings.

Perhaps because Marissa seemed to feel especially vulnerable as a learner, the high-demand environment both encouraged *and* discouraged her. Ideally, then, the high-demand class supplemented by outside-of-class help would be the best arrangement for her.

—ɯ—

As a teacher, I grappled with what my expectations of my students should be, and what they should be based on, but also with whether "expectations" expressed what students needed from me. It seems like a teacher could base expectations of a particular student on two different kinds of information—something about a group the student is a part of (racial, ethnic, religious, gender, etc.), or something individual about that student. If we have that choice, it seems clear we should pick the individual information—how the student has done in her previous grades, what her parents tell us about her, how she has done so far in our own class, what other professionals in the school can say about her, and so on.

The trouble is that it is not so easy to prevent group-based factors from affecting our expectations, especially in the area of race. And we are better armed to avoid these influences if we know what they are. There are three different kinds.[9] The most disturbing is when the teacher simply operates with a stereotype (say, of Latino students) that she has absorbed from the wider society or at her school. She may expect Latinos not to be good students because she just thinks that's the way they are. Obviously as teachers we should not typecast our students in this way. But we have to really be on our toes to avoid doing so. It is not enough to say, "I treat every student as an individual; I don't care if she's black, white, green, or purple," because stereotypes are all around us and they are more likely to affect us if we don't recognize them. We have to work to avoid common and pervasive stereotypes and not assume that our sincere desire to help all our students inoculates us against such ideas.

In a second type of group-based expectations, the teacher has had a fair number of Latino students herself, and she generalizes from her own experience. If on the whole these students have not been very high functioning in her classes, the teacher may expect a particular incoming Latino student not to do well either. This kind of generalization is somewhat preferable to pure stereotyping; at least it is based on actual experiences with the group in question. But it is still not right. It is wrong to generalize to the whole group (or to any specific member of it) based only on our individual experience.

In a third type of race-based expectation, the teacher is better informed and is neither channeling a common social stereotype nor over-
generalizing from her own experience. Rather, she knows relevant facts
about how different groups are faring. For example, she may be aware
of the racial achievement gap and may know some statistics that express the gap—for example, one sophisticated study shows that only 53
percent of Latino students who enter ninth grade graduate from high
school (the white figure is 75 percent).[10] Based on such statistics, she expects her own Latino students not to do as well, on average, as her white
students. Her expectations are group based, but they involve true generalizations and not just stereotypes. Let us say this teacher is careful not
to overgeneralize about the group in the way that stereotyping does. And
she recognizes that statistics record how things are in the present, not
how they have to be in the future, as stereotyping tends to do. Basically,
she knows that true generalizations can turn into or be used in a ste-
reotypic way. For example, someone who knows the statistic above can
form the stereotype that "Latinos are not good students." The teacher I
am imagining tries hard to avoid doing that.

It is important to know facts about how groups of students are doing as groups. We can't shun generalizations about groups just because
we are afraid they will keep us from seeing students as individuals. If
we know that the Latino dropout rate is substantially higher than for
whites, we want to devise policies in the school and in the world of education that address that disparity, and try to correct for it. If we know
that black and Latino kids sign up for advanced courses at a substantially
lower rate than white and Asian students, we can come up with ways to
encourage them to do so, and to help them be successful in those classes
(as I was trying to do). This point applies to behaviors that can have
a "cultural" dimension also. For example, some studies find that African American students watch more hours of television than otherwise
similar white students. And sometimes this behavior can be regarded as
"cultural," not in the sense of being part of the ethnic culture of African
Americans as a whole community, but as part of the social world of African American secondary school students.[11] But culture is changeable, so
knowing generalizations about groups' culture-based behavior can help
us figure out ways to change detrimental behaviors. Parents can turn off
the TV set, teachers can learn to engage the students better, and schools
can help parents enforce more constructive norms about TV watching.

So there are three different ways that group-based generalizations can
generate expectations of individual students in those groups—stereotypes,

teacher experience, and true group generalizations. Although the first of these is the worst basis of the three, we teachers should avoid forming expectations of individual students based on *any* type of group generalization. Why? Because individualized information about a student is a more reliable indicator of how that particular student is likely to perform than any information based on what that student's *group* does. It is a sounder basis for expectations of an individual student.[12]

Let's focus then on individualized expectations. Ronald Ferguson helpfully points to two distinct sources of individualized expectations. One is to look at the student's actual prior performance (in earlier classes, or so far in your own class). Although basing your expectations of your current students on their prior performance may avoid the problems with group-based expectations just mentioned, Ferguson points out a serious problem with doing so. It is that many black and Latino, or lower-income, students' achievement at a given level may not indicate their potential for future achievement. This is partly because socioeconomic disadvantages tend to depress performance but not necessarily potential.[13] Also, their past performance might have been depressed at least in part by the lower expectations previous teachers have had of them, based on either racial bias, inappropriate group generalizing, or previous performance.

So Ferguson proposes a different individual standard as optimal for teachers to base expectations on—the individual student's potential. If a student has not been performing to his potential, then future expectations based on his past performance will be pitched at a lower level than what he could accomplish. Guidance counselors at the high school would sometimes recommend students for my class by telling me, "Brian has been getting Cs, but I think he is ready for a new level of intellectual challenge." This message draws a clear distinction between what the student has done in the past and what he is capable of. We teachers need to be alert to when a student's previous record does not tell us all he is capable of. And "potential" expresses an important educational principle—that education should aim to enable every student to live up to his or her potential. This is one way to express what we mean when we say that education should provide "equal opportunity" to every student.

But tying expectations to potential is not such a simple matter. Previous achievement is concrete; we can point to it, we know what it is. But how do we know what "potential" is? What is the evidence of potential that does not somehow lie in previous performance?

—w—

Let's look back at the discussions with my five students to see if they can help us come up with some perspective on expectations and potential. What can we learn about "high expectations" from Norris? How do I view Norris's potential in light of his very inconsistent approach to his work? When he did turn in work, it wasn't bad. Does that mean that my expectation should be that he would turn in such work consistently? But all the evidence I had was that he had no commitment to doing this. He turned in work very seldom.

But since high school students can't generally be aware of the full consequences of school success and failure, perhaps their particular level of commitment to school should not be factored into expectations. Maybe the teacher should set expectations only to the highest quality of work she has some evidence for, not to the student's level of commitment. Thus, when Norris tells Justine he is not interested in school right now, I may need to take that as a challenge to engage him, or at least keep on him, and not let his perhaps short-sighted self-assessment rule the day.

So I can communicate to Norris that I have faith that if he applies himself to his work he can get a C in the course, possibly even a B–. But do I *expect* him to do this? No, I don't. That would be an expectation that flies in the face of the evidence before me. What I do have and can convey to him is a belief in that potential and a faith that he is capable of living up to it.

Is this belief a *"high* expectation," or a high anything? Not exactly. The work that I think Norris is capable of given his actual performance and that could deserve a grade of B– would not be of exceptionally high quality, or its grade would be higher. In communicating to students what we expect of them, and hope for them beyond those expectations, we have to stay grounded in what is aspirationally real to that particular student. A student will sense that we are not being straight with him if we propose a goal that seems way out of line with anything he has shown us. It's a challenging balance—pushing a student beyond where he has gone and expressing faith that he can do so, but not setting an unrealistic goal that would cause discouragement and perhaps a lack of trust in us. In any case, I don't think the language of "high expectation" is particularly helpful in dealing with such matters. What Norris seemed to need, if he was to be more successful, was someone constantly staying on him to get his work done. He was fortunate ultimately to find such a person in Leila.

In a sense, the issue of expectations did not arise with Antonine. She was already motivated to work hard; she just sometimes needed help, which she knew she needed, and knew to ask for. Of course, if I had communicated to her that I did *not* expect her to do very well, that might have undermined her degree of determination. But apart from avoiding low expectations, what Antonine needed from me was not so much high expectations but concrete help. She seemed to already have a commitment to educational standards appropriate for her, and only needed to be reminded of the educational goals she had set herself, including doing the best work she could in the class.

Antonine also seemed to have very definite ideas about environments that helped her do her work. She once told me about a cousin of hers who attended what she described as a private, "white, upper-class school." A white student at that school asked Antonine's cousin what she washed her hair with. Antonine and the cousin were annoyed by this racial insensitivity and ignorance; the cousin sarcastically replied, "We wash it with mayonnaise." ("What does she think we use?" Antonine exclaimed.) I said something favorable about CRLS in comparison to this school, but Antonine replied, "I don't like this school. A lot of the kids are too immature, like you think that when kids get older they get more mature, but here they don't get more mature, they get less mature." She said she would like to be able to go to a well-known, quite posh prep school in a Boston suburb, akin to the one with the racially ignorant white student.

In a later conversation, Antonine said she would not apply to UMass Boston for college because she knows too many CRLS students there, or who will be going there. She said, "I would just hang around with them and not do any work." Although Antonine does most of her assigned work, in class she is fairly easily distracted. She spaces out, talks to other kids. I often have to crack down on her. She evidently thinks that her own friends and peers are not a very good influence on her work habits. So in a way she herself could be one of the "immature" kids whom she sees as making CRLS a less-than-optimal place for students like herself. She is saying something like, "I don't want to be at a school with a lot of other kids like me." It is an admirable self-awareness to recognize that her social proclivities and peer group might be holding her back. She may be right in thinking that a new community where she doesn't know anyone would make it easier for her to focus. Maybe peer influence issues are much more central to Antonine's learning challenges, at least in this period of her life, than teacher expectations.

The learning problem Ebony presents also does not seem to be motivational or a belief in herself—issues affected by teacher expectations.

Rather, it is a racially grounded mental block that seems to involve an emotional component. The experiences Ebony wrote about in her journal were important learning events, as she saw racial discrimination up close, and learned an important positive lesson from her mother—that you do not let those incidents roll over you without standing up to that discrimination and challenging it. This lesson is emotionally healthy also. If you let the effects of injustice just sit with you and simmer, without doing anything about them, they can lead to self-doubt or an incapacitating resentment. Responding to injustice may involve anger in the moment, but the anger can be discharged through appropriate actions that challenge the injustice.

Still, as I mentioned, I wondered if Ebony had somehow internalized a general distrust of white people that was getting in the way of her learning. Something like this can happen with any subject that has a social or moral importance, but racial material is particularly fertile ground for generating various emotional and mental blocks. And I think it is fair to say that white students are most likely to experience these blocks. They often bring ways of thinking about American history, or about particular racial groups (including their own), that make it hard for them to take in accurate information about the extent of racial discrimination or the situation and experience of racial minorities. In my college classes many white students see discrimination as something that *used* to happen to black and Latinos, but doesn't much any more. What I'm seeing with Ebony is an analogous mind-set in a black student, one that formed an emotionally based, race-related obstacle to her learning.

As teachers, we can help students who are targets of discrimination to take their experiences in a constructive direction only if we are open to hearing about these experiences, and if are willing to teach about racial discrimination. Ebony may have come into the course with a lack of confidence that white people treat black people fairly. And this presented a challenge to teaching her, especially to me as a white teacher. But it did not seem to negatively affect Ebony's school commitments. Nor did she actually seem resistant to me as a white teacher. I say this in part because, in contrast, I had had black students in earlier years who were very resistant. Three young women actively challenged my knowledge and authority to teach the material in the course (but with two of them I ultimately worked out a reasonable modus vivendi). And with Ebony, you can see that learning about slavery actually helped to challenge her view. In the exchange I reported earlier, she is on her way to understanding the origins of slavery not as a conspiracy of white people against black people, but as an economic system that resulted in white people oppressing black people down the road. She isn't there yet, but she has started to break out of her mental constrictions. This is a learning obstacle that has little to do with "high expectations."

Does "high expectations" help us think about what Jacques needs as a student? His major obstacle to doing his best work is his learning disabilities. Schools now have a much better understanding than when I was in school of kids who have trouble turning their thinking into coherent writing, and of how to help those students. If I had had a better understanding of that issue myself at the time, I might have noticed earlier that Jacques needed learning disability accommodation and services. I don't think "high expectations" is very helpful for any of these issues. Learning disabilities require knowledgeable teachers to recognize them, and to know how to deal with them constructively. It is not an "expectations" issue.

I don't think the usual talk of "high expectations" helps us think about nurturing Jacques's intellectuality either. "High expectations" are generally focused only on school success (or even more narrowly on standardized tests). While intellectuality and school success overlap to some degree, they are two different things. In an earlier class I had an immigrant student, Selim, who seldom did his assigned work. But he was always looking for and finding public lectures in the area to attend, and reading things related to them. I was not as tuned in as I later became (by the time I taught Jacques's class) to figuring out this sort of thing. My point here is that taking ideas seriously in the way Jacques and Selim did, and in the way I was hoping to nurture in Jacques, is not the same as mastering the skills needed for school success. I think it would enrich Jacques's life, and make him a more constructive and imaginative citizen, if he were encouraged to pursue his love of ideas for its own sake, not only as part of doing well in school. The usual way "high expectations" is understood does not help with this.

How did, or should, I think about Jacques's "potential?" Thinking back, I realize that I was much less clear in my own mind about Jacques's potential than I thought I was about Norris's or Antonine's. His learning disabilities made it harder to see what he was fully capable of. They made what he wrote in his assignments less reflective of his underlying potential. Moreover, it seemed like Jacques was very much a work in progress. It was evident that he had greater intellectual potential than had been fully developed, and that was enough for me to try to nurture that intellectuality. But I couldn't know the extent of his potential.

Then this line of thought made me wonder about the way I had been thinking about Norris and Antonine. All I really knew about those two was that neither showed me specific evidence of Jacques's kind of intelligence. Because the class was intellectually demanding, apparently more demanding than courses these students had taken before, I took their potential essentially to be the best work they showed me. But I did not know whether some other teacher had seen evidence of a whole different aspect of their intellectual talent; or even whether their experience in the school as a whole had failed to tap into some capability they possessed, but maybe were not even themselves aware of. After all, there are a lot of forms of intellectual potential.

This thinking led me down another path. Suppose these students simply did not get enough nurturance of their forms of intelligence at earlier stages, and that meant one no longer saw any signs of them. Maybe by the time they were seniors in high school the potential they once possessed had become almost inaccessible to them.

Maybe we have to distinguish between two different forms of potential. One—"accessible potential"—is a potential that the student could realize in the present if she put forth special effort and were given a reasonable amount of support. It would still be a reach for the student, but she could do it. But another kind of potential—"almost inaccessible potential"—is something the student might have once had as accessible potential; but by now, because it has been suppressed or lain dormant for so long, it can no longer be reached with a reasonable amount of effort and support. It may still be there, but only an extraordinary amount of effort or an unusual set of circumstances can tap it. It is likely that it will never be realized.

But if the potential is almost inaccessible, can it or should it drive expectations? Shouldn't we be guided only by what we can see? I think we can draw two lessons from barely accessible potential. One is to always be willing to try new ways to stimulate students, so as to reveal sides of themselves that might not have been evident before; and in the process to always be on the lookout for signs of potentiality. We shouldn't ever think we have completely "gotten" a student—summed up her talents and possibilities. There might always be something that we missed. This guideline should especially be applied to students who may not be getting that stimulation elsewhere at school or may not have gotten it earlier.

A second point follows from this. It is to be aware of how the structures and expectations pervasive in the education system might be more likely to hide the potential of black, Latino, and poor and working-class students. So we should always do what we can to reverse this. It's a tall order, but ensuring equal opportunity for each student to develop her potential demands it.

There is another lesson in the fact that students may possess a potential that they don't develop or show in high school. That is the importance of "second chance" institutions—colleges such as UMass Boston that welcome older students who do not discover until some years after high school that they want to pursue further education. A real commitment to equality of opportunity demands greater public support for these alternative paths to developing students' potential, to reverse the spiraling costs of attending these institutions.

Finally, Marissa's situation also exposes a confusion in the language of "expectations." On the one hand, an expectation is something you believe will happen. If I *expect* a student to do well on a test, then I believe the student actually will do well. If I don't believe she will, then I don't expect her to. But "expectation" is generally used in education contexts in a different way—more like a goal you set for a student and believe she is *capable* of attaining, but not necessarily *likely* to do so. You want to communicate your fundamental faith in this capability (or "accessible potential"). So, then, what is the best way to help a student whom you have reason to believe is *not* likely to do well on a piece of work? I think you give her the help you think she needs to do as good a job as she is able, within her particular range of possibility. You express your confidence that she is capable of doing it *if* she puts forth her best effort. So you acknowledge it might be a stretch for her. You may feel she has not been putting as much into it as she could, or, like Marissa, has not been studying in the most effective way. But the language of "expectations" is not a helpful way to express this.

—m—

In this chapter I've tried to show that different students pose different learning challenges. Although we should want all our students to achieve at as high a level as they are capable, the constant invoking of "high expectations" does not generally help us come to grips with each student's particular situation. Ronald Ferguson helpfully alerts us to the danger of thinking that a given student will only do as well in our class as she has done in previous classes. Perhaps the student has just not been pushed hard enough, or given work that engages her intellect. And we particularly have to be on the lookout for this happening to black and Latino students.

9   Hair, Skin, and Pride
Moral Symmetry Revisited

Hair and skin color are very charged issues among American blacks, as is skin color among other groups and in many other countries. It is not easy to figure out how to teach about these matters, but I think we have to be prepared to. They are on the students' minds, and they are part of what race means in many societies. At the same time, because of the possibility for shame and shaming, talking about hair and skin color in mixed settings is perhaps even more perilous, especially for a white teacher.

I did plan a class discussion on skin color, but before recounting that conversation I want to relate an exchange about hair—which I had not planned to discuss in the class—that had taken place a few weeks before. Both conversations show how morally and personally complex the issues of hair and skin color are.

—⚉—

Mary, a postdoctoral student who sometimes observed the class, was demonstrating interview techniques for students to use in their racial empathy assignment (see appendix 2). Jean-Paul volunteered to be an interviewee. As part of the interview lesson, Jean-Paul said that late one night, a cop had stopped him for what seemed to him no reason. He was not sure the cop stopped him because he was black, but he couldn't think of any other explanation. (This was one of many occasions on which the black students did not conform to the stereotype that they are always quick to see themselves as a victim of racism.)

Someone in the class asked what race the officer was. Jean-Paul said he was Hispanic. I asked how he knew this. Jean-Paul replied, "He had an accent, and he had good hair." Then he ran his hands over his own hair and said, "You know, straight, not like my hair."

I was surprised to hear such a comment from Jean-Paul. He is a very charming, popular, and confident young man who seemed to me to have a good image of himself and to assume that he will be liked by others.

He is involved in community work with younger kids at a community center close to my house. He is a generous and sensitive member of the class, tuned in to what other students might be feeling. For example, one day because of absences, Behar, the immigrant student, was sitting by himself in his assigned seat, and all the other students present were on the other side of the horseshoe. Jean-Paul encouraged Behar to leave his assigned seat and join the others on the other side (which he did). Jean-Paul has a positive and optimistic self-presentation. His confidence is not at all obnoxious or smug. He just seems to have a very positive sense of himself. Of course I should not have been so surprised that an optimistic and positive personality might coexist with elements of internalized racial stigma. But I was.

Several of the black students (and perhaps others too—it was a bit chaotic and I am not sure exactly who spoke) were quite upset with Jean-Paul: "What do you mean, 'good hair'?!" Jean-Paul naturally became defensive.

> *Jean-Paul*: I just meant that *my* hair was bad hair. I'm not saying anything against your hair.
> *Mirvole*: But my hair is the same as yours, or it was before I did something to it. So if yours is bad then mine is too.
> *Antonine*: He's just talking about *his* hair. He isn't saying anything about yours.

I wondered how I should deal with this situation. I know that hair is a particularly sensitive issue for black women. A student from a previous class, Kayla, had once written a long description in her journal of the process black girls go through to straighten their hair, what it takes to maintain it, and how difficult that is. Kayla was informing me of something she thought I should know about and probably didn't. (She was right.) And she was also working out her ambivalent feelings.

I definitely did not feel as competent to weigh in on this area as I did other issues in the course, and was worried about treading on sensitivities. I avoided this problem because Mary had to finish her workshop on interviewing, and there were only a few minutes left in the class, so I brought us back to that, cutting off the hair discussion.

But I thought afterwards that the brief exchange among the three black students raised some morally interesting issues that might be worth taking up explicitly at some point. I think Antonine's defense of Jean-Paul was prompted primarily by her wanting to defend her classmate, but it might seem that this defense was pretty weak. Obviously, as Mirvole points out, the aspect of Jean-Paul's hair that he is referring to as "bad" is something others of his racial group share. So even if he doesn't think he is putting down their hair, what he says does imply a put-down. In addition, although the students did not say this explicitly, the idea that black people's curly or coiled hair is "bad" is clearly a racist idea. It emerges from just the kind of racist thinking about black people's visible physical characteristics that we saw in Thomas Jefferson, and that Walker challenged.

Yet, when I pondered this later, I thought that when Jean-Paul and Antonine said "I wasn't saying something about you" to Mirvole, they might have been onto a valuable moral insight about race-related issues of personal appearance. They might have been acknowledging that black people all have to contend with standards of physical beauty that devalue them. But they also might have been saying that they are not about to criticize the way that other black people deal with this devaluing, and do not want to be criticized for their individual ways of dealing with it either. While the racial terrain is very charged morally, as it involves the deepest issues of prejudice, acceptance, respect, and dignity, at the same time, morality can too easily slide into moralism in which we inappropriately generalize our own moral standards to others. Perhaps Jean-Paul and Antonine were rejecting that moralism and wanting to emphasize that dealing with race-related issues of personal appearance should be the province of each individual.

I was also struck by the black students' willingness to challenge one another on this sensitive issue in front of the nonblack students. I did not know whether Mirvole felt that Jean-Paul's remark was more shaming to her *because* it was said in front of nonblacks, and this is why she felt compelled to respond. But maybe not. Maybe the black students who spoke simply felt more comfortable in the class by this time, and could express what was on their minds even in a sensitive area.

I also didn't get to explore the idea Jean-Paul presented—that Latinos, who often also feel that fair skinned, European standards of beauty leave them out, have "good hair." I wondered if Cristina, Clara, and Tenzina had any feelings about Jean-Paul's remarks.

—⟶⟵—

This conversation about hair was an important backdrop to a conversation in a later class about skin color. We saw last chapter that David Walker was completely outraged that Thomas Jefferson would say that black people's skin color was "unfortunate." Walker replies, "As though we are not as thankful to our God, for having made us as it pleased Himself as they [the whites] are for having made them white."[1] I have the class discuss this.

> *Jacques*: So Walker is saying it's all right for us to have the skin color we have?
>
> *Jean-Paul*: Yeah, he says it's *good* that we have that skin color, that's the color that's *right for us*.

I am pleased that it is Jean-Paul who emphasizes that Walker thinks blacks' skin color is good, given his previous remark about hair. Maybe Walker is helping him rethink that view.

> *Jacques*: It's like, I'm tall, and someone says, "Yeah, you're tall" . . . that's just the way it is.

Jacques sounds to me more resigned than proud about his tallness. Maybe he is struggling to take on Walker's idea that all the characteristics God gave us are good, but isn't there yet. He may only be able to say that the characteristics are OK, not that they are positively good.

> *Me*: Is Walker saying *everyone* should be proud of their skin color—whites included?
>
> *Clara*: It should be the same. But pride in being white has a more negative connotation, because it is always connected to being superior.
>
> *Pema*: White isn't seen as negative. If you look in the dictionary, the definitions of *white* are all positive—like lightness, sun, purity. Black is connected with dark, something you're afraid of.
>
> *Adam*: Whites have power, and white pride is connected with that. But still, saying you are proud to be white isn't necessarily supporting white superiority.
>
> *Sherilyn*: If a white person said, "I'm proud of being white" my first reaction would be, "Are you saying you are better than me?"
>
> *Pema*: Even if you should be able to say you are proud of being white, if somebody said that to me, I'd react against it.

The students are struggling here with the symmetry issue—does pride in skin color have the same moral valence for all groups, as Walker's view that our skin color is a gift from God implies. Clara states the symmetry view: We all have a skin color. No one does anything to get it. You are just born with it. So it "should be the same" for everyone. Everyone should be proud of, or be able to be proud of, their skin color. But Clara recognizes that in the world she lives in, it isn't the same for whites and people of color. "White pride" seems to her to have a negative connotation, while black pride (she implies) doesn't. Why does white pride have a negative connotation? She says it is because it is connected to being superior, an idea she can assume most people in her world now reject (at least when presented with it explicitly). Pema challenges the idea that whiteness has a negative association. And she is right about how the dictionary defines the word *white*.[2] Adam accepts Clara's earlier point but is also looking for a way for there to be an acceptable white skin pride that does not have to buy into a false white superiority. Sherilyn and Pema don't accept that path. It is interesting that both of them put their points in terms of how they would personally react to someone's saying he was proud of being white. Pema even somewhat acknowledges that it should be all right to say this, but that, like Sherilyn, she would react negatively to a white person's saying it.

> *Tenzina*: Whether it's OK to say you are proud of your skin color depends on who is saying it; like if it's a racist friend of yours saying it, that is more suspicious. [Holding her arm up to foreground her skin color, she continues.] Asians don't say, "I'm proud of being yellow!" [General whooping and merriment at this remark, which manifests perfect comic timing, from a student who does not generally go for laughs.]
>
> *Pema*: Asians don't think of themselves as yellow.
>
> *Jacques*: Whites and blacks identify with their race. Asians don't.
>
> *Tenzina*: What are you actually proud of? In the case of blacks, it is empowering to take pride in your skin color.

The students are seeing that whether you take pride in your skin color is not just about a physical characteristic. It is filled with social meaning, and that might be why there are asymmetries. Tenzina sees that difference in terms of the individual who asserts the pride—a question of that individual's prejudice rather than of his racial group membership as Sherilyn, Clara, Pema, and Adam had said. But she also says that Asians don't take pride in being "yellow," the color-coded racial term historically associated with Asians (though no longer regarded as acceptable). Pema agrees. Jacques offers an explanation of this point by saying that Asians don't identify with a race, while blacks and whites do. So the students have noted several asymmetries—that white skin color pride is associated with a false superiority (though Adam does not think it has to) and so carries a negative connotation not carried by black pride, and Asian skin color pride doesn't get asserted, possibly because there is less racial identification among Asians.

In a journal entry around this time, Hannah voiced a symmetry slant on the issue of skin color and pride: "One question I have is why do many black people use items such as bleach creams and relaxers—to become more white? While white people get curly perms and go tanning—to become more black? Does the use of these products really indicate that both groups want to be something other than what they are? Or does the American society just look at caramel skin as the most beautiful color one can be? Or does the usage of these products indicate something more?"

These are fascinating questions. Hannah, a white and quite pale-skinned girl, looks out and sees blacks using products that seem to make them look more white, and white people doing something apparently similar to make themselves look like what could be regarded as more black. She also wonders if there is an American image of beauty that is in between these two, which each group is going for. I wonder if she is reflecting developments in her own generation that had only dimly penetrated my own radar. I would have thought that "American" styles of beauty were overwhelmingly white, as they were in my own childhood. I don't see fashion magazines or even watch television. But I realize that many of the iconic beauties of Hannah's generation—Shakira, Mariah Carey, Jennifer Lopez, Halle Berry, Beyoncé Knowles—are not white but not fully black-looking either, though some of them are racially black (or mixed) and are generally thought of that way.

But Hannah does not consider that the reasons whites want to darken their skin and blacks lighten theirs are entirely different and asymmetrical. As we have seen, and as Jean-Paul's remark suggested, "black looks" are not viewed as very attractive in the mainstream culture. So efforts to straighten one's hair and, especially, to lighten one's skin may be attempts to blunt the effect of that stigma by looking less black. But whites who wish to get a bit of color in their skin are not really trying to escape any stigma of racial whiteness; there is no such stigma, except in very unusual circumstances.

Hannah might still be right that American standards of beauty are undergoing some shift. The society does seem to be somewhat embracing of ethnically distinct ways of being beautiful. This is a very positive development. But this shift coexists with an older stigmatizing of blackness that, though perhaps weakened compared to earlier eras, is still very much with us. Two students who later in the term wrote an extra-credit assignment on skin color pride made this very point. Marie said that light-skinned black women are viewed more favorably within the black community, as seen in hip-hop, R&B, and other music videos, and that dark-skinned black women are not considered sexy, while dark-skinned black men are (within the black community). Sherilyn wrote in a journal that black female movie stars are seldom dark-skinned, but some males are.

I don't think it is surprising that a white high school girl like Hannah growing up in a racially and ethnically mixed peer community might be acutely tuned into the "multiculturalizing of beauty" while perhaps missing the asymmetries between white and black in altering one's skin color.

Returning to the class discussion, a bit later Pema tells a story about a dark-skinned male member of her family who was seen as "not good looking" by others, including his own wife. Pema makes the general point that affirmations of lightness and whiteness are harmful and hurtful. She has said in journals and occasionally in class that she had negative experiences with white students when in elementary school and relatively new to the country. She reported feeling that the norm that blond, blue-eyed girls defined the standard for what was cute and pretty was very hurtful to her. For one year of high school she also attended a sort of trade school for students who had trouble in the regular public schools. Even there, she said, the white students (who were hardly ever from middle-class families) were snobby and mean.

After saying some of this to the class, Pema adds, "I'm sorry, white people," in a good-natured sort of way. (Several students laugh.) While her remark carries some of her own racial resentment toward whites as a group, she seems to recognize that white students in the class might understandably be bothered by her expressing her thoughts and feelings about white standards of beauty. I appreciate Pema's civic respect here, and know she was working through her complex feelings about whiteness. This is a hard-hitting conversation as a whole, on touchy territory about racial symmetries and asymmetries, especially about who should be permitted to take pride in their skin color. But the conversation is still civil and it is constructive.

—⚏—

Harking back to Walker's religious take on questions of race and skin color, the conversation takes a turn toward a discussion of Jesus's skin color.

> *Sherilyn*: Jesus is big and dark. So how could Christians think God was white?
> *Tenzina:* But pictures of Jesus were white.
> *Antonine*: Bibles illustrated for black people show Jesus as dark.
> *Sherilyn*: God can be female too.
> *Jean-Paul*: God isn't that kind of image. He doesn't have eyes or a mouth.
> *Norris*: I'm a Christian, and God is whatever you see in God. So he can be dark or light.

I'm glad the students bring this religious dimension into the discussion. Not only is it an important part of Walker's argument and outlook, but many of the students, including all the ones who spoke in this exchange, are Christian. I am glad they are thinking through how their religion relates to these racial issues, as the class did in talking about Walker and nineteenth-century Christianity, and it reminds me that if we are to take race seriously, we teachers have to be prepared to discuss religion in our classes. Both are charged issues, and they're connected.

It is also interesting to me that some of the black students have seen Jesus portrayed as black or at least as dark. I wasn't aware of that. Sherilyn, Jean-Paul, and Norris move away from the issue of Jesus himself to the perhaps more general issue of the image of God, which would be significant for non-Christian believers also. Sherilyn and Jean-Paul say that God should not be thought of as having racial or indeed any physical characteristics at all. Norris says something slightly different—that you can always see yourself as made in the image of God. Both views reject the racist view of God as white, but Norris gives God a color if you want to see that in him, while Jean-Paul says God does not have a color.

I steered the conversation in a different though related direction.

> *Me*: Earlier in the semester we looked at the evolutionary origins of skin color and other phenotypic characteristics. Scientists are not completely sure why some people have lighter skin color than others,

but it probably has something to do with how close your long-ago ancestors were to the equator. I want to ask you a question about this. If your skin color is caused by natural selection, how does that affect how you should feel about it, comparing that to Walker's saying that you should be pleased with your skin color because you see it is as a gift from God?

Ebony: Walker's view doesn't make sense because it implies that you had all these people and they didn't have any skin color, and then God just said, OK, I'm going to give this group dark skin.

Tenzina: Not everyone believes the evolutionary view; and you get your skin color from your parents.

Adam [responding to this but more directly to Ebony]: God doesn't directly give you your skin color, but he puts the conditions that create your skin color.

Ebony's complaint makes a lot of sense to me. If we view God as giving people their skin color, it seems odd to picture a group of people without any skin color, then God decides what skin color to give them. Tenzina sidesteps this worry without addressing it by saying people inherit skin color from their parents. Adam makes a nice attempt at reconciling the religious and evolutionary outlooks. It reminds me of Francis Collins's *The Language of God*. Collins, the director of the National Institutes of Health and once the head of the government's genomic project, says that genetics, and the processes of random variation and natural selection that lead to humans' physical characteristics, should be seen as God's way of organizing the natural world—not that God directly produces each human characteristic.[3] (Collins believes in God, and is defending that belief. I wasn't sure whether Adam and Ebony were, or whether they were just working intellectually with the idea of God.)

There was only a minute left in the class and Anna returned to the topic of the lesson: "You don't have pride in your skin color, you have pride in your culture [the one that people of your skin color have]." This was a great point on the question of the social meaning of skin color and might have returned us to Smedley's sharp distinction between race and culture. But alas (as so often happens at these moments), the class was over.

—⚏—

After class Jacques came up to me and said, "You can have pride in your skin color if there's an ideology that says your skin color is bad, and then you can have pride to reject that ideology." I asked him if he thought that's what Anna was saying. He replied, "Yes, but it isn't a matter of your culture, it has to do with there being an ideology." This perceptive and sophisticated observation gave a new perspective to Jacques's remark at the beginning of the discussion. He had said Walker thought it was all right to be black, but Jacques resisted going further to say you should feel positively proud of being black. I had thought that remark meant that he was having trouble feeling positive about his dark skin color and his height. But I might have been misreading his view. What Jacques was saying in the after-class exchange was that you can't simply take pride in your skin color; you can only do so against a certain background, namely where there is a view commonly held by people in your society that there is something wrong with your skin color. You can say "No, there isn't anything wrong with my skin color" in the face of this ideology, and that is what pride can be—a rejection of shame about your color.

That very argument is developed by Randall Kennedy, a black law professor, in an article I use in my college class on race and racism. Kennedy echoes the views of Frederick Douglass, the great black abolitionist and former slave, that it makes no sense to take pride in something you had no part in creating. Douglass says, "The only excuse for pride in individuals is in the fact of their own achievements . . . If the sun has created curled hair and tanned skin, let the sun be proud of its achievement."[4]

Your skin color is not an achievement of yours, Kennedy and Douglass are saying, so it is unintelligible to take pride in it. But, Kennedy says, what you can do with regard to your skin color is to reject any stigmatizing of it—to say, "You may see my skin color as ugly or deficient, but it isn't, and I am perfectly happy to have this skin color." A religious view such as Walker's can help you adopt that position. Seeing one of your physical characteristics as coming from God can make it easier not to be ashamed of it. Of course, you can also reject the stigmatizing or shaming of your physical characteristics without believing in God.

But Jacques may have been right in that first class discussion to resist calling this rejection of shame "pride in one's skin color," although he did use the language of pride in the after-class exchange. Walker does not actually talk of pride, but of "thankfulness" to God for one's skin color, and being pleased with our skin color because of that. That is not really the same as pride, and it is possible that Kennedy and Douglass are right that pride can only be taken in actual accomplishments, not in mere physical endowments. That is a larger and more complex question.

Jacques was also right to distinguish his view from Anna's about culture. Cultures are things one can take pride in; they are, or can be, genuine human accomplishments. Anna is right about that. But pride in culture is not the same as rejecting shame in a physical characteristic that has been stigmatized in the society. Jacques is right on that point. What both Anna's and Jacques's views share is a recognition that "skin color" is laden with all kinds of social meanings; it is not a mere physical characteristic.

Jacques's view also explains an important asymmetry between black and white that the students have been exploring in the conversation. If pride consists in rejecting an ideology that stigmatizes your skin color, then blacks can have pride but whites can't. Why can't whites? Because there is no ideology commonly held in the United States that stigmatizes the light skin color of white people. Rather, light skin color is seen as desirable, a view that is a holdover from a racist ideology of white superiority. The asymmetry here is not only about blacks. Asians like Pema who have felt the sting of racial shame about their appearance would be in a position to take pride in their skin color (in this sense) if they too were able to reject the "white is beautiful" ideology that stigmatizes their group's appearance.

—ɯ—

Later in the conversation that day (and before Anna's remark at the end of the class), some of the students bring up skin color issues in other countries, often ones to which they have a personal connection, making it clear that the preference for light skin is by no means only an American phenomenon.

> *Leila*: Members of my family are racist against dark-skinned people. My father is Arabic and light-skinned and although he married a dark-skinned woman (my mother), his family prefers light to dark-skinned people.

I ask Leila where she thinks they got that preference from.

> *Leila*: My Arabic great-grandfather owned slaves, and that was where they got the idea that blacks were inferior.
> *Mirvole*: My grandmother is very light-skinned and she puts African people in a whole different category, and doesn't want to think

of herself as having African ancestry. With her grandchildren, she
would pinch their nose to try to give them a pointy nose.

Sherilyn [turning to both of these dark-skinned girls, she asks, very
nicely but pointedly]: Do the attitudes you just described reflect on
how those members of your families see you?

Leila: My aunt would say, "You're pretty but you're a little less pretty
than your cousin because you're a little bit darker." My cousin is
Lovelle's skin color.

Mirvole: My grandmother married a dark-skinned person.

As touchy as the subject of skin color is among blacks, and especially
black females, the girls seemed very matter-of-fact about these family
revelations, and about talking about their own and each other's skin
color. I was certainly struck by Sherilyn's direct question implicitly characterizing Mirvole and Leila as dark-skinned (which she herself isn't),
although, perhaps equally noteworthy, both girls had just characterized
themselves in that way. And for Leila to just casually use Lovelle, who
had not spoken during this conversation (and who does not speak much
in class), as a skin color prototype to clarify Leila's cousin's skin color,
did not seem a very usual thing to happen in class.

Certainly high school students' general uninhibitedness was partly at
work here—and it really enriched the conversation. I also think the students had gotten more and more comfortable with each other over the
three months the class had run. Finally, maybe the dominance of black
students in the class had also made them feel like it was a space where
they could speak with each other about touchy subjects without feeling
too self-conscious about nonblacks' reactions (including mine). (More
on this issue in chapter 11.)

In a way, as a society we should want to get to a point where we can
talk about each other's skin color without feeling like we are sitting on
a tinderbox. Skin color is a physical feature that varies among individuals, and there has to be a way of recognizing this in some teaching situations. This is not to deny that race and skin color matter. In this sense
saying we should aim to be "color-blind" or "color-mute" (seeing color
but not talking about it, in Mica Pollock's helpful coinage) is misplaced.
Indeed, the students are explicitly trying to understand the way skin
shade does matter, and matters somewhat differently in different societies. It's just that we can help students to understand the social meanings
attached to skin shade better if we can create a space where they can

refer to each other's skin color in the service of collective understanding, without embarrassment, shame, or oversensitivity.

I also think this sort of conversation was made both easier and more focused by the historical reading—Walker's defense of black appearance against Jefferson's demeaning of it—and perhaps by the scientific account of skin color from earlier in the course. If we plunge into a personally charged terrain not by asking the students what they think and feel, but by looking at what an authoritative or historically significant source says about the issue in question, that conversation can ease the way for the students to be more personally revealing. I am not saying that being personally revealing is the ultimate goal. Indeed, I think understanding the history and science is much more important for the students' learning and growth. But I also know that these issues are on their minds, and that it is valuable for them to give voice to and scrutinize their thoughts, while connecting them with the academic material.

10 Looking Back on Slavery

Racial Identity and Moral Self-Concept

Throughout the course the students were working out their own identities, as high school students generally do, but here the racial aspect of that identity was a central part of the challenge. After the end of the slavery unit, I decided to try to find out how they thought studying slavery had affected them (now that we had moved on to more contemporary events). In an in-class exercise, I asked them to write down some thoughts on this question:

How did our study of slavery affect how you think about

(1) yourself,
(2) your racial group,
(3) your moral and political values, and
(4) American history?

Cristina [Latin American father and white American mother]: It doesn't change the way I see my racial group much because I already knew that both the English and Spanish (which I guess are my racial roots) were both very much involved in the slave trade. Also because my Salvadoran roots are mestizo so it has a blurred effect on how I view it. I don't connect fully racially to being either race so I think it doesn't affect me much.

Cristina begins by identifying with both the English and the Spanish in her ancestry as groups that perpetrated slavery. It is not so common for Latina students to focus on the Spanish thread in their heritage specifically as an oppressive force. In the United States, Latinos are a relatively disadvantaged minority group, and it is much more common for them to identify with the Latin American dimension than the Spanish as a colonizing nationality.

But Cristina is tuning into and taking on an important theme in the class—that the Spanish were as deeply involved in slavery and the slave trade as the English/Americans, and that the English and Spanish practices of slavery were both quite brutal. She does say that she knew this prior to the class. But this particular exercise is heightening her recognition of the Spanish part of her heritage.

At the same time, Cristina also shifts from the encompassing "Spanish" identification to the more particular Salvadoran (her father's nationality) one, which she recognizes to be *mestizo*, a mix of European and indigenous ancestry. A mestizo identity is quite different from a Spanish one. Many persons of Latin American origin reject the designation "Hispanic" precisely because it does not acknowledge that mixed heritage. In particular, it erases the indigenous and African components.[1] Cristina's reference to the "blurred effect" on how she sees her race could just mean that because of the mixture, she can't identify with a single race. But it could also be more of a moral blurring—that her mixed ancestry as a Latina puts her on both sides of the slavery relationship, the Spanish slaveholder and the indigenous and African slaves.

However, in Cristina's last sentence, she distances herself from both of her ancestral identities (English and Spanish), rather than embracing them as she does at first. Cristina is here expressing the complexity of mixed identities in America at this time. Someone of her particular mix could say, "I'm white and I'm Latina; I'm both, and I identify with both communities, one that represents my mother and one that represents my father." Or she could say, "I'm neither white nor Latina really, because I'm a mixture of the two. So I don't really fit into either community." Taking the latter thought one step further, some organizations of mixed-race people are trying to create "mixedness" as a distinct identity of its own, different from either of the "component" races.[2] When Cristina adds, "It doesn't affect me very much," she may also be saying that she does not feel much responsibility for slavery, since her mixed background puts her outside either specific group of slavery perpetrators.

In my experience at the school, the mixed students do not generally take the path of a mixed identity *rather than* a "both/and" identity. They see themselves the way Cristina first stated—as both mixed and as both of the components in the mix (in Cristina's case, white and Latina). The exclusive mixed identity might seem to the student a repudiation of one or both of her parents and their heritage. Another reason for not privileging the "mixed" identity is that someone who is black and white, like Marissa, has a very different experience from someone like Tenzina, who is Asian and Latina, or like Cristina. "Mixed" as a primary identity downplays the way the particular racial components of your mix affect your experience of being mixed.

Of course, in line with a good bit of research, these high school students often see their identities differently in different contexts.[3] They don't necessarily assume a single racial or ethnic identity that they hold in every situation. We've seen that Marissa, for example, sometimes says she is just "black" but other times that she is "black and white." Perhaps when Cristina says she is "English and Spanish," that is the way she is thinking in the context of the class, where those two identities are very important in what we have studied. And maybe when she says at the end that she does not identify with either race, even though this seems to contradict her first statement, she is feeling her "in-betweenness"—like she does not identify at that moment with either of these slaving identities. Maybe Cristina can perfectly well have several identities simultaneously—white, Latina, Spanish, Salvadoran, mixed—some more salient in certain situations than others.

Two black students engage more directly with the personal identity aspect of the question.

> *Marie* [to 1: yourself]: It made me think of how I would react if all these things happened to me, would I be strong enough to survive. [To 2: your racial group] It made me think that I am proud of my racial group, we are a strong, determined people. It just made me love my race more. [To 3: your moral and political values] It doesn't really affect my moral and political values. It just made me enjoy and take advantage of my freedom.
>
> *Mirvole*: Oftentimes I think about my ancestors' struggle both on the journey and in the "New World." It forces me to step back and evaluate myself mentally and spiritually.

Sometimes teaching about slavery is criticized on the grounds that it will demoralize black students. But Marie's and Mirvole's reactions show us ways that students can pull something very positive from learning about slavery. Marie sees strength in adversity and is proud of black people, her people, for exhibiting that strength. It also makes her more aware of and appreciative of the freedom she herself has. At the same time, Marie places herself imaginatively in the slave's position and, in wondering how she would react, is drawing on historical understanding to ask herself that humbling question. Mirvole also reflects on and evaluates herself—something we teachers are always hoping to help our students do—and she does this on a foundation that she draws from reflecting on her ancestors' experience of slavery. I would have loved to know more about where Mirvole went with her "mental and spiritual" evaluation; but we have seen that Mirvole has a real capacity for moral self-examination and growth and I am sure that her journey will be a fruitful one.

Antonine puts a different spin on question 1:

> *Antonine*: In some ways, slavery does affect the way I think about my-self because I went through some struggles and I was always com-plaining about them like it was a big deal, but after I learned a few things about slavery, it made me realize that the slaves went through ten times more struggles than I could ever go through, but they never really complained. All they did was face reality and wait for the day when their struggles would end.
>
> [To question 2] I believe that most of the people of my racial group are and were educated enough to form alliances with other people to make life better for all African Americans.

I am pleased at this personal lesson Antonine has taken away, that studying about slavery, an experience she very much thinks of as about her people, puts her own personal struggles in a larger perspective. It helps her see that her own troubles may not be as significant as she sometimes experiences them to be. Of course, one challenge of maturity is to put your own troubles into a proper perspective, and studying his-tory is one way of helping achieve this.

On the other hand, I am disappointed in Antonine's portrayal of the slaves as "never complaining" and passively waiting for the day when slavery would be over. When I read that, I was sorry she was not re-membering the resistance to slavery in the different forms we had stud-ied it—slave rebellions, slave escapes, passive resistance, challenges (like Banneker's and Walker's) to racist ideas, and the abolitionist movement. These multiple forms of resistance were an important part of our study of slavery. I guess they had not become an active part of Antonine's thinking about it.

In her answer to question 2, however, Antonine seems to have learned one important lesson from our study of abolitionism, that blacks had al-lied with whites (and, in other contexts, with Native Americans) to, as she says, "make life better for all African Americans." She doesn't actu-ally connect this insight specifically with abolitionism, but in the con-text of the question, it seems reasonable to think that is where she is getting her point about alliances.

Sherilyn has a quite different reaction to question 1:

Sherilyn: No, not really. I don't take my study of slavery personal. I
know some of my black friends who when they started to study
slavery they start to hate all white people and it really got to them
but not to me. It's in the past and really does not change the way
I look at myself.

On the surface it looks like Sherilyn is rejecting the personal appropriation of slavery that Mirvole and Marie accept. But I don't think that
is what she's saying, because when Sherilyn writes "taking the study of
slavery personal" she seems to refer very specifically to hating white
people. That reaction is another concern sometimes expressed about
the teaching of slavery. At other times in the course Sherilyn has been
particularly sensitive to antiwhite hostility. Several times she has been
harshly critical of blacks who are hostile to whites as a group, or to particular whites, for what she feels is an inadequate reason. She has never
directed that criticism to members of the class, and in my experience
no black student has expressed a generalized hostility to whites, either
connected to slavery or not. Of course, perhaps they don't because they
would worry about my reaction as a white teacher. But in Sherilyn's case,
she has brought this point up in several different ways and contexts, and
she seems entirely sincere about it.

Still, it is not surprising, or even inappropriate, if one reaction a black
student of high school age has to studying slavery is to have feelings of
hostility and anger toward white people who perpetrated slavery. But
hostility toward white people in the present is an entirely different matter. There is no justification for being hostile to a *current* member of a
group because *past* members perpetrated some wrong. But some slavery-
related issues might blur that line between present and past, as when
current white students are uninterested in slavery, or take a "Why are we
spending so much time on this?" attitude. Jacques is the one student in
the class who said something along these lines—that it bothered him that
white students didn't want to learn about slavery, as if it weren't important. (He compared this with the Holocaust, which he thought current
white students were more willing to study.) He was upset with many current whites, but not with all whites, and his irritation was always based
on something they did or failed to do, not simply on their being white.

Perhaps some of Jacques's peers would, as Sherilyn reports, hate whites
in general. But just because a young person says, "I hate white people"

and feels that way in that moment, does not mean he hates white people all the time. In any case, I would hope that any teacher would find ways to teach students the basics of collective responsibility—that blame for causing harm attaches only to those who committed it, not to their descendants. But people can also be blamed for lending support to the perpetrators, and that includes passive support—the support of the bystander. And willingly benefiting from slavery, or other evils, is a prime way of providing that support. It is also not unreasonable to see the current advantages that whites have over blacks as a group as having their origins in slavery, and I implied this in the course, although we did not study this issue in any detail. Slavery can trigger an acute sense of current injustices suffered by blacks, and perhaps this is where some of the hostility can come from. In retrospect I wish I had spent more time on these complex issues of collective responsibility.

I did hope that my way of teaching about slavery, recognizing its historical and moral complexity, would put its racial aspect in proper perspective. We learned that slavery had been practiced by Africans and Arabs, before the various European groups, although only the Europeans fully developed it as a chattel system in which slaves had no socially recognized protections or rights, and slaveholders owned the offspring of slaves. We studied the African role in supplying slaves to the European slave traders (see chapter 6). I focused on the economic origins of New World slavery, to make it clear that slavery was not a white plot motivated by a desire to degrade and oppress black people, nor was it initially based on the idea that people of African ancestry were inferior. Students in the class were particularly struck by the fact that in the early colonial period, various populations (Native Americans, Irish, destitute English people) had been utilized in a slave or slave-like way. If students took all that in, it would provide an appropriate context for the racial element of U.S. slavery.

—⚏—

Two of the four white students answered the questions quite differently from the black students, and from each other as well.

> *Adam* [to 1: yourself]: It makes me reflect on how even today the white power structure oppresses and exploits non-whites. [To 2: your racial group] Without being hostile, I often point out the unfair fact that me being white gives me certain privileges in this society.

It's great that Adam so clearly recognizes the way that being white confers advantages and privileges on him, independent of anything he actually does. And his participation in groups that work on racial and other social justice issues gives him the experience of talking to whites about white privilege and their defensive reactions. Adam wants to do more than work out his own understanding of racial privilege; he wants to help other whites appreciate this as well. He knows that whites often don't recognize this privilege. It's just part of a "neutral" reality they take for granted. So Adam attempts to approach whites "without being hostile." His commitment to social justice is impressive, as is his grasp of some of its challenges.

> *Anna*: I grew up learning about slavery all throughout grade school, and beyond, so any effect the information might have had is already present in my mindset. Not that I'm tired of studying slavery in the slightest. I don't really think or identify myself that much with my racial group (not to say I identify with another racial group). So slavery doesn't really affect how I think about white people in general. Basically, I think that people of all races can do evil things.
>
> Studying slavery helps you to understand why certain people are in less than desirable circumstances even today. This can't help affecting political values of having empathy for the underclass.

Anna, who attended a progressive private school before coming to the public high school in her junior year, expresses a complicated range of sentiments here. As a white student, she begins sounding a bit like "Been there, done that." It is as if knowing a lot about slavery makes her less likely to see it as of concern. But then this does not sound right to her, and maybe she's afraid I will think she is not interested in the class, so she reassures me that she is not tired of studying slavery. But this does not translate immediately into the idea that studying slavery is important to her thinking. Rather, she says that she does not identify with white people in general, and she links this thought with slavery not affecting her view of white people. Her disidentifying with whites was a general theme in some of her other writing too.

But Anna's disidentifying with whites has a quite different character than something superficially similar in Adam's remarks. Anna sees herself as "beyond race" in some way; it just doesn't much matter to her, she thinks. Adam also sees himself as different from other white people, so he doesn't identify with them either. But the reason he doesn't is very different from Anna's. Adam thinks white people do not recognize the privileges they get from their race, whereas he does. So he very much knows he is white. He identifies with the category "white," but does not emotionally or personally identify with the people in that category. But Anna's way of not identifying with whites is closer to her thinking she is, or is trying to be, raceless, a kind of alternative to being white.

Anna elaborates on the idea that there is nothing particularly special about being white by saying that people from all groups can do evil things. Of course this is very true, and it is sometimes important to remind students, or anyone, of this perspective. In particular, discussions of racism do sometimes leave students with the misimpression that only black people, or blacks and Latinos, are victimized by racism, and this misunderstanding should be corrected. However, for Anna, this moral insight appears to fit with her minimizing the significance of race in general, and of her whiteness in particular. "People of all races can do evil things" could mean that people of all groups have to be particularly vigilant in combating such evil. That is a message I was trying to get across in the class. But you could also look at this statement in almost the opposite way: "People of all races can do evil things, so the white involvement in slavery and subsequent racial domination does not deserve distinct attention." It becomes a way of letting white people off the hook instead of increasing everyone's moral vigilance. But in our ongoing attempt to understand when the races are symmetrical and when they are asymmetrical, we have to acknowledge that white people in this country, at least are in a distinctive position in relation to slavery, and racism more generally. So while it is necessary to acknowledge that members of any group can be either the perpetrator or the target of racial wrongs, it is also true that whites, especially if one takes the historical record into account, are much more often the perpetrators. Anna does not directly deny this point, but she somewhat heads in that direction.

Anna's partial distancing of herself from responsibilities attached to her racial group sounds a bit like Cristina's earlier statement: "I don't connect fully racially to being either race, so I think it doesn't affect me very much." But I hear a possible difference; it feels to me that Cristina is more working through her complicated relationship to various parts of her identity, while Anna, though being quite conscientious in a general way, is following a pattern of white moral distancing from racism and race that is unfortunately fairly widespread among white Americans. It is an attitude that shows the need for courses such as this to be taught to white students on a much more extensive scale. It also highlights one of the trade-offs of the decision to limit white students to a minority in my class, in order to have a preponderance of blacks and Latinos.

And yet, shifting to a new paragraph, Anna links the current plight of "minorities" with slavery. I am glad she makes this connection, although as I mentioned, the course did not spend much time exploring the specifics of this link. Then Anna says that this connection must in some way encourage some sympathy for these minorities (referred to here as "the underclass"). Anna's use of the passive voice together with the use of academic terminology such as "underclass" seems quite distanced and abstract, and has a strikingly different character from most of the other students' writing in this exercise.[4] (This may simply reflect Anna's private school background, although even if it does, using such language might still reflect or encourage a psychic distancing.) Anna does not directly say that *she herself* has come to feel more empathy for disadvantaged minorities. Rather, she says that the learning can't help but affect such sentiments. This could mean that she herself does have that empathy and hopes that the study of slavery would encourage such empathy in other white students. But it is also possible that she is saying she thinks she *should* have more empathy for these minorities, but is not sure she does. Is this a step toward her developing that empathy?

However we interpret these remarks, Anna's complex sentiments well express her struggles with the material of the class, and her more general knowledge of the history of racism. She is pulled to distance herself from racial concerns, and to think that her whiteness does not really matter; at the same time, she is aware of continuing racial injustice and believes that she should care about it in some way.[5]

In this exercise, we see the students working through their moral identities in relation to their racial identity in light of studying about slavery. The three black girls in different ways relate their own personal struggles to their ancestors' struggles with slavery. Sherilyn is more concerned to distance herself from other black students, who she thinks use slavery in a negative way. The one Latina student who weighs in has learned important lessons in her schooling about her Spanish and English ancestors' role in slavery, and takes off from there into a complex locating of herself in relation to multiple identity categories. Finally, the two white students reflect on their white identity but in very different ways—Adam lodging a moral critique of white privilege and voicing the difficulty of getting other whites to acknowledge this, and Anna distancing herself from whiteness while ambivalently acknowledging its relation to racial injustice.

There is substantial variety within each racial group in response to the identity issues at hand. At the same time, there are notable general differences between the groups. These partly reflect the obvious asymmetries among a black identity, a Latina identity, and a white identity. We see again the importance of viewing each student as an individual, yet also acknowledging their racial group identities as part of that individuality.

11 The N-Word

*Boundaries and Community in
a Multiracial Classroom*

Most of this book documents discussions that occurred during one year, with one group of students. But a spontaneous discussion that took place among a different group of students who took the course a different year raised two important and seemingly distinct but actually related issues in such a striking way that I want to discuss it here. The two issues are the use of the "n-word" and the nature of community and communities inside a multiracial classroom.

In preparing for that offering of the course, I decided that I wanted to help my students think through the confusing but very charged terrain of the n-word. Black kids often use it, seeming to express affection or in-group solidarity. But should they? And if nonblack kids' black friends call each other "nigger" in friendship and affection, can the nonblack kids call those same friends "nigger" as a sign of *their* friendship? I found an article from *Emerge*, a black-oriented popular magazine of the time, that presented different points of view within the black community about whether it was all right for black people to use the word, and planned to use it for that offering of the course.

The summer before the course, I was at a meeting to discuss how parents, especially black and Latino parents, could be more involved in their children's education at the high school. The only parent at the meeting was Mrs. Pinderhughes, an African American. She had very thoughtful things to say about curricular issues. I mentioned my plan to use the *Emerge* article in my fall class. Mrs. Pinderhughes said she thought I shouldn't. She recognized the controversy over the use of the term, but did not think it was appropriate to teach that controversy to high school students. If I wanted to teach it in my Race and Racism course at the college level, that would be fine, she said. College students were mature enough to look at the issue academically. But in her view, the use of *nigger* in high school should be seen as a disciplinary and school climate issue, not an academic one. Teachers and school personnel should be figuring out how to stop students from using this word. They should certainly enforce a "no use" policy in their own classrooms.

I was quite taken aback. Unlike the questions of slavery, or black inferiority, I thought there were two sides to the n-word question, and perhaps more. So I had thought that providing a safe space for talking about an issue that was very much on students' minds could only be for the good. I never thought about the angle Mrs. Pinderhughes expressed. But I was inexperienced as a high school teacher, and I was white. I felt Mrs. Pinderhughes might be seeing something in the situation that I should heed. I also felt it was just safer for me as white teacher to take the path she was suggesting.

I'm not sure I was right about this. We teachers do need to listen to our students' parents. They may have a perspective we had not thought of before, especially if they are of a different race. At the same time, we are professionals and have to exercise our thoughtful and informed judgment. In the years since I taught my course, teachers' professional judgment and behavior have been under such attack that I would now be more hesitant to counsel deferring to parents. But at the time, while I was not entirely convinced by Mrs. Pinderhughes, what she said did make sense, and I took the *Emerge* article and the n-word off the syllabus.

But during a history lesson one October day that year, about six weeks into the semester, the students themselves started to talk about the word *nigger*. I tried to think of a way to change course, applying Mrs. Pinderhughes's disciplinary model. But I hadn't given any thought beforehand about how to do this, and in the moment I couldn't figure out how to stop the conversation, which was zooming along (as it so often did). Feeling guilty and a bit ashamed, I decided to just try to keep the talk moving in a productive direction.

Philippe, a vocal and engaged black student whom we met in chapter 7, started off:

> *Philippe*: There's a difference between *nigga* and *nigger*. No black person would ever pronounce the word as "nigger." So black youth aren't using a word adults disapprove of.

Philippe seemed to address this point especially to me, in a tone that assumed that I particularly needed to hear it (which I did—I wasn't aware of this distinction), and also that he could trust that I would understand his point. Black students dominated the early moments of the discussion.

> *Jocelyn*: I don't like to hear anyone say that word, no matter how you pronounce it.
> *Terri*: I don't either, but I don't think it's *wrong* of other blacks to use it if they want.
> *Kayla*: The word has a negative heritage but some black students feel they can use it in a way that doesn't involve that heritage.

At first, no nonblack students weighed in on this topic. This was not typical of our conversations in the class, but I'm sure these students recognized the perilous terrain here. Lionel was the first nonblack student to put in his two cents. Lionel was a sophisticated white student from an educated, progressive family in which race was often discussed. On an information sheet from the first days of the course, Lionel had written of what "white-phenotyped" people did to "black-phenotyped" people. Lionel was generally respectful and open in the contributions he made to discussions. He didn't use his intellectual sophistication to put down other students.

> *Lionel*: On that "negative heritage" idea, the word *nigger* is like *nerd* as portrayed in the film *Revenge of the Nerds*. In the film the group that had been stigmatized as "nerds" took the word and turned it into something positive that they could use among themselves, and to defy and stand up to the more popular and cool kids who looked down on them. At the end of the film the "nerds" triumph. Did any of you see the film? Do you agree with this comparison?

It was an insightful and imaginative contribution, I thought; but it also made me nervous. In my experience with college students, many black students do not readily accept that another group is experiencing discrimination or bad treatment comparable to that of blacks. They have a strong sense of asymmetry between blacks and nonblacks, especially whites. (Of course, other black students disagree, and fall more on the symmetry side. There is no uniform opinion on this, or any other, racial issue among blacks.) My worry was compounded by Lionel's analogizing the black case to something seemingly as trivial as "nerds." I was concerned that someone might be dismissive of his comparison, though

I had confidence that by this point in the semester, no one would do so in a harsh way.

In my anxious worrying in the few seconds before anyone spoke, I never anticipated what happened next. Murielle, a black student, was sitting in front of Lionel, in the inner horseshoe, her regular seat. Murielle seldom interacted with Lionel because he wasn't in her normal line of vision. She had not talked much in the class so far in the semester. She turned her head around toward Lionel.

> *Murielle*: Yes, it is like that. The way blacks use *nigger* is like the way the nerds in the film use *nerd*.

It was a very generous gesture on Murielle's part. I think she genuinely saw the point of Lionel's comparison. But I also wondered if she sensed that it was a pivotal moment in defining the class as a community. If a black student had rejected Lionel's comparison, this might well have felt to other members of the class, of every group, like drawing a bright line, cutting whites off from blacks, or perhaps cutting blacks off from nonblacks (or a third possibility, marking whites as separate from all students of color). Murielle's affirmation of Lionel's comparison had the opposite effect—reinforcing a sense of community in the classroom across racial lines.

The way community operates in these multiracial and multiethnic classrooms is quite complicated. It has some analogies with the debate over the n-word itself—who does and doesn't get to use that word, who is "in" and who is "out." I very much wanted the black students to feel comfortable speaking their mind, especially in contrast to other advanced classes where, as a small minority, they had reported feeling inhibited about doing so. I hoped that in my class they would not have to censor themselves, to feel that they had to carry the burden of "representing the race," or to worry that they were saying something the white kids might see as stupid. I had the same aspiration for the Latino students, who also had a small presence in the advanced classes, but their numbers in my class were only about 15 percent over the years, so their situation was never analogous to that of the black students. I wanted all of the students who might not have felt at ease in the advanced classes to feel more comfortable in mine.

Blacks understandably have a sense of solidarity as a disadvantaged and often stigmatized group that has historically had to pull together for support in the face of racism, and to change things for the better. Younger blacks, like my students, are not all tuned into this history, but they seem still to experience this sense of solidarity, or at least potential solidarity.

Because of this history and their numbers in the class, black students had the unique standing to draw a sharp line around themselves, to leave the boundary fluid, allowing and sometimes inviting nonblack students into the circle, or (something in between) to hold back from emphasizing themselves as a distinct group. No other group had that kind of power in the class. Black students were never a cohesive group—for instance, they did not generally sit together—so in fact they were infrequently in a position to make maximum use of this power. But another time I taught the course, seven of the eight black students were female, and six of them did tend to sit together. It did not seem an optimal arrangement. Too much of the "action" seemed to be concentrated in their geographical area, and I thought, though I was never sure, that there was a consequent diminished energy level everywhere else in the classroom. My teaching assistant that year and I never quite figured out whether to do anything or what to do about this seating issue. We were afraid that doing something about it would make everyone even more uncomfortable and the black students resentful.

In subsequent offerings of the class, the teaching assistants and I worked out a seating plan during the first week before any "natural" seating arrangement had established itself, and we made sure that there was no "racial clumping" in the seating pattern. I wanted the black students to have a sense of ownership in the class, but not to exercise that ownership in an exclusive way. Murielle's response to Lionel was a moment in which that vision was tested and realized.

I wanted the full class itself to feel like a community to all the students. I tried to help create this by attempting to bring all of the students out, asking them to speak in class, treating each one with respect and interest, and so modeling and encouraging them to do the same. I wanted them to feel they all shared something important, no matter what their racial or ethnic group—the adventure and challenge of learning this important material. I wanted the full-class community to complement the race-based one among the black students, not to replace it. The sense of community among the black students gave them a sense of ownership of the class, and buffered them against worries about their performance and how it might be viewed by other students. Claude Steele, whom we discussed in chapter 7, says that stereotype threat is reduced when minority students are present in a particular setting in substantial numbers. (We will further discuss the issue of diversity and numbers in chapter 12.) But I also needed all students to view each other as equal partners in the shared learning enterprise of the course, and to feel that special bond that comes from a class that is working well. I think the collective aspect of education has gotten lost in today's insistent focus on individual achievement. Interpersonal interaction in classes, and the ties between students that it involves and fosters, are important steps on the way to becoming participatory citizens in a democracy, especially in concert with those of different races and ethnicities.

Murielle's validation of Lionel's comparison between nerds and blacks helped to solidify the whole class as a community. After that exchange, other nonblack students felt safe venturing into the conversation.

> *Tariq*: You can't take a negative word and make it positive. I don't think anyone, including black students, should use that word.
>
> *Lisa*: The n-word is just racist no matter how you look at it. Nobody should use it.

Other nonblack students weighed in, and, though opinions differed, many expressed some version of Tariq's and Lisa's views.

Most of the black students gravitated toward the view that they themselves would not use the word; but at the same time, most did not think it right to be critical of other blacks who did. So there seemed to be somewhat of a racial divide on this issue, with the nonblacks condemning it across the board but most of the blacks thinking that the word could be used in a positive way to express solidarity or affection, even if they thought that looking at the big picture, you really shouldn't use it at all. That is, the nonblacks saw the use of the n-word symmetrically—either *everyone* should be able to use it, or *no one* should. The black students emphasized an asymmetrical dimension—that the word had different social meanings when used by different groups, to different audiences. They thought this difference mattered, although none of them directly addressed the question whether nonblacks should be able to use the word.

—⚭—

Another remarkable intervention changed the dynamic in this class discussion. Negasi had clearly been thinking very hard about all of what his classmates were saying.

> *Negasi*: I'm from Africa, and in fact from a country in Africa, Ethiopia, that slaves did not come from.

The high school had a significant number of students of Ethiopian ancestry, generally fairly recently arrived. It took me a while to recognize this group as a distinctive one within the larger black racial group, but I had come across an area on the first floor near the photocopy center (that I made extensive use of) where the Ethiopians hung out. I eventually realized that this group was speaking Amharic. Negasi himself spoke English without an accent, and he dressed similarly to the other black kids, at least as far as my weak sense of student attire could discern. He had never mentioned his African origins in class before and I was not aware of them.

> *Negasi*: Not only that, my country was never colonized by Europeans. So I don't think I can use the word. Only people whose ancestors were slaves and were oppressed have the heritage that allows them to use the word *nigger* in that positive way.

The spirit in which Negasi spun out this train of thought was remarkable. He was not holding himself above African Americans or trying to distance himself from them, as African immigrants in the United States sometimes try to do. (We discussed this phenomenon in chapter 5.) Nor was he taking pride in Ethiopia's not having been colonized or involved in the Atlantic slave trade. Rather, he was expressing a kind of regret that he could not be included within the community of legitimate users of the n-word.

Negasi's thinking was on a completely different track than the other students. The focus in the student-initiated discussion had been on whether it was ever morally acceptable to use the n-word. Negasi bypassed this question entirely. Instead, he had hooked onto the positive, community-affirming dimension of the n-word's use, which the other black students had acknowledged but were not focused on. And when Negasi thought through the criteria that allowed someone to be part of the community defined by the use of that word, to his way of thinking he, unfortunately, did not meet those criteria.

The response from several other black students was immediate. Several talking at once essentially said, "Look, you're a black male, people will see you as a 'nigger,' as much as they'll see us that way, and that's what counts. So you are inside the circle. You're one of us." No one directly engaged with Negasi's complex thinking about his origins; they were just saying this was irrelevant to the basic inclusion issue he had raised.

The moment was like the exchange between Murielle and Lionel earlier. In both cases, a student made a remark that had the potential to put him outside an important community in the class. And in both cases, responses from other students rejected that distancing, and brought the student into that community. A difference, of course, was that in Negasi's case, the community in question was of the black students alone, rather than the full class community. Another difference is that Negasi had explicitly expressed a concern about his own inclusion, and several students had essentially, and in the spirit of "let's be real," reassured him. In the Lionel case, the inclusion/exclusion dynamic was largely implicit, although Lionel did ask whether the other students accepted his characterization.

I did wonder afterwards what the nonblack students thought about the exchange with Negasi. I hoped the full-class community was strong enough to buffer them from any feeling of exclusion that the explicit assertion of black solidarity might have led to.

Sometimes educators are concerned by in-group socializing and solidarity by racial minority groups—an anxiety captured by the title (and substance) of Beverly Tatum's book, "Why Are All the Black Kids Sitting Together in the Cafeteria."[1] But as Tatum and many others have argued, there is a legitimate place for minority group solidarity and some degree of social separation in educational institutions. That place differs depending on the demography of a school. Where a minority group in the society is also a minority group within the school, and whites are a majority, there can be a greater need for a distinctive space and grouping. In a school like CRLS, where black students are the largest group but no group is a majority, there is not a majority-minority dynamic against which the minority needs to be buffered. Still, there is some value to all racial minorities in some degree of group support and distinctness. It behooves educators to help students of all groups recognize that value and learn to accept those group solidarities in their midst.

At the same time, it is equally vital for educators and other school personnel to encourage bonds across racial and ethnic groups, especially bonds that reflect educational values and shared learning. No student should be encouraged to find his or her entire social or friendship circle inside his racial group; and classes and classrooms should be places where students form attachments that can fully exist in tandem with any pull that the same-race group might exert.

The class was almost over. Philippe was clearly thinking hard about the issue of appropriate uses of the n-word as the conversation proceeded.

He presented a view that seemed to be the culmination of his thinking about the conversation.

> *Philippe*: Black kids often use "nigga" to mean "You're a cool guy, or an intelligent black man." But if they want to say that, they should just say it, rather than calling him "nigga."

Beautifully put, I thought. Overall it seemed to me an excellent conversation on a charged topic, and it advanced the sense of community in the class. I thought Mrs. Pinderhughes would actually be pleased to hear that no student in the class thought it was right to use the n-word themselves. I don't, of course, think that means that none of these students ever used the word. You can't immediately integrate a moral position you reach through a classroom discussion into your own behavior. But I felt sure the students would be more thoughtful about their own use of the word, and perhaps about their fellow students' use as well. The students did not directly take up the question whether it was ever all right for a nonblack student, and especially a white student, to use the word *nigger* as a term of affection for a black friend. It is fair to say that the drift of the conversation was very much against that view; the difference of opinion was only about whether blacks should use the word.

Mrs. Pinderhughes thought no one should say "nigger" (or "nigga," I'm sure she would include, despite Philippe's fine-tuned explanation), and that I should lend my authority to that view. I am still not sure if she is right or not. I think the students gained a lot from having to articulate and defend their own views, and hear each other's. I felt they showed a maturity in how they thought about this issue that Mrs. Pinderhughes seemed to believe you would find only among college students. In any case, you sometimes have to let the students take a discussion where they want to, and make the best of it. I hope I did that.

12 The Last Day

Students Reflect on Diversity and Learning

As teachers, we always want to know what our students are learning from their classes with us. I was particularly interested in how my high school students were taking in the somewhat unaccustomed subject matter, and also how the unusual racial and ethnic mix had affected them and their learning. I didn't gather feedback in any systematic way. But in my last three offerings of the course, I had the students discuss this issue on the last day of class. I also asked a few of them about it in my interviews the next summer [see appendix 3] and occasionally when I had contact with them in the years after they graduated. This chapter is based on all these various conversations.

Adam started off the last-day conversation with this observation:

> *Adam*: This material is touchy. So it's important to have racial diversity in the class because if you said something about another group, there would be people from that group to correct you if you were misinformed or had a misimpression.

I think many people would be surprised to hear this point of view from a white student. They would worry that in discussing race a white student might get jumped on for saying something critical about a minority group. They might express this by saying that an atmosphere of "political correctness" would keep white kids from openly expressing themselves in a setting in which whites were a minority. This common concern forgets that at least some white kids really want to learn about other groups, are aware that they may be misinformed about them, see a diverse class as an opportunity for members of those groups to correct these misimpressions, and can handle this material without getting defensive or feeling muzzled. I know the white kids in my class may not have been a typical cross-section of white students at the high school. But white students were definitely interested in the class. Every time the class was listed in the school course catalog, more than twice as many white students signed up as the number of places I set aside for them (25–40 percent). So I think we should at least approach courses like this with the initial assumption that studying racial material in a mixed setting will ultimately make white students feel enriched.

In any case, what Adam says is precisely what I would expect a teacher to aim for in a course of this kind. Adam joins personal to moral growth in seeing greater and more accurate knowledge as helping him have better relationships with other groups. Teachers should be able to help white students see that they grow from such knowledge. We have to provide a safe space for them to express their curiosity and sometimes voice their concerns, even when students of color might see the remarks as insensitive.

When I taught the course another time, a black student, Carmel, said something similar in the last day's conversation.

> *Carmel*: The class made me aware of other people and their similarities. It makes you reevaluate what you say. Something can seem fine to me when I'm thinking it, but when I say it someone else could be offended.

Obviously it is not only white students who recognize that they have something to learn about ignorance and stereotyping. Carmel beautifully expresses how something can seem fine when you think it, but when you say it, you can be surprised to discover that it offends someone.

In a conversation prompted by that discussion after that year's course was over, Lisa (whom we met briefly in chapter 11) spoke about stereotypes related to attire.

> *Lisa*: When I first came into the class, I though it would be a slacker class, because of the way a lot of the kids were dressed.
> *Me*: What do you mean about how they were dressed?
> *Lisa*: Like with baggy pants and stuff. But I decided to stay in the class and I'm glad I did. Before, when I would walk down the hall and see a group of minority kids, I would try to avoid making eye contact, even though I'm a minority [Latina]. I realize that these kids are intelligent now and that I had stereotypes of them that they weren't. The class taught me those stereotypes were wrong.
> *Me*: Since you say you are a minority, what do you mean when you are referring to "minority" kids?
> *Lisa*: I mostly mean black kids.

Lisa was very clear about the group she had been stereotyping, what stereotypes she had of them, and how the stereotypes affected and harmed her interaction with them. She also pinpointed the way the course helped her to dispel the stereotypes—through recognizing that the minority kids were intelligent, as shown by the intelligent things they said in class. And Lisa's experience reminds us that one "minority" kid can have stereotypes of another "minority" group. (This dimension may be implied in what Carmel said too, but it is not explicit.)

—⚉—

Several students referred specifically to studying history, and some in particular to what they had learned about slavery. Cristina noted that in many courses it doesn't really matter what the composition of the class is.

> *Cristina*: Especially in history courses, you have to cover so much material for such a long period that you don't have time to reflect on it, so you're not interacting with the other students, so it doesn't really matter. I liked this class because it gave me a chance to go into depth in a subject I already knew something about.

I have the impression that many AP history courses are as Cristina describes. They cover an enormous amount of material and leave little time for discussion and reflection. I had certainly emphasized in my course that you have to be able to reflect on history if you are to learn it in a meaningful way. And it is that reflection that is so enriched by differing experiences and perspectives, sometimes grounded in different backgrounds. Jessica, a student from the same class as Carmel, echoed my thoughts.

> *Jessica*: I had always hated history. It is taught in such an impersonal way. This course showed me that history is personal. It has to do with the reality of what you live with now.

I was glad that the history of race was alive for Jessica. Her use of "personal" to express this is interesting. She doesn't, I think, necessarily mean something about her own personal history connecting with the history we studied in the class. She just means that she sees the history as connecting with current reality. As I've mentioned, I did not particularly emphasize definite links between the history we were studying and specific phenomena in the present. I did not, for example, attempt to trace current disparities between white and black to past treatment of blacks by whites. That just wasn't the way I set up the course, although someone could well do so.

What I had tried to convey in the class is that the history of slavery and race were important *in their own right*. Just recognizing that "it was not always like this" is a deeply important thing to understand. Mirvole made this point in a conversation about the course after it was over.

> *Mirvole*: Before the class I always thought, race, it's just always been there, racism has just always been there. But then you broke it down . . . That's one thing that definitely stands out.

This historical point is especially important about racism since racism is an oppressive and destructive force. If you assume (without necessarily even thinking about it) that race and racism have always been with us, you're buying into a deep pessimism about the possibility of making the world better. Mirvole indirectly expressed this in our further exchange:

> *Me*: So you had thought race is like, it's always been there, it's just part of human nature?
>
> *Mirvole*: 'Cause I love that, I brought that, an article you gave us, to my mother, and she was like, wow, I think she made photocopies of it and like gave it out in church.

I think Mirvole was referring to one of the articles criticizing the idea of race from a scientific point of view. And she was saying that she and her mother were excited by this critique. And I am taking that excitement to include or imply a sense that we do not have to be imprisoned by race.

Some of the reflecting I had asked of the students—like whether they thought slave traders believed they were doing something wrong—was not meant to illuminate the present, but only the past.[1] Understanding your country's past, or the past of the slave societies of the Western hemisphere, doesn't have to provide insight on something specific in your present reality to be interesting and important to know.

I had hoped to encourage the students to see how fascinating, how intellectually compelling, the history of slavery and race in the Americas and elsewhere is. Both Cristina and Jessica seemed to be saying that reflecting on history—not just taking it in as facts or as a narrative to be accepted and learned for a test—made it more alive. And perhaps the students had not yet developed the idea of the value of "history for its own sake," so when they expressed their liking for a history course, they did so by saying how it helped them understand the present.

—⚏—

When I asked Pema (after the class was over) for one main idea she got from the class, she answered this way.

> *Pema*: That white people didn't specifically pick black people to, you know, put all their energy on, discriminate against. It just happened that way. It doesn't make the white people any less rude [morally bad], or whatever. Mostly black people think that they specifically picked black people to be rude against. But I think it's more like, it was a coincidence.

A year after the class, I asked her the same question (in an e-mail). This was her response (from the vantage point of a year into college).

> *Pema*: What I learned in your class made me realize that slavery was not started by the whites but has been around for ages. However, the slavery system long ago is different from what the white people did, which was worse. Also, I have realized through your class and other classes that race is not the big issue, class is. Racial discrimination was kind of born because of class.

This is a really interesting take on something that I have discussed in earlier chapters—that the English colonists picked the Africans not because they hated black people or wanted to oppress them but because they were the most available group (once the Atlantic slave trade was in full swing at the end of the seventeenth century). In the class Pema had expressed some hostility toward white people as a group. Her response here shows that a main point she took from the course counters one basis for that hostility—the idea that U.S. slavery was a product of white people looking for a way to oppress black people—and may be prompting her to reassess those feelings. Then Pema takes that point one step further, possibly influenced by courses she has taken in college. She moves slavery even further from race by saying that race is not the big issue—class is. It makes sense to see slavery this way when you shift from viewing it as a system of racial oppression to seeing it as a form of economic organization. It would be correct to say that slavery was "born of class." But I wouldn't say slavery was class *rather than* race—it was both, but in different ways—so I don't agree ultimately with Pema's saying class is the big issue, not race. I'd say they're both part of the big issue.

But in our conversation before she went to college, Pema did not let white people off the hook. She said that just because whites didn't have a conspiracy against blacks didn't make their involvement in slavery was any less "rude." And she echoed Tenzina's point (from chapter 6), which David Walker had emphasized, that American slavery was worse than ancient slavery. I had given the students a general framework for thinking about what made one form of slavery more onerous than another—for example, how grueling the work was, how often slaves were beaten, how destructive to family life, and so on—when we compared slavery in the United States to slavery in Latin America and the Caribbean. Walker had emphasized a further difference: that by saying that slaves were inherently inferior human beings—barely human, in fact—the American system dealt a harm to black people's dignity that had no parallel in ancient slavery. I appreciated Pema's struggles with these issues. Over the course of the semester she had really risen to the intellectual challenge of the course and of being a serious student. She seemed to have continued in that path in college.

—⁂—

In the class discussion on the last day, I shifted the focus and asked the students how the particular racial composition of the class affected them. I had in the back of my mind the Supreme Court's important 2003 decision about affirmative action, *Grutter v. Bollinger*. In its decision upholding certain types of affirmative action plans in college and professional school admissions, the majority opinion had used the idea of a "critical mass." Essentially what it said was that colleges had a very strong reason to make sure they enrolled a certain rough percentage of each major racial group (the "critical mass"), because members of a minority group would not feel comfortable participating in class unless that critical mass of their group was present.[2] Although college is not the same as high school, issues of learning and diversity apply to both.

> *Tenzina*: Being in a class of mostly white students doesn't by itself make me uncomfortable; but if I have an opinion that was different from theirs, I might be more reluctant to express it. I've been in mostly white classes, and I have felt this way in them.

Me: In those classes, was there "opinion homogeneity"? Did the white
kids tend to have similar opinions on things?
Tenzina: Sometimes.

What Tenzina says is partly, but only partly, in line with what the
Supreme Court said. Being in an all-white class does not by itself hinder
participation. But she is inhibited from speaking *if* she thinks her view is
out of line with what most of the white kids are saying.

There is a valuable message in Tenzina's view for teachers in classes
with mostly white students and just a few black or Latino, and possibly
Asian, kids. Even if those kids are talking, we can't be certain they have
broken through to a fully comfortable place. We have to pay close attention to what they are saying, and whether they ever voice opinions that
are at odds with a consensus among the white students. If not, they may
be muzzling themselves a bit.

When I brought up this same topic a different time I taught the course,
several black students said something really interesting. They said they
felt comfortable in the class because there were so many of them (eight
out of twenty-one that year). When I asked why, at first they said it was
because they thought the other black students would agree with them.
But as they explored the issue further in the conversation, they gave
up that view because they recognized that the black students so often
differed among themselves in their opinions. So the comfort factor for
them actually had little to do with opinion agreement.

The Supreme Court actually recognized this dynamic in its majority
opinion because it said that when a minority group had the critical mass
to feel comfortable participating in class, they would reveal differing
opinions within the group. Moreover, members of other groups would
then see that each group has internally diverse opinions, so they would
learn not to stereotype racial groups as having the same beliefs.

In other words, students' comfort level in class is affected not necessarily by agreement with other members of their group, but by the mere
presence of members of their racial group. Perhaps they had a confidence that their fellow black students would come to their defense if
they were attacked by a student from another group than if there were
only a small number of blacks in the class. There is something about the
mere presence of other members of your group that makes you more
comfortable—not necessarily something about agreement in opinion.

But the racial dynamics and demographics in my class were not really the same as what the Court had in mind in its opinion in the *Grutter*

case. Their idea of "critical mass" was 13 to 20 percent for blacks and Latinos (plus Native Americans) in total, the percentage at the University of Michigan under the affirmative action plan they were upholding.[3] My class had about that percentage of Latinos alone, and a much higher percentage of blacks, between 38 and 55 percent in the different years. Blacks were always the largest single racially defined group. *Maybe* the black students in the class described above would have felt a similar comfort level with a smaller percentage of their group. Perhaps eight out of twenty-one is above the critical-mass-for-comfort bar. Still, there is little reason to think that just because having seven fellow black students makes a black student feel comfortable, *two* other black students (the number if there were 15 percent blacks) would have the same effect. So what my black students from that class were saying about comfort might well have required a higher percentage than the Supreme Court was suggesting.

Another way to look at this is that there are different kinds of comfort, and the Supreme Court is talking about only one kind. Tenzina spoke to two of them—comfort in being in the class and talking (as long as you didn't disagree with the white majority), and comfort in offering a differing opinion. What the Supreme Court had in mind (although it did not explicitly say so) is closer to her second type, because they want students to feel free to say whatever is on their mind.

I had the impression that black students in all my classes often felt a third kind of comfort, different from Tenzina's two—a higher level that is more like feeling that you belong in that class, and the space of the class belongs to you. This higher level may allow for a deeper willingness to plumb difficult and touchy issues that an acute awareness of one's minority status in a white-dominated class would not. For example, I wondered if the black students would have felt as free as they did in my class to talk about hair, skin color, and the n-word (chapters 9 and 11) if they had experienced only the level of comfort that meets the Supreme Court's standard of critical mass. I cannot be sure, but there is a difference between that sense of belonging and the lesser but still significant feeling of ease when speaking in class.

Some white students also spoke to the comfort issue. Adam and Hannah said they did feel comfortable, but maybe that had to do with their having more experience in mixed groups, either in middle school or in organizations they were involved in, than some other white students. But Hannah also had a different experience, which she shared.

Hannah: I was in an African American literature class this semester, but when I got there, I was the only white student and I didn't feel comfortable. I was worried what the black students would think of me, although none of them actually said anything that made me feel uncomfortable. But I transferred out of that class and took this class instead.

Clara: Black students might make you feel uncomfortable—but not on purpose. You might just be worried that as a white person, or a non-black person, you might say something that would offend or upset the black students.

Is Hannah's experience similar to, symmetrical to, Tenzina's? Does she feel uncomfortable in an all-black class only because she might say something different that would challenge what the other students are saying? She doesn't articulate it that way, but the issue seems larger—more a feeling that the black students would think she didn't belong, simply because she was white. Clara helpfully adds a comment that is in the spirit of what Hannah says—that she might feel this way even if the black students didn't put out a vibe of exclusion aimed at making the white student uncomfortable. And that may be analogous to what sometimes goes on for the minority students in the AP classes; they may feel like the white students will think they do not belong, even if the white students do not do anything to put out this message.[4]

—⁓—

I wanted to continue exploring whether there were racial asymmetries in these different kinds of comfort and discomfort:

Me: Would a white kid in an all-black class feel uncomfortable in the same way as a black kid in all-white class?

Mirvole: It isn't the same; it would be different kinds of uncomfortable.

I pressed Mirvole to clarify but she said she couldn't explain it. I could tell that what Mirvole had on her mind in her remark about "different kinds of uncomfortable" was not whether the "intimidation" (in Clara's words) was intentional. I thought Mirvole's point was related to asymmetry. Time was running out, so I weighed in.

Me: Well, one thing some people might feel is that if the black student was the only student, she might be worried that the white students would think that she did not belong in the class, that she was not

a good enough student to be there; but no one would make that assumption about the one white student in the all-black class.

Mirvole: That's exactly what I meant.

Mirvole was focusing on a vulnerability that black students have and
that we had spoken about in class before, especially in the discussion of
Thomas Jefferson's views of blacks. It was another example of an asymmetry between racial groups. The asymmetry may have been hard to
see, since there was something analogous in the two situations—that
the student in the numerical minority within the classroom felt uncomfortable. Also, the symmetry framework tends to dominate discussions
about race. As we've seen, many people assume that what is right and
wrong when done to one group is always equally right or wrong when
done to another. So all that might make it hard to see the asymmetry
that Mirvole was getting at.

As Mirvole recognized, even if she couldn't articulate it in the moment, the quality of the discomfort was very different in a way that
mattered. Abdul, a student in Carmel and Jessica's class, expressed that
difference in something he once said in a discussion of AP classes.

Abdul: When I am in an advanced placement (AP) class with mostly
white students, I don't speak because I'm worried that people will
wonder if I belong in the class—if I am smart enough. I am worried
that they will take what I say to confirm their suspicions.

This is Steele's point about stereotype threat. Some minorities labor
under a suspicion that they are not smart enough; whites as a group do
not. That's why members of minority groups might feel that they don't
belong, or aren't sure they do, and why the kind of discomfort blacks
feel in a white-dominant class is not the same as what whites feel in a
black-dominant class.

It is interesting that it was Abdul who stated this point. Asian students
(as Abdul is) are not generally stereotyped as not intelligent. If anything,
the Asian stereotype goes in the other direction—they are often assumed
to be smarter than other groups, including whites. But scholars have
pointed out that the "model minority" stereotype is applied to some
Asian groups, defined by national origin, more than to others—roughly,
East Asians (Chinese, Japanese, and Koreans) and South Asians (especially Indians), but less so to Southeast Asians.[5]

But Abdul is Indian, a group to whom the model minority stereotype *is* applied, so this differentiation among Asians does not explain why he feels a threat of not being seen as smart in the advanced classes. There could be a class-related explanation. While Indian immigrants are, on average, one of the most highly educated of any immigrant group, defined by national origin, Abdul's parents are not well-educated, and have working class jobs.[6] In addition, Abdul's family lives in a large housing project where most of the residents are black or Latino. I think all this shaped the form of "minority" identity that Abdul took on.

Of course, a final reason that Abdul may feel vulnerable intellectually is that even if Asian students on average do not feel that vulnerability, this generalization holds at best only for the most part and still allows many exceptions, of which Abdul might be one.

These reflections on asymmetries in comfort require a qualification of the three levels I suggested earlier (comfort sitting in the class, comfort in speaking one's mind, and belonging/ownership). The asymmetry is already implicit in our discussion of the first two, since in those cases comfort depends both on being a minority (in that class) and on whether your minority group labors under a suspicion that you can't do the work, that you don't belong in an intellectually demanding class. But I think asymmetry applies to the "ownership" level also. I think that if your group is not accustomed to having ownership of an intellectually challenging space, then when you do, it feels different and has a different character than if your group *routinely* has ownership of such spaces—if that is what everyone, including you, expects.

To be sure, it is not as if the black and Latino students never had ownership of the class space at the high school. The black group, as the largest racially defined group in the school, was numerically dominant in many of the "college prep"–level classes. But they very seldom had that dominance in the advanced classes.[7] So I think maybe since none of the black students in my class would have had the experience of ownership in an advanced class before, that sense of ownership was something special for them; they implicitly felt the contrast with their other classes, both the less demanding ones in which they were a majority and, for some, the more demanding ones in which they were a minority. This is speculative; none of the students said this explicitly, although several of them had spoken of forms of discomfort in the demanding classes. But it is very much in line with there being important asymmetries between whites on one side and blacks and Latinos on the other.

—w—

Following the thread of diversity and comfort, Cristina took a different direction:

> *Cristina*: I feel more comfortable in a setting where there's more than one ethnic group there. When I begin to feel uncomfortable is when I'm with all one group. It isn't a lot of Latino kids that makes me comfortable, but whether the class is diverse overall.
> *Clara* [taking this point a step further]: I actually feel *un*comfortable in classes that are predominantly Latino.

Interestingly, the view of these two Latinas challenges the Supreme Court's reasoning in the *Grutter* case. The majority decision implied that Latinos need to have some number of Latinos in a class to feel comfortable participating. Much thinking about educational diversity presumes this identity-based approach—students are made comfortable or uncomfortable by the presence or absence of members of their own particular minority group. Yet Clara and Cristina's different way of experiencing classroom diversity may become increasingly typical. If a goal of educational multiculturalism is to have diverse racial and ethnic groups socializing and interacting across group boundaries in classes, clubs, sports teams, and schools, then students who grow up under that diversity regime may feel comfortable with the diversity itself—not only with groupings of their same racial or ethnic group. And indeed, like Clara, some of them will feel *more* comfortable with the general diversity than with their same-race group.

Since the first time I taught the course, I have heard a version of this reaction from various students. In that class I had two black students who went on to (different) historically black colleges after high school. They both wrote to me from college to say that they missed the diversity of CRLS. One said explicitly that he missed interacting with white people.

Some white students from my classes, who went on to predominantly white colleges (such as UMass Amherst), have also said that they missed the diversity of CRLS. Sometimes these students contrasted their experience at college with those of other white students at their same colleges who were from high schools that were proportionately whiter than the colleges. These non-CRLS white students often experienced these colleges as diverse because they were more so than their high schools. My ex-CRLS students were amazed that their fellow white students experienced these predominantly white colleges as so "diverse." For example, in 2008, UMass Amherst had 9 percent total black and Latino students combined, and 8 percent Asian students. This just makes the obvious point that comfort with diversity depends on what you are used to. But I do not think it is good for a white student to experience a 9 percent black and Latino student body as "diverse." That assumes "white America" as a norm, which is not accurate and is not a civically healthy way of thinking about the nation and its institutions (such as colleges). (Blacks and Latinos comprise about 27.5 percent of the American population, a figure that is growing.[8]) So if the overly segregated nature of our neighborhoods and schools produces this way of thinking, that is yet one more reason for trying to make changes in our school and neighborhood patterns so that people's lives are more intertwined with those of other races and ethnicities.

An interview with Sherilyn after she had graduated brought together a lot of these themes in an interesting way:

> *Me*: How did the racial breakdown in the class affect your experience of the class, as different from some other classes that you've taken?
>
> *Sherilyn*: It had an equal mix of equal people talking. Like you picked kids that weren't afraid to talk. . . Or weren't afraid to get into a conversation and expect different opinions from different cultures, you know what I'm saying? So it's like a spokesperson from a different culture, or a different way of living, or a different family, you know? Which is what I like.
>
> *Me*: You mean that a lot of people would talk?
>
> *Sherilyn*: So you weren't just hearing one *huge* group of African Americans and one *huge* group of white Americans . . . In our class, it was broken down into, like you weren't just black, I wasn't just black? You know? I was African American and Jamaican. There's a difference between me and Mirvole . . . like we were *individuals*. You know what I'm saying? And when you asked about race, you know, I wasn't just *black*.

Sherilyn isn't using the language of "comfort" to talk about her experience. But she is speaking partly to that issue, and she is bringing in a different dimension than the other students or the Supreme Court did. She is preferring the dynamics in my class, in which the ethnic subdivisions within the black group are recognized, to a class where the dynamic constructs blacks simply as a whole-race group and whites as a whole-race group. Students speak as blacks but not *only* as blacks—also as members of a particular ethnic/cultural group, like Jamaican or Haitian.

Sherilyn isn't talking about how the ethnic differences do or don't make her feel comfortable, but how they contribute positively to her learning. One interesting way she speaks to this is by saying the students are "spokespersons" from their groups. We teachers are frequently warned *not* to treat individual students as spokespersons from their racial ethnic groups. It is good advice, because we want to treat each student as an individual. To say to a student, "Sherilyn, what is the black (or Jamaican) point of view on this question?" Or "How do you as a black (or Jamaican) student see this question?" is to deny them space to speak as an individual.[9] But Sherilyn's response also reminds us that in many educational situations, as we discussed earlier, students are individuals but they are also members of groups, and there is no contradiction between these two perspectives. Indeed, when Sherilyn says that in our class the students were "individuals," she seems actually to mean, at least in part, that they were not just members of *racial* groups, but *ethnic* subgroups of those racial groups. I think that is a cautionary note about overemphasizing students as "individuals, not only members of groups." In many settings, students *want* to speak as members of racial or ethnic groups. We have to make it their choice to do this; we can and sometimes should invite it, but should not force it on them.

> *Sherilyn*: We were talking about something that with the wrong group [i.e., class], it could have been very sensitive, hard to get through. We were talking about race, we were talking about the way other people look at you, the way people talk about you; you know . . . stereotypes.

Sherilyn notes (in the earlier segment) that the students in the class weren't afraid to talk. I can't tell if she thinks I actually hand-picked students who I thought had this willingness, or if she just means that's who ended up in the class. But she says that they were interested in each other's backgrounds and expected that to be part of what they were contributing. And here she says the class had conversations about all these sensitive issues that, with a different group, might well not have worked. And yet we did it, and it did work.

I'm glad Sherilyn brings this feature of the class out so explicitly. And I am sure she is right that with some other group of students, these conversations would not have happened. But I do not agree with her implication that there was something very distinctive about this group. I think that most students, when placed in a setting where they are trusted and respected, where the teacher is interested in what they have to say and makes the space in the class safe for them to speak, will generate conversations comparable to the ones that Sherilyn values so much.

CONCLUSION

The Personal, Moral, Social, and Civic Values of Integrated Education and Diversity

After reading this account of my class, I hope some teachers (including college professors) will think, "Maybe I could teach a course like this"; parents, "I wish my son/daughter could take a course like this"; and citizens, "I hope young people get to take a course like this." The two main elements that made the class such a rich educational experience were the mix of kids in the class and the racial curriculum. You could have the student mix without the curriculum and the curriculum without the student mix. Each would still provide great educational benefit. But when you have a racially mixed class engaging with race as a curricular subject, it is a very special combination.

Public discussions about the value of education increasingly focus on the individual student's academic skills, and how they contribute to his or her college or job readiness and upward mobility. An even narrower focus is student test scores, which are increasingly treated as the standard of educational accomplishment. But traditionally education, especially public education, has been recognized to serve other important purposes. It has aimed to enhance students' personal growth (including intellectual growth beyond its instrumental value for economic success), to contribute to their moral development, to improve their social relations, and to develop their capabilities as future citizens. Schooling contributes to the social good in helping to produce moral persons and responsible, informed citizens.

When students come to have respectful and engaged conversations with peers of other races, learning to listen and to express themselves across the racial divide, this is a moral step forward, and it is personally enriching as well. Students learn to treat others with respect across divisions that often inhibit people from achieving that respect. They learn to be more accepting, welcoming, and appreciative of differences, rather than hostile, fearful, prejudiced, or resentful of them. This is more than mere tolerance. My students did not merely tolerate one another.

Respect and appreciation are core moral attitudes and, especially in the face of potentially divisive differences such as race, they define a higher moral standard than tolerance—one we should look to our schools to help students achieve.

These classroom exchanges and engagements also help students develop the intellectual tools to identify and criticize stereotypes, and to understand the forces in society that affect the well-being of different groups. The ability to analyze the factors in society and history that contribute to social inequality and social division naturally, if not inevitably, informs and encourages a sense of social justice. Thus the development of such abilities is not only intellectual, but also moral and civic.

Learning in racially integrated environments also enhances students' social development. It enables richer interpersonal relationships with a wider range of peers than students have if they take classes primarily with those of their own race or attend schools with little diversity. These relationships do not have to be intimate friendships to be personally enriching, although hopefully some close friendships do emerge in these contexts. Even in-school friendships that do not carry over to the student's life outside of school can be significant relationships.[1] But these social and moral benefits require more than just hallway contact. The different groups have to take part in ongoing shared activities, especially learning together in the same class. Remember Lisa's recognition that she had had no meaningful contact with significant groups among her fellow students at the high school and held uncorrected stereotypical views of them (chapter 12). It took the shared classroom to turn those anonymous "others" into fellow students for her.[2]

Courses like mine also help develop students' civic capacities. I have emphasized the critical thinking dimension that we saw in the class's moral discussions and also in assignments such as that on Walker and Jefferson (chapter 7). Critical thinking helps citizens analyze social phenomena and evaluate public issues and policy proposals connected with them. Other civic capacities are also involved, for which both the composition of the class and the curriculum are important. Race remains a major source of disparity in access to education, health, a decent job, a decent income, a home in a good neighborhood, and other aspects of life in the United States. So, if civic engagement aims (among other things) to improve the lot of all U.S. citizens and to create a more just society, understanding racial issues and being able to discuss them intelligently and productively with fellow citizens is an absolute necessity. Yet, as Attorney General Eric Holder noted, Americans in general are neither adequately informed nor capable of having in-depth conversations about race, most especially with persons of other racial groups (introduction). In a revealing study of people now in their forties who graduated high school in 1980, the authors find that whites in this group hold two contrasting views about racial inequality. The first sees blacks and Latinos as to blame for their disadvantaged state. The second group is "uncomfortable with such an explanation, even if they are not sure exactly why." The authors say that the second group is typical of the white graduates of racially mixed schools, while the first is more typical of whites who did not attend mixed schools.[3]

The whites in the integrated schools group are a bit better tuned in to racial reality than the nonintegrated schools group. But their views are still pretty superficial in terms of a real understanding of the racial history of the United States and its legacy for the present—of slavery, segregation, discrimination, and ongoing prejudice. The authors of the study report that the 1980 graduates of integrated schools say that despite the sincere attempt to bring students of different races together in the schools and classes they attended, racial issues were almost never part of the curriculum nor discussed in other contexts in those schools. This is no doubt part of the reason for these graduates' superficial understanding of race in American society, compounded by the absence of public conversation after they left school.[4]

Courses that deal with race—not only ones like mine in which the entire curriculum concerns race—and also have a racially diverse group of students offer the best setting to develop race-relevant civic knowledge, skills, and capability. As Adam and Carmel said, in the mixed class you might say something you believe about other groups, and their reaction might lead you to reconsider, to think that maybe you didn't have it right (chapter 12). Comparatively speaking, as a group, whites have the greatest civic (and moral) need to learn about race, as they are the most likely of all racial groups to have misinformed and stereotypical views.[5] So teaching racial material even to an all-white class would be very valuable. But embedding that curricular learning in the experience of hearing from students of different racial groups and engaging with them is most likely to make that learning stick.

Such mixed classes contribute to developing civic capability in another way as well. They help provide a foundation for a sense of civic attachment to a broader group of future fellow citizens of our national political community than one finds in one-race-dominant schools. By learning to see fellow students of different races as peers in the classroom and as part of the shared activity of learning together, the students gain a much greater ability to feel that people of different races are bound up with them in society, that they all have a shared fate. The interpersonal and collective dimension of learning has received too little attention in the current insistent focus on individual attainment. Our discussion of community in classrooms (chapter 11) pointed the way to a connection between in-class community and a future sense of civic attachment across racial and ethnic divides.

Thus when these diverse classes work well, they contribute to the students' moral, social, and civic development. In doing so, they help the individual student live a better, richer, more fulfilling life in all kinds of ways, as education at every level should contribute to. But all these aims of education garner little attention in today's public and policy discussions of "educational reform."

These moral, social, civic, and personal benefits accrue to members of *all* racial groups—all students are enriched by an education that puts them in productive and engaged connection with one another. But this racial symmetry is not meant to deny important asymmetries in the benefits of integrated education. Black and Latino students have more to gain from integrated education and more to lose from separation and isolation. They acquire more social capital from going to school with whites than whites do with them. Because whites as a group have more resources and are thus better connected to successful outcomes in work and society, knowing how to work with, interact with, and understand white people helps blacks and Latinos achieve occupational success.[6] This asymmetry is a product of our unjust social order of racial hierarchy. If our society were more truly equal, benefits of interracial contact would be more symmetrical. While acknowledging these asymmetries, I want to reemphasize that the moral, social, personal, and civic benefits of integration very much accrue to all students, including whites.[7]

—⁜—

I suggested that we have lost touch with this broader set of benefits to individual students that education in diverse settings devoted to learning about that diversity itself, can and should promote. Equally striking is how we have lost touch with the benefits *to society* of educational integration and diversity. These benefits are implied in the civic purposes just mentioned. A society that is both democratic and pluralistic requires citizens who understand and appreciate democratic and diversity-embracing values, and who develop capabilities that enable them to live by and promote the realization of these values. Justice Sandra Day O'Connor, the author of the affirmative action decision discussed in chapter 12, said after she retired from the Supreme Court that the testing regime fostered by No Child Left Behind "has effectively squeezed out civics education because there is no testing for that . . . We can't forget that the primary purpose of public schools in America has always been to help produce citizens who have the knowledge and the skills and the values to sustain our republic as a nation, our democratic form of government."[8] The civic purposes of education have also been affirmed by many state courts interpreting their constitutions in the past twenty-five or so years, in cases establishing a right to a "sound basic education," understood in part as preparing the student to be a citizen.[9]

In this spirit, Wells and her coauthors express some of the collective civic benefits of integrated schooling:

> [V]irtually all of the graduates we interviewed said that attending desegregated public schools dispelled their fears of people of other races, taught them to embrace racial and cultural differences, and showed them the humanness of individuals across racial lines. In comparing themselves to peers and spouses who did not have similar integrative experiences, they are quick to note how much more comfortable they felt in multiracial settings or in places there they are a minority.[10]

As our society becomes more and more diverse, there is an increasing need for its citizens to gain this sense of shared humanity, appreciation of diversity, and greater comfort, ease, and trust with those who are different. We can hope that many of them will follow my two students who said they were more comfortable with diversity itself than with classes mainly of their own ethnic group (chapter 12). In its 2003 affirmative action decision, the Supreme Court cited "better prepar[ing] students for an increasingly diverse workforce and society" as an important reason to ensure racial diversity in higher education.[11] Diversity-friendly capabilities enable citizens to better appreciate how their fellow citizens' group identities affect their life experiences and outlooks, while also rendering them better able to see these fellow citizens as individuals.

This "seeing as individuals," which I have discussed several times in the book (e.g., chapters 2, 12), is emphasized in the court's majority opinion. But the opinion does not sufficiently emphasize the complementary civic and intellectual goal—understanding ethnic and racial groups *as groups* and the ways that "race matters" to the prospects, well-being, and experience of members of those groups.[12] Nor does the opinion recognize that appreciating the actual historical and social experiences of particular groups contributes to recognizing the individuality of members of those groups.

Race is indeed, as the court emphasizes, only one important form of social difference that constitutes "diversity." But it is one that poses distinctive civic challenges and should inform particular civic ideals. On the one hand, as we have seen, race is still a major axis of inequality in virtually every life domain. The United States has not come near to delivering on the American promise of equality for all racial groups, notwithstanding great strides since the segregation era. On the other hand, we hear little about these racial disparities from our president and elected representatives, despite President Obama's eloquent delineation of racial inequality in his 2006 book *The Audacity of Hope*.[13] As opinion polls suggest (see note 5), for the most part whites as a group are invested in not seeing injustice, and in being reassured both that they are not to blame for and have no responsibility for the injustices that might exist. They are not eager to hear about racial injustice, especially from a black president.[14] This is an unfortunate situation that we need to change, and education can help us do so.

We need to be educating a new generation of young people of all races who will recognize race as an important public issue; who will understand the complexities of the issue, with a foundation in basic racial literacy that courses in several different high school subjects can help to provide; who will have some commitment to racial justice, recognizing that existing inequalities offend against moral and political principles of justice and equality for which the nation allegedly stands; and who will have some practice in discussing racial issues in a respectful and constructive way with future citizens of all races. My students learned why race is such an especially touchy topic, generating discomfort, misunderstanding, and strain; and, partly through that understanding, they took some steps toward engaging with it productively. If our society is to function well as an increasingly multiethnic democracy, more citizens must develop these capabilities, in the way that only schools can do, so that down the road a black or Latino president (or a white or Asian one) can talk frankly about racial inequality.

The need to promote constructive interracial contact, engagement, and understanding through integration in neighborhoods, schools, public spaces, and workplaces is little recognized in policy and judicial decisions. And despite the increasing diversity, Americans continue to live separately from one another, with whites and blacks the most segregated groups (a state of affairs harmful to both groups but much more so to blacks), and Latinos and Asians no less segregated than in 1980.[15]

In the education world, integration has increasingly moved off the policy agenda. Superficial attention is paid to racial disparities in education. But the set of interrelated measures actually needed to address those disparities—in addition to integration (by race and class), at least a reduction in poverty and in overall economic inequality, early childhood education, increased pay for teachers in schools with high concentrations of low-income students, training of such teachers to see these students as capable of greater achievement than they might have already shown, school funding formulas tied to student population needs rather than local tax base, more demanding classes for blacks and Latinos—are seldom put on the table.[16] The United States is currently as unequal a society as any in the developed world, and as unequal as it has been since before the Great Depression, and this general inequality has intensified inequalities between whites and blacks and Latinos.[17] Yet the impact of this general inequality on disparities of educational access is barely discussed outside of particular academic circles.[18]

As a high intellectual demand class primarily for blacks and Latinos, my own course was aimed at the disparity in intellectually demanding courses. That issue is not intrinsically related to integration. Demanding classes can be offered in largely segregated minority schools, and they should be more often than they are. But the two issues often come together in integrated schools because the high intellectual demand courses in such schools tend not to contain minority students in sufficient numbers. Integration in school buildings must be accompanied by integration inside classrooms.

—∿—

One bright spot on the current scene pushing back against this retreat from integration is that in December 2011, the U.S. Departments of Justice and Education clearly and forcefully recognized the civic and educational importance of integrated education and diversity, in a joint set of guidelines the two departments issued "on the voluntary use of race to achieve diversity and avoid racial isolation in elementary and secondary schools." The guidelines say at the outset:

> As the Supreme Court has explained, elementary and secondary schools . . . are "pivotal to sustaining our political and cultural heritage"; they teach "that our strength comes from people of different

races, creeds, and cultures uniting in commitment to the freedom of all." Racially diverse schools provide incalculable educational and civic benefits by promoting cross-racial understanding, breaking down racial and other stereotypes, and eliminating bias and prejudice.[19]

The political context of these guidelines is important to note. In 2007, in one of the most important school integration cases since *Brown* (in 1954), the Supreme Court struck down two student assignment plans that had been utilized by their districts to achieve a degree of racial integration in their schools (often referred to together as the *PICS* cases).[20] Use of individual students' racial identities has been perhaps the most common way that districts committed to in-district racial integration keep their schools from becoming too segregated. But the court's decision in the *PICS* cases greatly reduces the scope of permissible integrative efforts that rely on students' racial identity. In 2008, the Bush administration issued a set of guidelines for school districts in light of the *PICS* ruling. Its guidelines emphasized the restrictions on employing individual students' racial identities, and on that basis discouraged districts from undertaking race-conscious integrative efforts.[21] What the Obama administration has done is to supplant the Bush-era guidelines, which have remained in place until the present, with a highlighting of the aspects of the *PICS* decision that affirm the importance of racial integration in primary and secondary school to the civic health of the nation and the mutual enrichment of students. Clearly a product of Eric Holder's tenure at the Department of Justice as well as pressure from civil rights groups to provide an alternative interpretation of the *PICS* ruling, the guidelines lay out in some detail ways that districts can engage in integrative policies within the letter of the ruling, drawing mainly from Justice Kennedy's controlling opinion in the case.

For example, a district may use nonracial factors, such as parental education, socioeconomic status, and the socioeconomic character of a student's neighborhood, as proxies for racial ones. The district could, for instance, assign individual students to particular schools based on family socioeconomic status, where a lower SES is more likely to mean the student is Latino or black. The guidelines also permit a district to rely directly on racial information, such as the racial character of neighborhoods or elementary schools, in order to site new schools, redraw school zones, create feeder elementary and middle schools for middle and high schools, or give preference to students from certain neighborhoods in admission to a particular school. The use of this type of racial information is regarded as in the spirit of the *PICS* ruling because it does not directly make use of an individual student's race to assign her to a school.[22]

Supreme Court decisions are important civic texts, shaping and often reflecting both policy and public discourse. The *PICS* decision has drawn a tremendous amount of commentary and is indeed a civic text for our times. I want to highlight a few of its many elements, but let me first describe its basic holding. Four justices declared that the achievement of racial integration is not a compelling state interest but mere "racial balancing," which they take to be unconstitutional.[23] Four other justices declared that the two districts' integration plans were constitutional (and more generally upheld the use of student racial identity in student assignment in order to support integration). The ninth justice, Anthony Kennedy, formed a five-justice majority with the former group to rule against the two districts and to reject the use of individual student racial identity, but joined the latter four to affirm the importance of racial integration as a vital public purpose. As Kennedy powerfully states: "This Nation has a moral and ethical obligation to fulfill its historic commitment to creating an integrated society that ensures equal opportunity for all of its children."[24] It was for the most part Justice Kennedy's opinion that formed the basis of the overall decision, and therefore of the Departments of Justice and Education guidelines.

Chief Justice John Roberts wrote for the four who ruled against the two districts' plans and rejected racial integration as a compelling state purpose. One portion of Justice Roberts's opinion addresses the issue of diversity, noting that the *Grutter* (affirmative action) decision had said that achieving diversity was an important goal that permitted higher education institutions to take race into account in admissions policies, subject to various constraints. But the cases in which that compelling goal has been affirmed—*Bakke*, *Grutter*, and *Gratz*—have all been at the postsecondary level.[25] As part of his discussion of diversity, Roberts said that the *Grutter* court "relied upon considerations unique to institutions of higher education."[26] This observation is part of the chief justice's argument that the court's support for diversity in higher education does not extend to the K–12 level and thus to the *PICS* cases.[27] I am not equipped to assess the constitutional question about the implied reach of the *Grutter* decision. But it is very much worth noting that, on their own merits, diversity-based arguments are actually *more* compelling at the primary and secondary level than they are in the context of the selective colleges and universities that employ affirmative action programs.

This is so for several reasons. First, K–12 students would gain the benefits of integration and diversity (and thus of policies that support them) for many more years than do college students—twelve compared to four (though more for the smaller number who go on to postgraduate education). Second, the earlier in their lives that students' worlds are integrated, the more the students will be able to reap integration's benefits—for example, the more "natural" it will seem to them to live in a world of diverse groups and individuals, and thus (everything else being equal) the deeper their investment in such a society. In his dissent in the *PICS* decision, Justice Stephen Breyer (on behalf of the four who favored upholding the desegregation plans) speaks to part of those rewards, though only in relation to black students. Summarizing a large number of studies of school integration, he says that: "(1) black students' educational achievement is improved in integrated schools compared to racially isolated schools, (2) black students' educational achievement is improved in integrated classes, and (3) the earlier that black students are removed from racial isolation, the better their educational outcomes."[28] (I have argued in this chapter for a much broader range of benefits—personal, social, moral, and civic—to the individual student and to society than Breyer mentions here.)

In addition, if we couple our thinking about educational diversity with residential diversity, recognizing that residential segregation is a major cause of school segregation (and the reverse causality holds as well), then attempts to make our neighborhoods more racially heterogeneous as part of promoting school integration would contribute to the broader impact of integration on K–12 students, compared to students in affirmative action colleges.

Third, many more students are potentially affected by integrative policies at the K–12 level than the comparatively quite small number of students attending affirmative action institutions. Obviously only a subset of K–12 students go on to higher education, and a smaller percentage of them attend colleges selective enough to practice affirmative action,[29] which they can do by having a significantly higher proportion of qualified applicants than the number of places. Colleges can then select among their applicants partly on the basis of race in the ways that the *Grutter*, *Gratz*, and *Bakke* decisions said were (and were not) permissible as part of an affirmative action program.[30]

Finally, the socioeconomic diversity within all racial groups that can be part of integrative policies at the K–12 level is much more extensive than that secured by higher education affirmative action. Although in the early years of affirmative action (the late 1960s and 1970s) the economic gap between blacks and Latinos admitted under those policies and whites at those institutions was much greater than it is now, increasingly, the blacks and Latinos who are brought in under affirmative action admission policies are from fairly well-to-do families. (This shift is due partly to the success of the early affirmative action programs in helping to create a black middle class whose children are now among the major beneficiaries of current affirmative action policies.) So, as many observers have noted, racial diversity at selective colleges increasingly brings much less socioeconomic diversity in its wake.[31]

Integration at the K–12 level is not restricted, as college admission is, by students' scores and grades, which tend to correlate with SES status. So a much broader economic spectrum of all racial groups is, or can be, included in K–12 integrative policies.[32]

One might reply that by talking of *SES* diversity in the context of *racial* diversity, I am bringing in an extraneous element in the comparison of higher education and precollege education. But this is not so. Although race and class are not the same, they are deeply intertwined with one another—not only in the relatively less advantaged class position of blacks and Latinos compared to whites, but also in the way "diversity" in ethnoracial contexts is generally understood. That is, the value of educational ethnoracial diversity resides partly in differences in societal experience and position strongly related to advantage and disadvantage that generally cannot be neatly divided into a race part and a class part.[33]

All these factors explain why the diversity at high schools like CRLS is so much greater than what almost any of my students went on to experience in college, and certainly than what is found at the affirmative action colleges. Many more high schools (and primary schools) could attain a comparable diversity if our politicians and policy makers recognized the value of doing so, as the Departments of Justice and Education guidelines encourage them to. They would have to attack housing segregation in order to more fully achieve that diversity, and a further civic advantage of the diversity issue at the primary/secondary level is that it shines a spotlight on housing segregation.[34]

—⁂—

So the pure diversity argument is actually stronger at the K–12 level than the college/university level, contrary to the spirit of the chief justice's argument. But I want briefly to note two other civically significant features of the majority opinion in the *PICS* cases; these draw on the court's jurisprudence of the past twenty-five or so years, which has deeply constrained our society's ability to meet what I regard as its responsibility to rectify its legacy of past racial discrimination and to create truly equal educational opportunity in the present.

Let me begin with a brief account of the Louisville, Kentucky, plan that the court struck down. Under that plan, a majority of students attended schools in their neighborhoods, but all students could apply to a range of schools across the district. Criteria for selection included student performance, family hardship, available space, and a race-based consideration requiring schools to have a black student population of no less than 15 percent and no more than 50 percent. This was hardly a rigid quota, and the system treated (the student's) race as one of several factors in assignment. When the plan was challenged in federal district court (the challenge that eventually landed at the Supreme Court), that court agreed that the school district "had demonstrated compelling reasons for its use: (1) a better academic education for all students; (2) better appreciation of our political and cultural heritage for all students; (3) more competitive and attractive public schools; (4) broader community support for all schools [in the district]."[35]

The first element to note is that, in rejecting this seemingly quite educationally sound practice, the Supreme Court majority wildly inflates the alleged harm of employing individuals' racial categorizations in general, and specifically in order to rectify wrongs caused by racial discrimination. Justice Kennedy refers to race-based student assignment policy this way: "Crude measures of this sort threaten to reduce children to racial chits valued and traded according to one school's supply and another's demand" and "Reduction of an individual to an assigned racial identity for differential treatment is among the most pernicious actions our government can undertake."[36] Justice Roberts, citing an earlier case, echoes this: "Distinctions between citizens solely because of their ancestry are by their very nature odious to a free people whose institutions are founded upon the doctrine of equality."[37] *Any* assignment policy in which some schools are oversubscribed will disappoint some families and children. The solution is to try to make all the schools in the system as high quality as possible, so that no child loses out by not getting her first choice. Race-based assignment is a perfectly plausible way of

contributing to making all schools as good as possible, by trying to ensure a reasonable degree of racial balance in them all, and the district
court found Louisville largely successful in doing so.[38] Such policies do
not "reduce" a child to a "racial chit" any more than I did when I worked
with guidance counselors to have a racial balance, including a minority
of whites, among the students in my class.[39]

Also, districts do not assign racial labels arbitrarily to students, as
Kennedy's statement implies, but simply use identities that parents select for their children, which in turn presumably reflect the generally
accepted criteria for assigning racial identities in our society, while still
leaving for some room for individual choice in the matter. These racial
and ethnic identities are indeed often important to people, and it is hard
to know what Roberts is talking about when he says they are "odious to
a free people." People of all races and ethnicities in the country regard
themselves as free and equal citizens and don't necessarily see the fact
of their race and ethnicity, whether officially acknowledged or not (e.g.,
on the federal census) as detracting from that equality. True, not all such
persons are in fact treated equally, as my students recognized, but the nature of the departure from equality is not mere classification by ancestry,
or even mere differential treatment on those grounds—but rather actual
unequal treatment. These are not "crude measures," and the assignment
policies at issue that are based on them are hardly "among the most pernicious actions our governments can undertake." The extreme rhetoric
of these justices appears to bear little relationship to the situations being
adjudicated in the *PICS* cases.

Chief Justice Roberts, writing for the conservative plurality of four,
revises history beyond recognition in a misplaced castigation of using
students' racial identities when he implies that the harm black students
suffered in the segregated schooling systems of the 1950s, to which the
court was responding in its landmark *Brown v. Board of Education* case,
"was not the inequality of the facilities but the fact of legally separating
children based on race on which the Court relied to find a constitutional
violation of that case." Roberts also says, "Government action dividing
people by race is inherently suspect because such classifications promote
'notions of racial inferiority and lead to a politics of racial hostility.'"[40]
This inability or unwillingness to see the vast difference between racial
classifications put in service of ideologies and practices of inferiorization,
exclusion, and second-class citizenship, and innocuous classifications
used as one of a number of factors to help create integrated and equal
school systems is a sad commentary on current American jurisprudence.

What the *Brown* court struck down was the district's operation of inferior, segregated school systems for black students, not racial classification in abstraction from such uses. The *Brown* court was indeed also concerned about the stigmatizing of black students as inferior and unworthy to attend schools with whites. But this stigmatizing was a product of the racially prejudiced intentions on which the segregated systems were based, and the ideology of black inferiority expressed in those intentions, not a product of bare racial separation, as Justice Roberts implies.

Similarly, Louisville's use of racial classification in its integration program was not premised on nor could it plausibly be seen as contributing to notions of "racial inferiority," as the chief justice implies it did. When the district utilized a student's racial identity as one factor in denying the student's parents a preferred school, the district was not declaring the student inferior—as the districts operating segregated schools in 1954 *were* indeed doing—but was merely serving the purpose of ensuring that schools did not become segregated, a goal residents in the district had agreed was an important one, according to the district court. Nor does the plan "legally separate children based on race," but rather brings them together on that basis in a way that benefits students of all racial groups.

Thus the majority in the *PICS* cases, and especially the four-justice conservative plurality, failed to recognize or credit the elementary racial asymmetries that I tried to teach my high school students and that they often recognized on their own.[41] The justices put consigning a black student to a black school because it was not thought that black students deserved as good an education as white ones on the same legal plane as denying a white student her (parents') school preference in order to maintain an integrated school system. Justice Roberts explicitly and decisively rejects the significance of racial asymmetry in the last sentence of his opinion—widely quoted in the media when the decision was announced—which he clearly takes to summarize and reinforce the main thrust of his opinion: "The way to stop discrimination on the basis of race is to stop discriminating on the basis of race."[42] This has a nice ring to it, and sounds almost like a tautology; but it is actually completely misleading. Suppose the statement is reframed to capture the two different meanings of "discrimination" at play: "The way to end inequality in education is to stop using students' racial identities" in educational policy. Obviously, given the multiple causes of racial inequality in our educational system, merely refraining from using students' racial identities will go nowhere toward reducing inequality; indeed, since (as in the *PICS* cases) that principle deprives districts of the best available way to integrate schools, it is more likely to exacerbate it. Again, the failure to credit social and historical racial asymmetries is blinding the chief justice to the facts and their appropriate policy implications.[43]

Indeed, invoking some prior decisions, the chief justice affirms explicitly that correcting for these historical, asymmetrical injustices is not a compelling state purpose: "[A]n effort to alleviate the effects of societal discrimination is not a compelling interest" and "Societal discrimination, without more, is too amorphous a basis for imposing a racially classified remedy."[44] Given this way of thinking, together with the wildly inflated idea of the harm caused by mere racial classifications (independent of their use), it becomes very difficult for governmental and private actors to adopt racial justice as a policy goal requiring (as it must, to some degree) race-targeted programs. This is as Roberts and the conservative four wish it to be. I note only that in his dissent Justice Breyer (speaking for all four dissenting justices) vigorously disputes both prongs of this disabling of racial justice policy, and specifically of school integration in service of racial justice.

The conservative four's outlook leaves us with the irony that the achievement of *diversity* in education is viewed as a "compelling state interest" but *equality* is not. This irony is acutely present in Justice O'Connor's opinion in the *Grutter* case, where O'Connor virtually says that universities have a compelling interest in making sure that white students get to hear about the experiences of racial discrimination suffered by black, Latino, and Native American students, but that universities (and other governmental and private actors) cannot try to reduce or rectify that discrimination in their admissions policies. But certainly part of the point of having students hear about experiences of disadvantage and discrimination is to nurture a sense of social justice that will hopefully lead students to want to change their society and its institutions so as to minimize those inequities and that discrimination in the present and the future. This is certainly an important part of how I saw the educational value of the racial diversity in my own class, and it seems that recognizing the civic importance of diversity must rest at least partly on that pedagogical goal.

The court's understanding of the value of diversity as not essentially related to racial equality is also revealingly expressed in what the court, in its *Grutter* decision, saw as the harm of stereotyping. The harm highlighted in its opinion is that of leading students to fail to recognize the internal diversity in the opinions of members of a different racial group. In chapter 1, we saw that this "misrecognition" aspect of stereotyping was indeed important, but was not the only harm that stereotyping could cause. The other harm we mentioned was that of *stigmatizing* a group—attributing negative characteristics to it—the harm that we also investigated in relation to stereotype threat in chapter 7. This harm is much more closely tied to inequality, because stigmatizing a group as inferior or incapable helps to rationalize that group's disadvantaged position, and at the same that position helps to feed the stigmatizing stereotype. That the court failed to note this inequality-related harm of stereotyping is part of its severing the benefits of diversity from equality—and indeed, as mentioned earlier, its more general failure to foreground the benefits of learning about the character and experience of multiple racial groups as groups present in the school and classroom, not only about the variety of individual opinions within those groups.[45] Justice Roberts's opinion in the *PICS* cases very much reinforces this narrowing of the harm of stereotyping, as part of demoting the correcting of "societal discrimination" as a vital public purpose.

The *PICS* decision is only the most extreme in a series of judicial rulings that have relieved school districts from mandates to integrate as well as pulled some of the ground out from under districts that have or had voluntarily attempted to.[46] Overall, school segregation has been steadily increasing for the past several decades. In 1980, 63% of blacks attended predominantly minority schools (down from 77% in 1968, as a result of integrative policies). In 2000 that number had risen to 72%. The number of black children attending schools more than 90% minority fell to 33% in 1980 (from 64% in 1968), then rose to 37% in 2000. The average non-Hispanic white student now attends schools that are 75% or more white.[47] Some evidence suggests that overall, as of 2006, Latino students were the most educationally segregated minority group in the country.[48] As these statistics suggest, the class of 1980 that Wells and her coauthors studied turns out to be something of a high water mark of school integration. They comment:

> What we learned . . . is that efforts to desegregate public schools for a short time in the mid-twentieth century [from the late 1960s until the early 1980s] were simply the beginning of what should have been a long and comprehensive journey toward a more integrated society—a

journey that has been aborted instead of expanded since that time. We write this book wondering when and if our leaders will ever wake up to the rapidly increasing diversity of this country—now that only . . . 58% of the school-age population are non-Hispanic whites—and recognize that the ongoing racial segregation in housing and now increasingly in our public schools needs to be addressed.[49]

—⁂—

In addition to resegregation and anti-integration effects of judicial de-cisions, another contributor to the increasing disappearance of racial integration from education policy is connected to the corporate and privatizing educational reforms of the 2000s and 2010s. These currents of reform have all but abandoned a robust sense of public schools as a public trust, serving a public good. Hochschild and Scovronick comment on these currents: "The push for vouchers is mainly part of a broader attempt to redefine the relationship between individuals and the state, to make people think more like consumers in a market than citizens in a democracy."[50]

Parents understandably want what they take to be best for their child. However, if more and more parents buy into a consumerist mentality by thinking about this "best" almost entirely in terms of providing their child a competitive advantage over other children whose parents are thinking in the same way, this shortchanges their child's moral and civic development, and, in the mix, a love of learning for its own sake.[51] Some parents may indeed desire racial diversity in their children's education and social world. Others may be indifferent to it. Yet others may seek ho-mogeneity as providing comfort for the child, or, especially in the case of some white parents, because they may associate diversity with infe-rior schooling. It is true that when racial integration and diversity func-tion as they should inside schools and classes, they indeed pull the child outside her comfort zone. That is the whole point of making sure that students encounter those of different backgrounds, experiences, and heritages, a goal of American public schools ("common schools") going back to their inception in the nineteenth century.[52] Integrated schools and classes (and neighborhoods) are the best venue for students to learn a sense of ease and comfort with difference that they would not neces-sarily learn at home, and that helps position them to become democratic citizens of their future increasingly diverse society. Such a venue changes the nature of their comfort zones.

Justice Breyer states the connection between integrated education, democracy, and citizenship well: "[T]here is a democratic element . . . It is an interest in helping our children learn to work and play together with children of different racial backgrounds. It is an interest in teaching children to engage in the kind of cooperation among Americans of all races that is necessary to make a land of three hundred million people one Nation."[53]

The larger point here is that we cannot depend on parental preference to do the civic and educational work of matching children to schools and their demographics, and of ensuring that schools are committed to robust civic education with the diverse populations I have been arguing for. The civic purposes of schooling cannot be beholden to parental predilections. As the historian David Tyack says, "All citizens, not just parents, have a stake in the civic education of the next generation."[54] Turning education into a consumer good is bound to weaken citizens' sense that they have that stake. That sense of a common good entrusted to a democratic public that nurtures it—and education as a vital common good—is threatened by an overextension of consumerist and market ways of thinking beyond their proper domains.

When the Louisville case discussed earlier came before the district court, that court recognized the civic value of the integration plan devised by the district and applying to all its schools:

> Louisville's voluntary integration of its schools has . . . encouraged continued public support for educational excellence and equity across the district, "invest[ing] parents and students alike with a sense of participation and a positive stake in their schools and the school system as a whole."[55]

This shared commitment to equity and excellence is weakened by the charter school movement and market reforms in general, notwithstanding the individual charter or private schools that may do a terrific job of civic and moral education or that have a strong commitment to equality and integration.[56] Losing this sense of public education as a public good, something from which the society as a whole benefits, is bound to exacerbate existing inequalities, weakening even the inadequate corrective mechanisms we now have in place to help the disadvantaged. But more than that—the point I wish particularly to emphasize from my experience teaching my high school course—is that privatized, consumerist, and market mechanisms, ideas, and sensibilities wear away the deeply civic purpose of education, one on which we are entirely dependent if we are to educate our next generation to rise to the challenge of running and peopling a diverse, democratic society. And so we need to do our best to create schools (and neighborhoods) that have mixed populations like Cambridge Rindge and Latin High School, and to make sure the classes in those schools do not resegregate the students. This must be seen as an urgent policy imperative. Nothing less than the viability of our multicultural democracy depends on it.

APPENDIX 1

The Students

Below is a list of the students featured in the book. Each student is identified by a quote, along with racial and ethnic information. Ethnicity is based on parents' national origin. An asterisk indicates students whom I know to have immigrated to the United States. (I did not have this information for every student.)

Abdul (South Asian: Indian): "When I am in an advanced placement class with mostly white students, I don't speak because I'm worried that people will wonder if I belong in the class—if I am smart enough." Chapter 12.

Adam (white): "I think there are survival instincts that make us suspicious in a society like ours, because racism is so, like, embedded." Chapter 2.

Anna (white): "Being prejudiced is being ignorant about the groups you are prejudiced against, and lumping groups together." Chapter 5.

Antonine (black: Haitian): "I thought you'd be a black guy, Professor." Introduction.

Behar (white: southeastern European): "What I learned about [Thomas Jefferson] has created in me great confusion about this character and I really don't know if it is right to say that Jefferson was one of the most prominent Americans." Chapter 7.

Bernadette (black: Haitian): "I'm surprised any white students would sign up for a course called 'Race and Racism.'" Introduction.

Carmel (black: Haitian): "The class made me aware of other people and their similarities. It makes you reevaluate what you say." Chapter 12.

Clara (Latina): "I think [African slave traders] thought of it as a business, and if it had been going on for years, why would they question it?" Chapter 6.

Cristina (mixed race: Salvadoran and white): "When they say stiff *white* hips, it means they are insulting all white people." Chapter 4.

Ebony (black: African American): "Listening to this discussion, I guess I am changing my mind." Chapter 4.

Esteban (Latino: Dominican): "I would take the opportunity to meet them and teach them." Chapter 4.

Hannah (white): "If you walked into a room of people you didn't know and they were all naked, who would you sit next to?" Chapter 2.

Jacques (black: Haitian): "I think we are naturally curious." Chapter 2.

*Jean-Paul (black: Haitian): "She's *black*??!!" Chapter 3.

Jessica (white): "This course showed me that history is personal. It has to do with the reality of what you live with now." Chapter 12.

Jocelyn (black: African American): "I don't like to hear anyone say that word, no matter how you pronounce it." Chapter 11.

Julia (mixed race: African American and white): "In this class, everyone cares about what everyone else has to say." Introduction.

Kayla (black: Haitian American): "The word has a negative heritage but some black students feel they can use it in a way that doesn't involve that heritage." Chapter 11.

*Leila (black: Tanzanian): "Before I studied slavery, I did not care about the past much and I never thought slavery was as bad as it sounded like." Chapter 6.

Lionel (white): "The word *nigger* is like *nerd* as portrayed in the film *Revenge of the Nerds*. Do you agree with this comparison?" Chapter 11.

Lisa (Latina): "The n-word is just racist no matter how you look at it. Nobody should use it." Chapter 11.

Lovelle (black: African American): "Personally, I'm not afraid or suspicious of people who are different from me." Chapter 2.

Marie (black: Haitian): "Selling someone who is already a slave is still wrong because it is wrong to begin with." Chapter 6.

Marissa (mixed race: African American and white): "The people you feel comfortable with when you are young are the ones you feel comfortable with when you're older." Chapter 2.

Mirvole (black: Haitian): "The Africans, the African traders, knew what was going on on those boats. They knew how bad those conditions were and they still sold their own people there. It was totally wrong." Chapter 6.

Murielle (black: Haitian American and African American): "Yes, it is like that. The way blacks use *nigger* is like the way the nerds in the film use *nerd*." Chapter 11.

Negasi (black: Ethiopian): "Only people whose ancestors were slaves and were oppressed have the heritage that allows them to use the word *nigger* in that positive way." Chapter 11.

Norris (black: Jamaican): "I won't just make fun of somebody, but if he hits a bad note . . . I'll just say it." Chapter 4.

Pema (Asian: Tibetan): "If you look in the dictionary, the definitions of *white* are all positive—like lightness, sun, purity. Black is connected with dark, something you're afraid of." Chapter 9.

Philippe (black: Haitian): "There's a difference between *nigg*a and *nigg*er. No black person would ever pronounce the word as *nigg*er." Chapter 11.

Sherilyn (black: African American and Jamaican): "Common sense tells us that it is wrong to be suspicious, but if you have learned to be fearful, it's hard to ignore those ideas." Chapter 2.

Tariq (Middle Eastern): "You can't take a negative word and make it positive. I don't think anyone, including black students, should use that word." Chapter 11.

Tenzina (mixed race: Cambodian and Peruvian): "If you see your parents turn away from certain kinds of people, you kind of learn to be suspicious without knowing it." Chapter 2.

Terri (black: African American): "I don't think it's *wrong* of other blacks to use [the n-word] if they want." Chapter 11.

APPENDIX 2

Syllabus, Readings, and Assignments
for "Race and Racism"

Each week's classes (four per week) were divided between intellectually very demanding historical/scientific material (three days) and more accessible material—contemporary sources and videos (one day). I list the historical/scientific and the contemporary/video material separately to make it easier to follow the chronology of the former. The interspersing of the contemporary material was somewhat random so which week it was assigned doesn't matter. Later in the term, meetings on group projects provided a break from the historical material.

HISTORICAL AND SCIENTIFIC MATERIAL

Scientific critique of race

Jared Diamond, "Race without Color," *Discover*, October 1994.

Daniel Blackburn, "Why Race Is Not a Biological Concept," in *Race and Racism in Theory and Practice*, ed. Berel Lang (Lanham, MD: Rowman and Littlefield, 2000).

American Anthropological Association, "Statement on Race," 1998.

Slavery before race—the ancient Greeks [lecture]

What is the idea of "race"? Are we naturally fearful of physical and cultural differences?

Audrey Smedley and Brian Smedley, *Race in North America: Origin and Evolution of a Worldview*, 4th ed. (Boulder, CO: Westview, 2012), 21–27.

(Note that the page references here are not to the edition I used in class but to the most recent 2012 edition. The text is pretty much the same, only slightly updated.)

English treatment of the Irish before English colonization of the New World

Smedley, 52–62.

> Smedley sees the English domination of (and view of) the Irish in the twelfth to the fifteenth century as the beginning of or dry run for their treatment of conquered peoples and slaves in the Americas—and first steps toward the idea of "race."

Spain under Muslim and Catholic domination, and beginnings of "race" in reference to Jews

Smedley, 62–70.

> When the Muslims dominated southern Spain, they were relatively tolerant of Jews and Christians. But when the Christians retook Spain, they forced Jews and Muslims to convert. In the Inquisition (fifteenth century), the Catholic church began to suspect converted Jews and looked in their bloodlines for evidence of their being "secret Jews." This is one of the first manifestations of racial thinking—that important characteristics are carried "in the blood."

Beginnings of Spanish and Portuguese exploration and colonization, and plantation slavery on the Canary Islands [lecture]

> I had an excellent map of the Atlantic slave trade routes and nations, so these lessons about the geography of colonalization and slavery were more vivid to the students.

Columbus and early contacts and later conflicts between English colonists and Native Americans

Smedley, 73–81, 85–90.

> Early wary but not totally hostile relations between the colonists and various indigenous tribes disintegrate over time, with Metacom's War of 1675 (aka King Philip's War), a turning point in the colonists' developing the idea of Native Americans as "savages."

The English encounter with Africans before slavery (seventeenth century)

Smedley, chapter 5, "The Arrival of Africans and the Descent into Slavery," selections.

Ira Berlin, *Many Thousands Gone: The First Two Centuries of Slavery in North America* (Cambridge, MA: Belknap Press of Harvard University Press, 1998), chapter 1 (selections).

Africans in America, PBS series, Orlando Bagwell, executive producer (Boston, MA: WGBH Television, 1998), DVD.

Danny Duncan Collum, *Black and White Together: The Search for Common Ground* (Maryknoll, NY: Orbis Books, 1996), chapter 2, "Revolt Before Race."

All four sources chronicle the complex status of Africans in the early years of the British colonies, where they were occasionally landowners (even occasionally owning slaves), often indentured servants or slaves, but slaves were not treated very differently from (white or black) indentured servants. The mass use of African slaves beginning in the late seventeenth century began the "descent" Smedley refers to in her chapter title, and Africans were deprived of all legal or social standing that they had possessed in the earlier (mid-seventeenth century) period. Berlin and *Africans in America* focus attention on Anthony Johnson, one of the first Africans in the colonies, a fascinating character who became a respected landowner and owned a slave, but whose descendants illustrate the "descent." Imported Irish and poor English people, as well as some Native Americans, were utilized as slave-like labor until the slave trade (until then controlled mainly by the Spanish and Portuguese) brought the possibility of solving the labor problem through mass importation of Africans to the British colonies. Bacon's Rebellion of 1676 uniting "blacks" and poor "whites" against the planter class in Virginia (and Native Americans) was a turning point in spurring laws raising the status of even poor whites decisively over blacks. The ideology of Africans as an inferior, barbaric, and degraded population was not yet developed (that is, the idea of "race" had only just begun), and the skills and knowledge of African labor were recognized. Smedley emphasizes developments in the idea of race. Berlin emphasizes changes in the lives and situations of Africans (and their descendants) in the colonies.

Field trip to "Black Heritage Trail"

We toured an area of Boston where the free black community of the antebellum (pre–Civil War) period lived, and where resistance to slavery (e.g., sheltering escaped slaves) joined with the abolitionist movement.

Why enslaved Africans became the main labor force in the English colonies, instead of Native Americans, Irish, and poor English

Peter Kolchin, *American Slavery, 1619–1877*, revised and updated (New York: Hill and Wang, 2003), 3–13.

Further develops the argument mentioned just above, emphasizing cost savings and ease of controlling a population (the Africans) who could not escape by blending into the urban population (as English and Irish escapees could), did not know the terrain (as Native Americans did), and were intentionally thrown together by the slave owners with people from other ethnic groups who did not speak their language.

Changes in slaves' lives from the charter generation (seventeenth century) to plantation slavery (developed in the eighteenth and nineteenth centuries)

Berlin, chapter 5, "The Tobacco Revolution in the Chesapeake," selections.

> The slaves are subjected to new levels of violence and humiliation. Previous rights and opportunities (e.g., to work one's own plot of land) are taken away.

The African role in the slave trade; the experience of captives in Africa and on the slave ships

Gary Nash, *Red, White, and Black: The Peoples of Early North America*, 4th ed. (Upper Saddle River, NJ: Prentice Hall, 2000), 140–150. (This book is now in a 6th edition, published in 2009.)

O. E. Uya, "The African Involvement," from *African Diaspora and the Black Experience in New World Slavery* (Lagos, Nigeria: Third Press, 1992), 65–70.

Olaudah Equiano, *The Interesting Narrative of the Life of Olaudah Equiano or Gustavus Vassa, the African* (1789), in *The Classic Slave Narratives*, ed. Henry Louis Gates Jr. (New York: Mentor, 1987).

Slavery in the Portuguese and Spanish colonies, and comparison to the English colonies

Smedley, 139–145.

Nash, 155–166.

> Differences in slave experience in these different colonies; why the Portuguese/Spanish populations became so much more mixed (among indigenous, Africans, and Europeans) than in the English colonies; and how this affected the ideas of "race" in those colonies and the countries they became.

Slavery and the growth of U.S. ideology of race

Smedley, 149–153.

> Slavery, in connection with other currents of thought (Christianity and the Enlightenment), is central to the development of the idea of race.

Guest speaker on slavery and race in the French Caribbean, especially Haiti

A slave experience in the Caribbean

Mary Prince, *The History of Mary Prince, a West Indian Slave* (1831), ed. Sara Salih (New York: Penguin, 2000).

> We spent several days on this excellent slave narrative, which also deals with the British abolitionist movement. I had students prepare by selecting particular passages to read aloud in class and comment on.

Thomas Jefferson, his views about blacks, and Banneker's challenge to Jefferson

Smedley, 177–181.

Benjamin Banneker, "Blacks Are Not Inferior to Whites" (1791), Banneker-Jefferson Letters: www.infoplease.com/t/hist/banneker-jefferson/1/html.

David Walker's challenge to Jefferson, and his condemnation of and arguments against slavery

David Walker, *Appeal to the Colored Citizens of the World,* selections from preamble and chapter 1 (1830), ed. Peter Hinks (University Park, PA: Pennsylvania State University Press, 2000).

The abolitionist movement in the U.S.

William Lloyd Garrison, "The Great [Constitutional] Crisis" (1832), in *Against Slavery: An Abolitionist Reader,* ed. Mason Lowance (New York: Penguin, 2000), 112–117.

Indian and Black slave resistance in the Spanish, French, and Portuguese colonies; the Seminoles and their role in slave escape and resistance in the U.S.

William Loren Katz, *Black Indians: A Hidden Heritage* (New York: Aladdin Paperbacks, 1997), 33–47, 49–62.

Escaped slaves, sometimes in cooperation with indigenous people (some of them slaves also), revolted against the Spanish and French slave masters, and sometimes set up "maroon" colonies in the Caribbean and parts of Latin America. Role of Seminoles, a U.S. Native American group that welcomed escaped black slaves.

Slave rebellions in the United States: Stono, Prosser, Vesey, Turner

Nathan Huggins, *Black Odyssey: The African American Ordeal in Slavery,* with a new introduction (New York: Vintage, 1990), 210–227.

Louis Agassiz and racial science in the nineteenth century

Smedley, 227–229, 233–237.

Nineteenth-century debate between monogenists (humans were created by God as a single species) and polygenists (multiple creations). Influence of Agassiz, a revered Harvard scientist of the mid-nineteenth century, in the development of racist thought. Brief discussion of impact of Darwinism on racial thought.

Asians and U.S. naturalization law in the early twentieth century

Ian Haney-Lopez, *White By Law: The Legal Construction of Race* (New York: NYU
Press, 1996), 79–92.

> Discussion of fascinating *Ozawa* and *Thind* cases of 1923, at a time when U.S.
> law said that only whites could naturalize (a 1790 law, not fully rescinded un-
> til 1952). Ozawa, a Japanese immigrant, claimed he was white; the Supreme
> Court said scientists say Japanese aren't Caucasian and so aren't white. Thind,
> an Indian immigrant, then claims that since he is Caucasian, he should be able
> to naturalize, as white. Court, reversing previous argument (of the same year),
> says being Caucasian does not make you white. For contemporary students,
> the cases raise issues of pride, heritage, skin color, immigration, white suprem-
> acy, and the role of race in American history.

CONTEMPORARY MATERIAL

Rachel L. Swarns, "'African-American' Becomes a Term for Debate," *New York
Times*, August 29, 2004.

> African immigrants, African Americans, and the appropriate terminology.

Ward Churchill, "Let's Spread the 'Fun' Around: The Issue of Sports Team Names
and Mascots" and "In the Matter of Julius Streicher: Applying Nuremberg
Precedents to the United States," in *From a Native Son: Selected Essays on Indi-
genism*, 1985–1995 (Boston, MA: South End Press, 1996).

> Gives arguments against using Native American names for sports teams.

Skin Deep, directed by Frances Reid, 1995, DVD.

> Excellent documentary about twelve college students from different racial
> groups, colleges, and parts of the country. The first part of the film is about
> each student's individual story; in the second part they are brought together
> for a weekend of discussion of racial issues and their own experiences.

Correspondents of the *New York Times*, *How Race Is Lived in America* (New York:
Times Books/Henry Holt, 2001):

> - "Growing Up, Growing Apart." Three middle school girlfriends of different
>   races go to (the same) high school and find racial forces making them drift
>   apart.
> - "Best of Friends, Worlds Apart." Two Cuban friends, one dark skinned, one
>   light skinned, immigrate to the United States and find the U.S. racial order
>   separating them and challenging their friendship.
> - "Reaping What Was Sown on the Old Plantation." An African American Na-
>   tional Park Service guide on a Louisiana plantation tries to figure out the
>   best way to educate visitors about slavery. A descendant of the plantation
>   family is not pleased.

Tim Walker, "Something Is Wrong Here: Denver Students Confront Racial Track-ing at Their High School," *Teaching Tolerance*, Fall 2002, 38–43.

Describes a Denver high school with a similar demographic to CRLS and in which there are a disproportionate percentage of whites in the high-level classes. The article explores possible explanations.

RACE—The Power of an Illustion, produced by California Newsreel, 2003, VHS.

ASSIGNMENTS

1. *Reading questions:* Every reading was accompanied by several questions to guide the students through the complex material and to give them a further in-centive to do the reading. The students had to answer a third of the questions on a given day's reading. They had to show their answers to the teaching assistant before class started (so they could not write the answers in class) and turn them in at the end of class. I checked their answers against the numbers the teaching assistant gave me and commented on their particular answers. Individual answers were not graded; students were graded only on making a reasonable attempt to answer the question, not on getting it right.

2. *Educational autobiography* (400–800 words): "Write an essay about your edu-cational history, experiences, aspirations, and hopes." (Assigned the first week.)

3. *Racial incident description* (discussed in chapter 4): "Describe an incident in-volving race in some way, and involving people you know, that did not work out well. Write about how a bystander to the incident might have intervened in a constructive way." (Assigned second or third week.)

4. *Race and science essay* (500–800 words): "Explain three different scientific criticisms of our system of racial classification, drawn from our three readings."

5. *Journals:* There were four journals, one targeted to a specific reading and the other three completely open. In the open ones, the students could write about racial issues in their own lives, bounce off the readings, or talk about something that happened in class, or anything racial.

6. *Racial empathy essay* (500–800 words): A complex, several-stage assign-ment that spanned a six-week period (starting about a third of the way through the semester). The students had to find someone of a different race to interview about their racial experiences and their outlook on racial issues. The class gener-ated questions to ask (in six categories that I devised) and I compiled them; each student was encouraged to come up with questions of their own as well. They interviewed their subjects in two stages. In the first stage, they transcribed the in-terview in a coherent way and turned that in, with suggested follow-up questions for the next interview. I gave feedback on this "organized transcript," generally suggesting some more follow-up questions or asking for clarification on particular

points and issues. In the second stage, the students did a follow-up interview. They then wrote an essay in the interviewee's voice, and added their own reflections on what they had learned about the interviewee's racial group that was surprising to them, what they learned about race and racial issues, and "what you learned about yourself."

7. *Acting white/acting black essay* (300–500 words): The essay assignment asked students to explain what they and their peers mean when they say someone is "acting white" or "acting black," and then to examine whether the use of these expressions is harmful, hurtful, or damaging to the people who are accused, the people who do the accusing, or anyone else overhearing the use of the expressions. (Assigned seventh week.)

8. *Mary Prince essay* (500–800 words): The students had a choice of two essay questions on Mary Prince's slave autobiography, one on Mary's developing consciousness about whether slavery *itself* (or only especially harsh treatment within slavery) is wrong; the other about developments over time in how Mary responds to how she is treated. (Assigned thirteenth week.)

9. *Banneker/Walker essay* (500–800 words): "Describe and analyze three different arguments that Banneker or Walker uses against Jefferson's arguments that blacks are inferior." (Assigned nineteenth week.)

10. *Final group project:* This was a very complex activity that ranged over the last two and half months of the term. First, my TA and I created three-person groups, with kids of different races in each, although we did not call attention to this fact. The groups had to pick topics to work on, drawn from a list of topics we had generated in class and to which I added. I did not allow more than one topic to be picked twice, which meant that some groups did not get their first choice, but I think all got their first or second choices. Here is a typical list of topics:

- Use of stereotypes by CRLS students
- The racial achievement gap at CRLS
- Race, ethnicity, and the social world of CRLS
- Mixed-race identity
- Race and racism in two different countries (Japan and Haiti)

Once the groups were formed, I gave them time to meet in class—one class period per week in December and early January (until their presentations). The groups also had to meet outside of class, and some of them found it difficult to find a time that all members could meet, or at least sometimes used that as an excuse for why they did not meet. The groups had to turn in weekly reports (rotating who wrote them) on what they had accomplished, and what they were aiming at.

The final week of the course was devoted to presentations by the groups, which had to be at least twenty minutes, had to involve something visual, and had to make use of research that had been done on the topic beyond interviewing. The audience for the presentations, besides other students in the class, included other adults, mostly from inside the school but occasionally colleagues of mine from outside. The evaluators graded the presentations according to a protocol I created.

The individual student's grade for the presentation was a combination of a group grade and a grade on the individual's role in the group presentation.

I think the groups were a good learning and interpersonal experience for all the students. But the interaction was often quite difficult. A few of the groups had real interpersonal crises that I had to resolve, generally through conferring with individual students in the group. (The TA and I tried to pick groups that contained at least one student who seemed to us exceptionally responsible, hoping that person would keep the group relatively on target.)

11. *Final project individual essay* (no more than five pages): After the group presentations, on the last day of class each student had to turn in an essay reflecting on and examining her or his group's process, assessing the dynamic within the group, saying honestly what the interpersonal challenges were and how the group attempted to deal with them, and describing what the individual student felt he/she contributed to the group and learned from the project.

12. *Exams:* One exam six weeks into the semester, one midterm, and one final.

APPENDIX 3

A Note on Methodology

Philosophers do not usually have "methodologies" in the sense that people in education and social science are accustomed to. So let me simply describe how I gathered the material for this book.

In my college courses, I occasionally write down a particularly striking event or exchange that took place in class. I did this the first time I taught the course Race and Racism at Cambridge Rindge and Latin High School. Over time I became more methodical about my record keeping and preservation of material. The most important innovation was that after a given class session was over and I left the school building, I dictated into a mini cassette recorder what I remembered of what had transpired. For the class that is the primary focus of this book, I taped such notes for a third to a half of the class sessions, generally capturing discussions that were particularly striking for some reason or other. These notes were sometimes augmented by notes from pre- or postclass discussions with students, phone calls, or debriefing conversations with my teaching assistant.

In addition, a research assistant, Mary Casey, sat in on about half the classes, and I was able to consult her notes for the book.

At the end of the course I asked if any students were willing to give me a portfolio of all their work in the course, and about half the students agreed. I also kept all student work that was submitted by e-mail.

Finally, I conducted interviews with slightly less than half the students in this class during the summer after they graduated. I also interviewed three students from another class a few months after the course ended.

This is the material that forms the basis of the book. As I said, the book only presents snapshots from the course; many exciting things happened in the class that did not make it into the book.

NOTES

INTRODUCTION

1. In recent years, since I taught the course, more white professional families have kept their children in the system through high school.
2. The speech was given in February 2009, in relation to African American History Month: www.justice.gov/ag/speeches/2009/ag-speech-090218.html.
3. Sheryll Cashin, *The Failures of Integration: How Race and Class Are Undermining the American Dream* (New York: Public Affairs, 2005), 14.
4. "Color blindness" can have several meanings beyond those mentioned here. For example, it can refer to a social ideal in which a person's race has no impact on her life chances. For fuller discussion of color blindness, see Lawrence Blum, *"I'm Not a Racist, But . . .": The Moral Quandary of Race* (Ithaca, NY: Cornell University Press, 2002), chapter 4; and Elizabeth Anderson, *The Imperative of Integration* (Princeton, NJ: Princeton University Press, 2010), chapter 8.
5. Martha Nussbaum, *Cultivating Humanity: A Classical Defense of Reform in Liberal Education* (Cambridge, MA: Harvard University Press, 1998), 173.
6. Amy Stuart Wells, Jennifer Jellison Holme, Anita Tijerina Revilla, and Awo Korantemaa Atanda, *Both Sides Now: The Story of School Desegregation* (Berkeley, CA: University of California Press, 2009), 9.
7. Not everyone agrees on this terminology, but I use "African American" to refer to blacks whose ancestry in the United States goes back to the slave era. And "black" refers to anyone whose ancestry is primarily from Africa since about 1500. So Haitians, Haitian Americans, Jamaicans, Caribbean Americans, and African Americans are all black, but differ in ethnicity or nationality. I use "Latino" (and "Latina"), rather than "Hispanic," the more common and official designation, to emphasize the Latin American roots of this group of students.
8. Cambridge Public Schools Student Data Report, School Year 2009–2010, 5.
9. Deborah Meier, *The Power of Their Ideas: Lessons for America from a Small School in Harlem* (Boston, MA: Beacon Press, 1995), 4.

CHAPTER 1

1. I didn't differentiate between race and ethnicity yet but just let the students relate to the two as they chose.
2. The idea that stereotyping is an inevitable product of using categories is a common one in social psychology. To give one example: "A long tradition has conceived of stereotyping as an automatic and inevitable consequence of categorization." Loretta Lepore and Rupert Brown, "Category and Stereotype Activation: Is Prejudice Inevitable?" in *Stereotypes and Prejudice*, ed. Charles Stangor (Philadelphia, PA: Psychology Press, 2000).
3. See Silvio Torres-Saillant, "The Tribulations of Blackness: Stages in Dominican Racial Identity," *Latin American Perspectives* 25(3), May 1998: 126–146.

CHAPTER 2

1. American Anthropological Association Statement on "Race," May 17, 1998: www. aaanet.org/stmts/racepp.htm.
2. Jared Diamond, "Race Without Color," *Discover*, November 1994.
3. This version of the general argument is drawn from the introduction to *Revisiting Race in a Genomic Age*, eds. B. Koenig, S. Lee, and S. Richardson (New Brunswick, NJ: Rutgers University Press, 2008), 1.
4. Although almost all scientists in the relevant fields agree that the classic idea of race is false, some of them want to hold on to the language of "race" to mean something different—something like "relatively isolated breeding populations." Others think there is enough of a match of genetic difference with traditional races to retain a careful, situational use of "race." In fact the post–Human Genome Project lay of the land concerning scientific and medical uses of "race" is pretty complicated, beyond the scope of this book. (For more readings on this question, see appendix 2.)
5. The reader may have heard the idea that race is a "social construction (or construct)." And you might think that what I have said so far means that that is the way I presented it to my students. But I chose not to use that language, since I think this idea of social construction is ambiguous and confusing. What I did was to talk about the "historical construction of race," by which I meant the process that our readings (and especially Smedley and Berlin) described, by which the idea of race was created over several centuries in the United States, and in the Western hemisphere more generally. And I distinguished this process from the falsity that scientists attributed to the "classic" idea of race, which they generally agreed continues to inform current ways of thinking about race. I discuss the idea of "social construction" in more detail in an essay, "Racialized Groups: The Socio-Historical Consensus," *The Monist* 93, no. 2 (April 2010): 298–320.
6. I defend this view of "racism" in my book *"I'm Not a Racist, But . . . :" The Moral Quandary of Race* (Ithaca, NY: Cornell University Press, 2002).

CHAPTER 3

1. Smedley's *Race in North America: Origins and Evolution of a Worldview* (Boulder, CO: Westview, 2012) is now in a fourth edition, cowritten with Brian Smedley (Smedley's son), and the page numbers I give in the appendix are from that edition.

CHAPTER 4

1. The students assumed, as did I, that even though the dance may well have been Latin-themed and in theory aimed at students from all groups, in fact the attendees were primarily Latino, and the Latino students in some significant way regarded the event and space as theirs.
2. Dorinda Carter provides an excellent discussion of ways that black students can feel, or be made to feel, "hypervisible" in classes in which they are a minority. It can happen if we wrongly assume that just because a student is black, she already knows, for example, about slavery or segregation. And it denies the student her individuality as a learner. At the same time, Carter makes it clear that it

is wrong to adopt a totally "color-blind" stance toward one's minority students. Dorinda J. Carter, "On Spotlighting and Ignoring Racial Group Members in the Classroom," in *Everyday Antiracism: Getting Real About Race in School*, ed. Mica Pollock (New York: New Press, 2008), 230–234.

3. We do not know if the white couple in the original incident had been invited to the dance or not.

4. Weissbourd notes that many nonblack children who operated in integrated settings "described black children—and black children sometimes describe themselves—as . . . more honest, less hypocritical, more independent-minded, more willing to assert their view, and less concerned about popularity than about respect in comparison with their peers." Richard Weissbourd, *The Parents We Mean to Be: How Well-Intentioned Adults Undermine Children's Moral and Emotional Development* (Boston, MA: Houghton Mifflin Harcourt, 2009), 186–187. Janie Ward has made the same point about African Americans. Janie Victoria Ward, *The Skin We're In: Teaching Our Children to Be Emotionally Strong, Socially Smart and Spiritually Connected*, chapter 3, "The Bricks and Mortar of Building Strong Children" (New York: Free Press, 2000).

CHAPTER 5

1. Rachel Swarns, "'African-American' Becomes a Term for Debate," *New York Times*, August 29, 2004.

2. Although racial and national origin restrictions on immigration that had been put in place earlier (1924) were lifted in the Hart-Cellar Immigration and Nationality Act of 1965, it is fair to say that the U.S. Congress did not anticipate then how many non-Europeans (that is, nonwhites) would actually take advantage of the new access. It would not be right to see the 1965 congress as extending open arms to the nonwhite peoples of the world.

3. For a succinct summary of the government's role in promoting segregation and inequality related to housing in the period prior to the Fair Housing Act of 1968, see Elizabeth Anderson, *The Imperative of Integration* (Princeton, NJ: Princeton University Press, 2010), 68.

4. On the role of housing and federal housing policy in giving whites (including the offspring of the European immigrant generation) advantages over blacks, and in exacerbating wealth disparities between whites and blacks, see Melvin Oliver and Thomas Shapiro, *Black Wealth/White Wealth: A New Perspective on Racial Inequality*, 10th anniversary edition (New York: Routledge, 2006).

5. Ira Katznelson, *When Affirmative Action Was White: An Untold History of Racial Inequality in 20th Century America* (New York: Norton, 2006), 121. Katznelson provides great detail about the way that the New Deal and postwar welfare programs that benefited all were entirely racially compromised by the power of Southern Democrats in the Democratic coalition that passed these programs, assuring that they would be administered in a racially discriminatory manner, whether this was built into the legislation itself or not. Douglas Massey summarizes the argument: "[A]lthough Southerners [in Congress] favored the New Deal's populist economic programs, they did so only to the extent that the programs did not challenge the racial status quo . . . Traditionally black occupations were not covered by the Social Security Act; labor legislation was written

to allow segregated unions; states were delegated authority to exclude African Americans from receiving veterans benefits; and bureaucratic rules were written to prohibit black families and black neighborhoods from Federal Housing Association and Veterans Administration loans." Massey, "The Past and Future of American Civil Rights," *Daedalus*, Spring 2011, 41.

6. The fascinating history by which various what we now think of as white immigrant groups from the 1880–1920 period came to be accepted as "white" is told in works such as Jennifer Guglielmo and Salvatore Salerno, eds., *Are Italians White? How Race is Made in America* (New York: Routledge, 2003); David Roediger, *Working Toward Whiteness: How America's Immigrants Became White: The Strange Journey from Ellis Island to the Suburbs* (New York: Basic Books, 2006); and Matthew Frye Jacobson, *Whiteness of a Different Color: European Immigrants and the Alchemy of Race* (Cambridge, MA: Harvard University Press, 1999). A foundation of these groups' being seen as white is that the 1790 Naturalization Act granted naturalization only to "free white persons." While the contours of that category were not spelled out at the time, it got interpreted to include immigrants from Europe. So even when the Southern and Eastern European immigrants were not, or not immediately, accepted socially as "whites" by native-born whites, they had official standing as whites in light of this act. The works just mentioned describe the process by which these groups came to be seen socially as white.

7. It is true that Latinos or Hispanics can be of any race; but increasingly that group as a whole is seen as a "racial minority" by others. And many see themselves as a single and nonwhite group, as indicated, for example, by their choosing "other" (e.g., on the federal census) when asked for their race where the other options are "white," "black," "Asian," and "Native American." On the 2010 census, 36.7% (18.5 million) out of a total of 50.5 million Latinos/Hispanics selected "other" (and 3 million others picked "black"). www.census.gov/prod/cen2010/briefs/c2010br-04.pdf, p. 14.

8. There are other factors affecting mobility for the post-1965 immigrants compared to the 1880–1920 ones that have nothing to do with race or discrimination. For example, in the earlier period there were many blue-collar jobs that immigrants without education could get and that, with unionization, were decently paid and provided a foundation for their children to advance. There are far fewer such jobs now, and contemporary immigrants, like natives, generally need some education to make a decent living.

9. Mary Waters, *Black Identities: West Indian Immigrant Dreams and American Realities* (New York: Russell Sage, 1999).

10. Kasinitz et al. put it this way: "The central cleavage in American life was once clearly between whites and non-whites. Today there is mounting evidence that it is between blacks and non-blacks." Philip Kasinitz, John Mollenkopf, Mary C. Waters, and Jennifer Holdaway, *Inheriting the City: The Children of Immigrants Come of Age* (New York: Russell Sage, 2008), 368.

11. In an important study of immigrants in New York City from 2007, Philip Kasinitz and his colleagues find this worry pervasive among English-speaking Afro-Caribbeans: "West Indians feel that African Americans have been hurt by their awareness of their stigmatized status as well as by pervasive discrimination. They

want to protect their children from this negativity and discrimination." *Inheriting the City*, 305.

12. In her study of second-generation black Caribbean immigrants to New York, Mary Waters finds that the second generation tends to go in one of three different identity directions: (1) hold firmly to an ethnic identity that distinguishes themselves from African Americans, generally experiencing this as a cultural difference, while seeing themselves, in contrast to their parents, as very much Americans; (2) embrace an immigrant identity that connects them very strongly to their parents and distinguishes them strongly from American youth, including African Americans; (3) embrace an identity that is not firmly distinct from African Americans—either as a "black" pan-ethnic identity (as Jean-Paul and Jacques do), or as African Americans themselves. Waters, "Race, Ethnicity, and Immigration in the United States," in *Social Inequalities in Comparative Perspective*, eds. Fiona Devine and Mary Waters (Oxford, UK: Blackwell, 2004).

13. Kasinitz et al., *Inheriting the City*, 352.

14. Richard Alba and Victor Nee, *Remaking the American Mainstream: Assimilation and Contemporary Immigration* (Cambridge, MA: Harvard University Press, 2003), 209–210.

15. Cynthia Feliciano, *Unequal Origins: Immigrant Selection and the Education of the Second Generation* (El Paso, TX: LFB Scholarly Publishing, 2005), 46. Feliciano uses a measure according to which 71% of Haitian immigrants are better educated than Haitian nonimmigrants. Feliciano looks at the immigrants at age twenty-two, ensuring that most or all of their education was acquired in their home country (p. 46). Mexicans have the lowest such immigrant advantage of all the groups (.2 on her index), although Puerto Ricans, who may or may not rightly be counted as an immigrant group, are lower, with an educational disadvantage (–.06).

16. Feliciano, *Unequal Origins*, 35. The percentage of natives with a bachelor's degree or higher was 33% in 2010; among immigrants it was only 5% points lower, and among naturalized citizens, it is actually higher than for natives—35%. (U.S. Census Bureau, "Native and Foreign-Born Populations by Selected Characteristics, 2010.") By comparison, the figure for blacks is only 19.8%. (These figures count persons twenty-five or older.)

    Comparing immigrant blacks to native-born blacks, the former category has 75.1% college attendance, the latter 60.2%. (The discrepancy with the bachelor's degree figures are accounted for by the large numbers who attend some college but do not graduate.) Amy Lunday, "Immigrant Blacks More Likely to Attend Elite Colleges," *Johns Hopkins University Gazette*, August 17, 2009, www.gazette. jhu.edu/2009/08/17/immigrant-blacks-more-likely-to-attend-elite-colleges.

    The relatively high level of education of immigrants overall, given that so many come from countries a good deal poorer than the United States, is in a small degree due to preferences given to certain "employment-based immigrants" in the Immigration Act of 1990, somewhat enhancing a similar preference in the 1965 Hart-Cellar Act for professionals with baccalaureates or advanced degrees and "aliens of exceptional ability in the sciences, arts, or business" See C. Gordon, S. Mailman, and S. Yale-Loehr, *Immigration Law and*

Procedure (Albany, NY: Matthew Bender, 1997), 3–31. (Immigrants falling within the preferred categories specified by the act are capped at 40,000 out of 700,000 overall legal immigrants per year.)

17. If you compare immigrants by continent, Africans are the most highly educated of all immigrants—more than Europeans and Asians. Eugene Robinson, *Disintegration: The Splintering of Black America* (New York: Doubleday, 2010), 71.

18. Kasinitz et al., *Inheriting the City*, 352–353.

19. See W. J. Wilson, *More Than Just Race: Being Black and Poor in the Inner City* (New York: Norton, 2009). "For many West Indian immigrants, low-paying jobs are actually seen as 'good' jobs, when one considers the wages they would receive in their home countries" (86).

20. On low-income blacks resenting but accepting low-wage work, see Wilson, *More Than Just Race*, 86.

21. "Class Acts," *Boston Sunday Globe*, June 19, 2011, B8. The accompanying article recognizes the immigrant advantage: "It's no coincidence that, year after year, so many Boston High School valedictorians are the children of immigrants, or immigrants themselves. Just getting into this country, especially from places that are poorer and troubled, requires the kind of resiliency that shoots kids into the stratosphere. And every day, their parents confront them with potent examples of guts and self-sacrifice." Yvonne Abraham, "Brighton High to Harvard: She's Defying, Altering Labels," B1.

22. I have been focusing here on African Americans, as they are the group whose achievement gap with whites is most often attributed to cultural failure in comparison with immigrant groups. But it is important to note that the achievement gap also holds between whites and Latinos, and some of the dynamics in the two cases are similar. However, there are some noteworthy differences. For example, Mexicans make up 64% of Latinos and have among the lowest levels of education upon immigration. For a good discussion of the situation of Latino students, see Patricia Gándara and Frances Contreras, *The Latino Education Crisis: The Consequences of Failed Social Policies* (Cambridge, MA: Harvard University Press, 2009).

23. Racial and racist ideologies can also be found among non-Europeans. John Dower in *World Without War: Race and Power in the Pacific War* (New York: Pantheon, 1987) documents Japanese racial thought in the run-up to and during WWII. In this thinking, Japanese were racially superior to all other groups (including other Asian groups, such as Chinese, who were seen as race-like groups). So hostility to all groups other than one's own is not confined to Europeans, although Europeans developed and implemented this mode of thinking much more than any other racial group.

24. I discuss distinctions between subvarieties of prejudice in more detail in "Prejudice" in H. Siegel, ed., *The Oxford Handbook of Philosophy of Education* (New York: Oxford University Press, 2009).

25. Abigail Thernstrom and Stephen Thernstrom, *No Excuses: Closing the Racial Gap in Learning* (New York: Simon and Schuster, 2003), 84. All citations from this book are on page 84.

26. Frank Wu, *Yellow: Race in America Beyond Black and White* (New York: Basic Books, 2002), especially chapter 2. Stacey Lee, *Unraveling the "Model Minority" Stereotype*, 2nd ed. (New York: Teachers College Press, 2009). The "model minority"

stereotype is complex because while it often generates hostility toward Asians, it is also frequently used against blacks and Latinos. It is generally thought to imply that blacks and Latinos are inferior, that they are not "model." It does not imply that blacks and Latinos are *inherently* inferior, but rather *culturally* inferior; the point of the model minority idea as applied to Asians is that blacks and Latinos are not doing well and it is their fault for not acting like the model Asians. So the stereotype also has the effect of fomenting black and Latino hostility toward Asians.

27. Waters, *Black Identities*, 60.

28. In his important book on black solidarity, *We Who Are Dark: Philosophical Foundations of Black Solidarity* (Cambridge, MA: Harvard University Press, 2005), Tommie Shelby draws this distinction between "thin" and "thick" blackness. He claims that some racial prejudice and discrimination is triggered by thin blackness alone. It is therefore an instance of whole-group prejudice. I am emphasizing here ways that prejudice is not triggered by thin blackness alone but only when other characteristics (poor, male, African American ethnicity) are also present. Shelby does not deny this, but I don't think he leaves sufficient room for it in his discussion of how antiblack racism operates.

29. A group can have both positive and negative associations that distinguish it from other ethnic subgroups within their larger racial group. For example, earlier Haitian immigrants (in the 1980s and perhaps later as well) were associated with AIDS.

30. Although I have focused in this chapter on significant differences between immigrants and natives of the same racial group in relation to blacks, the more general issue of sensitivity to ethnic differences within racial or pan-ethnic groups is important in relation to Latinos and Asian Americans as well. For example, the image of the high-achieving Asian or Asian American student is much less applicable to Cambodian, Hmong, and Lao groups than it is to Chinese, Japanese, Koreans, and Indians. The former groups tend to become invisible in light of the model minority stereotype. Of course, it is also true that no single ethnic group should be painted with a broad brush of attributions like high and low achieving; there is always great internal variety, as we have seen. But there are genuine group differences among ethnic subgroups of a larger group, and we need to be sensitive to these in relation to all groups. For an insightful discussion of all these issues, see Lee, *Unraveling the 'Model Minority' Stereotype*.

CHAPTER 6

1. Recent scholarship by Vincent Carretta suggests that Equiano was actually born in the colonies (probably South Carolina), not in Africa. So the Africa and Middle Passage portion of his memoir does not reflect his own experience, although the experiences he describes are probably (according to Carretta's account) drawn from his attempt to portray that experience accurately, based on what he learned from other slaves and from other sources. Vincent Carretta, *Equiano the African: Biography of a Self-Made Man* (Athens, GA: University of Georgia, 2005).

2. Patrick Manning, "Slavery in Africa," in *Africana: The Encyclopedia of the African American Experience*, eds. Kwame Anthony Appiah and Henry Louis Gates Jr. (New York: Basic Civitas Books, 1999), 1720.

3. There was a course in African American history at the high school, offered by two different instructors, where the students might also have gotten a deeper presentation of American slavery.

4. In his best-selling 1995 book, *The End of Racism*, Dinesh D'Souza uses this moral complexity in a totally misleading way. Citing the fact that a few blacks themselves owned slaves and that the slave system was driven by economic goals, he adds the irrelevant point that not all whites owned slaves, and that not all blacks were slaves (there were about 250,000 free blacks on the eve of the Civil War) to suggest that slavery was not a "racist institution." See Dinesh D'Souza, *The End of Racism* (New York: Free Press, 1995), chapter 5, "An American Dilemma: Was Slavery a Racist Institution?" In fact, D'Souza essentially concedes the account of slavery that I provided in the class and that Smedley's text explains; but he tries to frame this account as if it did not involve whites exploiting and oppressing blacks and using a racist ideology to rationalize doing so.

5. April 23, 2010, A23.

CHAPTER 7

1. Theresa Perry, "Up from the Parched Earth: Toward a Theory of African-American Achievement," from *Young, Gifted, and Black* (Boston, MA: Beacon Press, 2003), 105. There do appear to have been some changes in white attitudes about black intelligence over the past thirty-five years or so, with fewer whites explicitly avowing that blacks are innately inferior in intelligence. Lawrence Bobo reports a 1994 survey in which 46% of whites said blacks were "less intelligent" than whites, but he also says that these whites were more likely to see that quality as a product of environment and cultural differences than in earlier eras. "Racial Attitudes and Relations at the Close of the Twentieth Century," in *America Becoming: Racial Trends and Their Consequences*, volume 1, eds. National Research Council, Neil Smelser, William Julius Wilson, and Faith Mitchell (Washington, DC: National Academies Press, 2001), 278. Howard Schuman, Charlotte Steeh, Lawrence Bobo, and Maria Krysan, *Racial Attitudes in America: Trends and Interpretations*, revised edition (Cambridge, MA: Harvard University Press, 1997), report comparative data on a slightly different framing of the question. In 1977, 74% of whites denied racial differences in "in-born intelligence," a figure that went up to 90% in 1996 (p. 353, note 37). There is an extensive scholarly controversy over how to interpret changes such as these in avowed white attitudes. Some say that certain forms of prejudice are too stigmatized to be directly expressed, so the degree to which actual prejudice has gone down is probably not as great as the reduction in admitted negative racial views. There seems also to have been a shift from biologistic to "cultural" versions of prejudice and stigma—essentially saying that blacks are not biologically or genetically inferior, but have cultural deficiencies that produce the same behaviors and underperformance. For example, Schuman et al. present evidence that many whites believe "blacks do not try to get ahead" as an explanation for why blacks do not have greater incomes than they do (*Racial Attitudes in America*, 306). Although culture is changeable while biology is not, at the same time, "culture" is sometimes misunderstood to be something so deeply embedded in the character of a group that it functions as

an unacknowledged stand-in for genetics, a point nicely made by the historian George Frederickson in his *Racism: A Short History* (Princeton, NJ: Princeton University Press, 2002), 7–8.

In any case, Perry's statement remains true historically, and even those proposing the most favorable interpretation of the polling data allow that there is widespread belief in black deficiency related to intelligence. And the 1994 best seller *The Bell Curve: Intelligence and Class Structure in American Life* (New York: Free Press, 1994), a scholarly book presenting what the authors, Richard Herrnstein and Charles Murray, regarded as solid scientific evidence of genetically based differences between blacks and whites, shows that Perry is capturing something that is still very much with us. (The book is still selling very well; it was ranked 4,905 on Amazon in March 2012.)

2. Steele provides both a history of, and his and his colleagues' current thinking and research about, the idea of stereotype threat in *Whistling Vivaldi: And Other Clues as to How Stereotypes Affect Us* (New York: Norton, 2011).

3. Perry, "Up from Parched Earth," 49–51.

4. Thomas Jefferson, *Notes on the State of Virginia* (1787), ed. Frank Shuffleton (New York: Penguin, 1999), 145.

5. Banneker-Jefferson letters: www.infoplease.com/t/hist/banneker-jefferson/1.html.

6. I have not been able to find out if Banneker had read *Notes on the State of Virginia* before writing this letter. He does not refer to Jefferson's views that blacks are inferior.

7. Philippe may have gotten this view from a reply Jefferson made to Banneker's letter, which was published at the time (1791) along with Banneker's letter, and which the students had read.

8. Religious historian Albert Raboteau says that the St. George's incident "is undoubtedly the most famous event in African American religious history" in *Fire in the Bones: Reflections on African-American Religious History* (Boston, MA: Beacon Press, 1995), 80. My account of Methodism is drawn from Raboteau's book.

9. Peter Hinks, ed., *David Walker's Appeal to the Coloured Citizens of the World* (University Park, PA: Penn State University Press, 2000), 61, 62.

10. There has been a long-standing suspicion of foul play in Walker's death, considering his powerful antislavery stance, message, and influence. But Hinks, in his biographical account of Walker accompanying his edition of the *Appeal*, says the evidence is that Walker died from the outbreak of consumption of that year, as did his young daughter (p. xliv).

11. Hinks, *Appeal*, 3.

12. Hinks, *Appeal*, 17. Hinks summarizes Walker's point of view about Jefferson's expressed viewpoint about black inferiority: "Walker believed that one of the most urgent assignments for African Americans now was to attack and refute this nefarious doctrine, because it was the ideological centerpiece of American racism" (xxvii).

13. See Jeannie Oakes, *Keeping Track: How Schools Structure Inequality,* 2nd ed. (New Haven, CT: Yale University Press, 2005). Grouping students by prior achievement is sometimes called "ability grouping." This is misleading in that prior

achievement often reflects inferior prior instruction or other inferior educational opportunities rather than, or at least in addition to, "ability."

14. On the racial civic knowledge and engagement gap, see Meira Levinson, *No Citizen Left Behind* (Cambridge, MA: Harvard University Press, 2012).

15. John Ogbu, *Black American Students in an Affluent Suburb: A Study of Academic Disengagement* (Mahwah, NJ: Lawrence Erlbaum Associates, 2003), 79.

16. Hinks, *Appeal*, 14.

17. U.S. Census Bureau, "Income, Poverty, and Health Insurance Coverage in the United States, 2010," 5.

18. This point must be modified somewhat for health disparities. Some differences in the incidence of medical conditions may have as one component of their causes some average genetic differences between different racialized groups. But it is very important to recognize that the causes of health disparities can have a strong environmental dimension that reflects how different racialized groups are treated in society, not their underlying genetic differences. Racial differences in health insurance, treatment by health professionals, and stress in one's environment are all nongenetic differences that can contribute to health disparities between racialized groups. (Chapter 15 of the fourth edition of Smedley's book, written by Brian Smedley, summarizes this argument.)

19. It is important to recognize that many of the kinds of arguments Walker used against Jefferson do not apply directly to the more sophisticated forms of racist thought that one finds, for example, in *The Bell Curve*. The authors, Herrnstein and Murray, claim only statistical differences between groups, which allows that many blacks will be superior to many whites, a viewpoint that is not part of Jefferson's thinking, and thus not to the target of Walker's concerns. Jefferson implies that *all* blacks are inferior to *all* whites, although perhaps he is not entirely clear on this point.

    Showing why the more sophisticated *Bell Curve*–like views are false would have taken much more time in the class than I had, given the way I set up the course, although it would have been worth doing. I would have had to teach the students some statistics and statistical reasoning. (At the time I was teaching at the high school, there was an elective course in research methods and statistics.) I chose not to take on that more complex challenge.

20. Here are Steele's own words on his view: "You have to have some sense of identity comfort in a situation to thrive in it. You have to feel comfortable in order to learn and prosper. I have to be in a situation where my prefrontal cortex is solely devoted to the education task at hand, and not to some semi-conscious calculation about how people are regarding me and about what the consequences for my life will be at every turn." Henry Louis Gates Jr., "A Conversation with Claude M. Steele: Stereotype Threat and Black Achievement," *Du Bois Review* 6, no. 2 (Fall 2009): 258.

21. To clarify an important aspect of Steele's view: He thinks that stereotype threat is actually strongest among those students who are most successful, because those are the students who most identify with the domain of academic success. He argues, and the research he cites seems to support this, that if a student is alienated from school, stereotype threat will not affect him. You have to care to be affected.

CHAPTER 8

1. The language of the "achievement gap" has to be used with caution. For example, although there are average differences between racialized groups, there are also significant ethnic differences in school achievement within those racial groups. For example, Chinese Americans do better, on the average, than Cambodians. Stacey Lee, *Unraveling the 'Model Minority' Stereotype*, 2nd ed. (New York: Teachers College Press, 2009), 14.

2. Ronald Ferguson, *Toward Excellence with Equity* (Cambridge, MA: Harvard Education Press, 2007), 128.

3. For more detailed discussion of the nature of stereotypes and their difference from accurate generalizations, see L. Blum, "Stereotypes and Stereotyping: A Moral Analysis," *Philosophical Papers* 33, no. 3 (November 2004): 251–290.

4. Skin color mattered in these early years of U.S. slavery, but not in a racial way. People with European features could escape and blend into the city populations. People with African features were immediately spottable as escapees from some form of labor bondage. It was a social control issue, without a racial implication that the slave population possessed distinctive psychological and mental characteristics. That ideology was developed later, over the next century and a half (eighteenth and first half of the nineteenth century).

5. It is not that blacks and whites were really *equals* in the abolitionist movement, only partners. Many abolitionists opposed slavery for moral reasons but still did not really think of blacks as equal to whites in all fundamental ways. But radical abolitionists, such as William Lloyd Garrison, whom we studied, learned from black abolitionists (like David Walker, whom I discussed in chapter 7) to be genuine racial egalitarians.

6. As we saw in chapter 3, by "primordialism," Smedley means the view that hostility or animus towards people who have different phenotypes than you is built into human nature, and is thus universal across cultures and historical periods.

7. Ferguson provides evidence for the importance of student-teacher relationships, especially for black and Latino students, in *Toward Excellence with Equity*, chapter 6, "What Doesn't Meet the Eye."

8. Jeannie Oakes, *Keeping Track: How Schools Structure Inequality*, 2nd edition (New Haven: Yale University Press, 2005), summarizes the research on tracking. This research is usually used to show why integrating schools by class and race benefits the disadvantaged members of those groups. But the point of the research does not fundamentally have anything to do with race and class. If a student, no matter what his race and class, who has always been in low-demand classes is placed in a high-demand one, he will generally do better work, though he may need extra support.

9. My discussion of different types of group-based expectations of individual students is drawn partly from Ferguson, *Toward Excellence with Equity*, 117ff.

10. Patricia Gándara and Frances Contreras, *The Latino Education Crisis: The Consequences of Failed Social Policies* (Cambridge, MA: Harvard University Press, 2009), 23.

11. Ferguson reports these findings (*Toward Excellence*, 169–171). Although he also finds no direct correlation between television watching and grade point average,

he hypothesizes a way they could be connected that does not show up in the direct correlation. He says, "It is difficult to believe that watching television for three or more hours each day can be as inconsequential as these findings suggest" (170).

12. Although basing expectations of individuals on racial group information is not right, that is not to say it is necessarily or usefully thought of as racist. Only the stereotype-based expectations should be considered racist; and even then it is the stereotype itself, not necessarily the teacher who is employing it, that is racist. The teacher might just be accepting a stereotype without thinking about it, or not even recognize she is using it, since stereotypes so often work unconsciously. Statistically valid generalizations are not in themselves racist (though they can be put to a racist use), even if they seem to make a group look bad. And generalizations from one's own experience are not racist either, even if they are ill-advised and damaging to students.

   The lesson here is that we can do racial damage without being racist in our hearts and thoughts. The area of expectations is a perfect example of this. It is well known that on average, black children begin school with a deficit in key academic areas, such as vocabulary. (George Farkas, "How Educational Inequality Develops," in *The Colors of Poverty: Why Racial and Ethnic Disparities Persist*, eds. Ann Chih Lin and David R. Harris [New York: Russell Sage, 2008], 109, summarizes the evidence.) If teachers keep tailoring their expectations to how blacks are doing as a group, they will then always expect less of black students. And since we are assuming that expectations have some effect on performance, they will actually be contributing to the achievement gap, even if they in no way intend to do so. That is racial damage we must try to avoid. It is scant comfort to know that we can bring about such a bad result without having racist thoughts or feelings behind it. At the same time, we need to be careful about throwing around the word *racism* when we are diagnosing what is going wrong in the area of race. (I give a fuller argument to this effect in my book *"I'm Not a Racist, But . . .": The Moral Quandary of Race*, especially chapters 1 and 3.)

13. We will see later in this chapter that socioeconomic factors can sometimes depress potential too.

CHAPTER 9

1. Peter Hinks, ed., *David Walker's Appeal to the Coloured Citizens of the World* (University Park, PA: Penn State University Press, 2000), 14.

2. OED's fourth definition of "white" is "morally or spiritually pure": www.askoxford.com:80/concise_oed/white?view=uk. Older dictionaries, such as *The Random House Dictionary of the English Language*, 2nd ed., unabridged (New York: Random House, 1987), have "slang: decent, honorable, dependable," as in "That's mighty white of you," an expression I have definitely heard.

3. Francis Collins, *The Language of God: A Scientist Presents Evidence for Belief* (New York: Free Press, 2007).

4. Randall Kennedy, "My Race Problem—and Ours," *The Atlantic Online*, May 1997, www.theatlantic.com/issues/97may/kennedy.htm, accessed 2/5/10. The Douglass

quote is in "The Nation's Problem," in *African-American Social and Political Thought, 1850–1920*, ed. Howard Brotz (New Brunswick, NJ: Transaction Publishers, 1992), 316.

CHAPTER 10

1. As the students had learned, the Spanish had enslaved indigenous peoples before and during the same period as the African slave trade. All of Latin America is to some degree a mixture of African, indigenous, and European; but the degree differs greatly from one area to another. *Mulatto* is a word generally used for a European/African mix (*mulato* in Portuguese), and *mestizo* for a European/indigenous one. But that meaning is not strict, and sometimes *mestizo* is used to encompass a mix of all three, if the indigenous is a larger part of that mix than the African, as in Mexico and Guatemala.

2. The attempt by these organizations of mixed-race persons to create a "multiracial" identity category, as well as the (unsuccessful) attempt to persuade the Census Bureau to recognize it on the 2000 census, is helpfully discussed in Ronald Sundstrom, *The Browning of America and the Evasion of Social Justice* (Albany, NY: SUNY Press, 2008), and Kimberley McClain DaCosta, *Making Multiracials: State, Family, and Market in the Redrawing of the Color Line* (Stanford, CA: Stanford University Press, 2007).

3. See, for example, Mica Pollock, *Colormute: Race Talk Dilemmas in an American School* (Princeton, NJ: Princeton University Press, 2004), for the way high school students foreground different identities in different contexts.

4. And the language of "underclass" (a word I never used in the class, but also did not explicitly critique) is a bit dehumanizing and certainly distancing. It is significant that William Julius Wilson, who made the term popular in his influential book *The Truly Disadvantaged: The Inner City, the Underclass, and Public Policy* (Chicago, IL: University of Chicago Press, 1987), subsequently repudiated it. W. J. Wilson, "Studying Inner-City Social Dislocations: The Challenge of Public Agenda Research: 1990 Presidential Address," *American Sociological Review* 56, no. 1 (1991): 1–14.

5. In their superb book exploring the current attitudes of students who graduated from racially mixed high schools in 1980—the high-water mark for national attempts to promote school integration—Amy Stuart Wells and her coauthors find a duality very similar to Anna's in many of the whites they talked to. They had some grasp, not always very firm, of racial injustice, but were also drawn to a "color-blind" way of thinking about race that did not acknowledge stark differences in racial groups' social and economic well-being. The slight difference between Wells et al.'s white subjects and Anna is that Anna's distancing from whiteness is not exactly the same as the proactive philosophy of "color-blindness." Anna does not reject an outlook that can acknowledge continuing racial injustice. Amy Stuart Wells, Jennifer Jellison Holme, Anita Tijerina Revilla, and Awo Korantemaa Atanda, *Both Sides Now: The Story of School Desegregation's Graduates* (Berkeley, CA: University of California Press, 2009), especially chapter 4. The authors also point out that on an interpersonal level, the "color-blind" mind-set was often helpful to the white 1980 graduates in

helping them get past their fears and prejudices directed toward their fellow black students, and blacks in general, even though it also helped blind them to larger injustices.

CHAPTER 11

1. Beverly Daniel Tatum, *"Why Are All the Black Kids Sitting Together in the Cafeteria?" and Other Conversations About Race* (New York: Basic Books, 1997).

CHAPTER 12

1. Of course I hoped and assumed that the moral reflection the students engaged in with regard to historical events would help them develop general capabilities that they could apply to current issues. The development of this moral thinking was indeed a central aim of the course for me.

2. The Supreme Court's opinion in *Grutter v. Bollinger et al.* (539 U.S. 306 [2003]) dealt with other issues besides the comfort/critical mass issue, but I am interested in that particular one here. (I will discuss some of the others in the conclusion.) The court's thinking on any publicly debated issue has a large impact on popular thinking, even apart from the specific laws and policies that it forbids or allows. As I am finishing up this book, the affirmative action case *Fisher v. University of Texas at Austin* is on the Supreme Court docket and will be decided in the next months. Whatever its outcome (more on this issue in the conclusion), the articulation of the "critical mass" idea at the Supreme Court level stands and has become a part of popular thinking in the world of higher education. Even if the court rejects some race-preference policies based on it, even ones validated in *Grutter*, it is not likely to reject the educational significance of the idea of critical mass itself.

3. To clarify the complex Supreme Court decision: there were two different affirmative action cases the court was ruling on at the same time. It ruled that the affirmative action program at University of Michigan's Law School was constitutionally acceptable (in *Grutter v. Bollinger*), but that the affirmative action program at the University of Michigan's undergraduate college was not (in *Gratz v. Bollinger* 539 U.S. 244 [2003]). The figures I give in the text are for the undergraduate program. Even though the Supreme Court ruled against the program that resulted in these percentages, their reason for doing so did not deny that these percentages constituted a "critical mass," and the undergraduate context seems to me more comparable to high school than is a law school. That is why I am citing the figures for the college.

4. It must be said that in many situations the majority group *does* put out the vibe that members of the other group do not belong.

5. Ways that this "model minority" stereotype is false, damaging to Asian Americans, damaging to blacks and Latinos who are compared unfavorably to this stereotype, and damaging to relations between Asian Americans and these other groups are discussed in Frank Wu, *Yellow* (New York: Basic Books, 2002), and Stacey Lee, *Unraveling the "Model Minority" Stereotype: Listening to Asian American Youth*, 2nd ed. (New York: Teachers College Press, 2009).

6. In Cynthia Feliciano's study of the educational attainments of immigrant groups, discussed in chapter 5, Indians are the third highest among the thirty

groups she examines. Cynthia Feliciano, *Unequal Origins: Immigrant Selection and the Education of the Second Generation* (El Paso, TX: LFB Scholarly Publishing, 2005), 46.

7. "College prep" was the name of the course level lower than honors or advanced. Most courses at the high school were college prep.

8. In the 2010 Census, blacks were 13.6% of the population and Hispanics 16.3% (with 2.4% of Hispanics saying they were black).

9. Notice, however, that there is an important difference between these two questions. The first one explicitly asks the student to think about a general group point of view (of a group she is a member of) and report that view. The second question asks the student to decide how she is to report her own view, albeit as a member of that group.

CONCLUSION

1. Amy Stuart Wells, Jennifer Jellison Holme, Anita Tijerina Revilla, and Awo Korantemaa Atanda, *Both Sides Now: The Story of School Desegregation* (Berkeley, CA: University of California Press, 2009), 124.

2. Sports and other extracurricular activities are also venues in which students can have the extended contact with one another that permit and generally encourage the moral and social growth that integrated education can provide. But of course the classroom remains the most important such venue since it embraces all students.

3. Wells et al., *Both Sides Now*, 124.

4. "With no forum or dialogue in which to make better sense of the racial differences they experienced every day, many of these graduates walked away from high school with fairly superficial understandings of race and its role in American society, understandings that would not lead to challenging the racial status quo." Wells et al., *Both Sides Now*, 135.

5. To take just one indication of this knowledge deficiency in whites, consider that in a 2008 poll, 61% of white Americans said that blacks have achieved equality; 21.5% more said they will soon do so. Lawrence Bobo, "Somewhere Between Jim Crow and Racialism: Reflections on the Racial Divide and America Today," *Daedalus*, Spring 2011, 29. Remember that as we saw in chapter 7, in 2010 the median white household income was $54,620; Hispanic, $37,759; and black, $32,068; so at least on that one very important measure of well-being, we are far from equality. As a philosopher I am of course aware that there are differing and competing conceptions of equality, so that what some recognize to depart from it, others see as exemplifying it. But I do not think any plausible account of equality would regard as equal a society in which the racial gaps in education, health, income, wealth, and occupational attainment are as great as they are in ours.

    I agree with Wells et al.'s statement about whites overall: "White Americans want to think about race only on the individual level—how individuals treat each other—but many, especially those who have had cross-racial friendships and experiences, sense that there are broader, society-level explanations for the ongoing racial inequality" (129–130). We should look to our schools to give students the tools to begin providing those explanations, so they can do more than "sense" them—and to be able to handle the complex race-related emotions involved in coming to grips with the moral implications of these explanations. These involve (among other things) a recognition that although these white students themselves may have done nothing to harm anyone of another race, all of us live in a society that inherits a still inadequately corrected history of injustice—so it is all our responsibility to support efforts to remedy that history by correcting for these stark disparities in the present.

6. As Jeannie Oakes and Richard Kahlenberg have argued, when working-class students are educated with middle-class students, it tends to help close the academic skills gap between the two groups (by bringing the less advantaged groups "up")—a class-based effect with a racial impact. Oakes, *Keeping Track: How Schools Structure Inequality,* 2nd ed. (New Haven, CT: Yale University Press, 2005); Richard Kahlenberg, *All Together Now: Creating Middle Class Schools Through Public School Choice* (Washington, DC: Brookings Institution Press, 2003).

7. Elizabeth Anderson spells out in convincing detail the ways that everyone, whites included, benefits from integration in all domains of life, including education, and that blacks and Latinos benefit more because of their disadvantage in social and economic location. *The Imperative of Integration* (Princeton, NJ: Princeton University Press, 2010). In particular, Anderson articulates the purely instrumental advantages to whites in being able to function more effectively in multiracial workplaces, a point not emphasized in my focus on moral, social, civic, and personal growth benefits.

8. Cited by Pedro Noguera and Richard Rothstein, "Educational Accountability Policy in the New Administration," Economic Policy Institute policy memorandum, December 19, 2008 (no citation given for O'Connor quote). O'Connor is cochair of the Campaign for the Civic Mission of Schools.

9. For a discussion of these cases, see Michael Rebell, *Courts and Kids: Pursuing Educational Equity Through the State Courts* (Chicago, IL: University of Chicago Press, 2009). The report "Guardian of Democracy: The Civic Mission of Schools," produced by the group of which Justice O'Connor is a cochair (see previous note), also emphasizes that state constitutions generally emphasize the civic importance of education (Silver Spring, MD: Campaign for the Civic Mission of Schools, 2003), 11.

10. Wells et al., *Both Sides Now,* 5. In a study of Cambridge Rindge and Latin seniors in 2002, a large number said that attending the school had helped them understand and be more comfortable with students of other racial and ethnic groups. Civil Rights Project, *The Impact of Racial and Ethnic Diversity on Educational Outcomes: Cambridge, MA, School District* (Cambridge: Harvard University, 2002), 6–8.

11. *Grutter v. Bollinger et al.* 539 U.S. 306 (2003), 9 (O'Connor opinion).

12. Elizabeth Anderson nicely summarizes the evidence of the positive effects of integrated experience on whites' greater understanding of blacks as a group: "The political opinions of whites who have more black neighbors, coworkers, and fellow churchgoers are less influenced by antiblack stereotypes than the opinions of more segregated whites. In general, the more diverse individuals' networks of political discussion are, the better informed they are of the grounds for their own and others' opinions *and* the more tolerant they are of opposed

political views. These facts suggest that more racially tolerant opinions generated under conditions of integration do not represent an oft-decried cowardly submission to imperious demands of 'political correctness' but reflect a more informed and conscientious thought process in light of a normatively legitimate democratic pressure to form opinions that can be justified to a diverse public." *Imperative of Integration*, 133. Although Anderson is focusing on whites and blacks, her reflections here would apply to all racial groups.

13. Barack Obama, *The Audacity of Hope: Thoughts on Reclaiming the American Dream* (New York: Three Rivers Press, 2006), 232. As a presidential candidate, Obama also gave an excellent speech on race in March 2008, though only in response to a controversy that he could not ignore, caused by remarks of a former minister of his, Reverend Jeremiah Wright. President Obama gave another important speech on race in 2009 at an NAACP convention. (See discussion of Obama's views in these speeches in Tommie Shelby, "Justice and Racial Reconciliation: Two Visions," Race in the Age of Obama, volume 1, *Daedalus*, Winter 2011, 100–102.) But on the whole, Obama said almost nothing about racial inequality in his first term in office.

14. There is reason to think that some of President Obama's universal, or race-neutral, initiatives and accomplishments, such as raising the minimum wage and the Patient Protection and Affordable Care Act, were part of a conscious strategy to help blacks and Latinos, without calling attention to that fact, as these policies are disproportionately beneficial to the lower-income segment of the population. While such race-blind measures are an essential part of reducing racial disparities, they are unable to fully address them. (For a discussion of Obama's investment in these race-blind programs and their limitations, see Shelby, "Justice and Racial Reconciliation," 101–106.)

15. John R. Logan and Brian J. Stults, "The Persistence of Segregation in the Metropolis: New Findings from the 2010," census brief prepared for US2010 Project. Black/white segregation (the separation of those two groups from each other) has only very slowly declined since 1980. It should be noted that whites are the most segregated racial group in part because they are the largest such group. But this does not keep their segregation from having deleterious effects on themselves, and on groups from whom they are segregated as well.

16. Rebell, *Courts and Kids*, shows that funding formulas have become more equal as a result of the cases he discusses, but they are still far from adequately tied to student need, which would require greater funds for concentrated poverty districts (for teacher pay and wraparound social services, for example) than for wealthy districts.

17. Wealth disparities by race have also substantially worsened since the Great Recession of 2008–2009. In 2009, blacks had a median net worth of $5,677 per household and Hispanics $6,325, while whites had $113,145. "The disparities are three times the gap that existed three years ago." Reid Epstein, *Politico*, July 26, 2011, reporting on a Pew Research Center study from July, 2011. "These lopsided wealth ratios are the largest since the government began publishing such data a quarter century ago." Pew Research Center, "Wealth Gaps Rise to Record Highs Between Whites, Blacks, and Latinos," http://pewresearch.org/pubs/2069/housing-bubble-subprime-mortgages-hispanics-blacks-household-wealth-disparity.

The report adds, "Moreover, since the official end of the recession in mid-2009, the housing market in the U.S. has remained in a slump while the stock market has recaptured much of the value it lost from 2007 to 2009. Given that a much higher share of whites than blacks or Hispanics own stock—as well as mutual funds and 401(k) or individual retirement accounts (IRAs)—the stock market rebound since 2009 is likely to have benefited white households more than minority households."

18. As of March 2012, as I am finishing up this book, there has begun to be a small but welcome increase in public attention to the impact of increased overall inequality on education. An important scholarly collection, Greg J. Duncan and Richard Murnane, eds., *Whither Opportunity? Rising Inequality, Schools, and Children's Life Chances* (New York: Russell Sage, 2011), has been discussed in several media articles—for example, Lesli Maxwell, "Achievement Gaps Tied to Income Found Widening," *Education Week*, March 7, 2012.

19. "Guidance on the Voluntary Use of Race to Achieve Diversity and Avoid Racial Isolation in Elementary and Secondary Schools," Civil Rights Division, Department of Justice, and the Office of Civil Rights, Department of Education, 2011.

20. The two cases are *Meredith v. Jefferson County Board of Education*, 548 U.S. 938 (2007) and *Parents Involved in Community Schools v. Seattle District No. 1*, 551 U.S. 701 (2007). They were decided in a single opinion.

21. The Bush administration document, written by Stephanie Monroe, has been withdrawn from the historical Web site and is very difficult to find. I have an account of it only from other sources.

22. I am not providing a full summary of the guidelines' recommended paths for school districts, but only trying to give a sense of their character and to emphasize that the Obama administration sees substantially greater possibilities for, and certainly much more decisively expresses a commitment to, integrative policies than did the Bush administration. I mean also to foreground the guidelines' highlighting of the civic and educational value of integration and diversity in education. One other important difference between the two is that the Bush guidelines said that a district had to actually implement "race-neutral" policies (e.g., using SES as a proxy for race) and only if that did not result in a reasonable degree of integration could the district make use of (permitted) race-conscious policies. By contrast, the Obama administration says that the district could move directly to a race-conscious policy if it could make a plausible case that a race-neutral alternative would not work, without having to attempt it. (Again, the race-conscious policy still could not make use of individual students' racial identities as a basis to assign them to a school.)

23. Syllabus (an official summary of the *PICS* decision), 5; Roberts (writing for the four rejecting racial integration as a compelling state interest), in PICS, 551 U.S. at 23.

24. Kennedy, 17, also quoted by Justice Breyer in his dissent, 38.

25. *Regents of the University of California v. Bakke*, 438 U.S. 265 (1978); *Gratz v. Bollinger*, 539 U.S. 306 (2003); *Grutter*, 539 U.S.

26. Roberts, 16.

27. Roberts, 17. I am talking about the standing of diversity as an educational and civic value in these Supreme Court decisions without taking on all the legal

ramifications of the idea of a "compelling state interest," an important legal concept in this area.

28.   Breyer, 39. Justice Breyer specifically claims that the benefits of diversity are as compelling at the secondary level as in higher education (54). This is part of why he talks here about the benefits to black students of integration at the pre-college level.

29.   Between 20% and 30% of colleges practice affirmative action, according to William Bowen and Derek Bok, *The Shape of the River: Long-Term Consequences of Considering Race in College and University Admissions* (Princeton, NJ: Princeton University Press, 1998), xxxvii–xxxviii.

30.   This is not to say that affirmative action institutions actually have a great deal of racial diversity, or that less selective institutions that do not practice affirmative action lack it. Indeed, the point we saw in chapter 12 is that even with affirmative action, many colleges are not very diverse; and depending on their location, state universities—especially other than the "flagship" campuses—and community colleges are on the whole much more diverse than selective colleges. UMass Boston is much more racially diverse than UMass Amherst, Boston University, and Harvard. Although with their increasing cost (UMass Boston is currently about $12,000 per year for tuition and fees), one might accurately say that the increasing inaccessiblity of public universities to lower-income students, caused by a precipitous diminishing of state support over the past thirty years, has resulted in diminished economic diversity among their students, and, more important, the pricing out of low-income students who used to be able to attend these universities. (In the mid-1980s, UMass Boston students paid less than $1,000 a year). This economically based exclusion also diminishes black and Latino numbers at these institutions, but they are still generally more racially diverse than affirmative action institutions in their same states.

31.   Michael McPherson and Morton Owen Schapiro, eds., *College Access: Opportunity or Privilege* (New York: College Board, 2006) is one of several books decrying the increasing skewing of attendance at selective colleges (as well as of college completion rates more generally) toward upper-income students and away from lower-income students. In 2003, 3% of the students at the 146 most selective schools came from the bottom income quartile, and 6% from the next highest quartile (that is, 9% from the bottom half of the income spectrum). john a. powell and Rebecca High, "The Common Schools Democracy Requires," in *Lessons in Integration: Realizing the Promise of Racial Diversity in American Schools*, eds. Erica Frankenberg and Gary Orfield (Charlottesville, VA: University of Virginia Press, 2007), 277. See also Walter Benn Michaels, *The Trouble with Diversity: How We Learned to Love Identity and Ignore Inequality* (New York: Metropolitan Books, 2006).

32.   Selective "exam schools" like Bronx High School of Science in New York and Boston Latin School in Boston function more like colleges in this respect than like regular high schools (although the degree to which exam schools can practice affirmative action has been greatly reduced by legal rulings; e.g., in *Wessmann v. Gittens*, 160 F.3d 790 [1st Cir. 1998]).

33.   In any case, even if the value of racial diversity could be separated from that of socioeconomic diversity, institutions that are diverse in both ways thereby gain greater diversity benefits than those diverse on only one dimension.

34. A November 2011 study shows a tremendous growth in income-based residential segregation from 1970 to 2009. If neighborhoods are categorized into "high income," "middle income," and "low income," the percentage of families living in either high- or low-income areas increased from 35% to 56% in that period (so "middle income" decreased from 65% to 44%). Sean Reardon and Kendra Bischoff, "Growth in the Residential Segregation of Families by Income, 1970–2009," US2010 Project (Brown University and Russell Sage Foundation), November 2011. Income-based residential segregation tends to correlate partly with race-based segregation, since race tends to correlate with income. The Reardon-Bischoff study also shows that blacks are increasingly segregated by income within their own group; that is, poor blacks are increasingly segregated from middle-class blacks. But this development does not translate into middle-class blacks being increasingly integrated into middle-class white neighborhoods. Middle-class blacks are more likely to be in neighborhoods with poor whites than with middle-class whites (Reardon and Bischoff, 23.)
35. Citation from the district court's opinion in Powell and High, "The Common Schools Democracy Requires," 279–280. Breyer affirms the district court's assessment, in PICS, 551 U.S. at 34.
36. Kennedy, 18, 15.
37. Roberts, 38, citing *Adarand v. Pena* 515 U.S. at 214.
38. "Racial balance" seems a perfectly innocuous way of referring to ensuring that schools have a reasonable racial mix among their students, in light of the demographics of the school district. In jurisprudence since the *Bakke* case in 1978, this expression has taken on a stigma as something constitutionally impermissible. In my reading of some references to it, it sometimes denotes a goal defined by a specific percentage of different racial groups for which no coherent reason is offered—as if the actor in question (a school district, a business) had a bare preference for such-and-such percentage of whites, such-and-such of Latinos, and so on, resting on no consideration of justice or reasonableness. I do not know that any standard public or private actor has sought racial balance in this somewhat arbitrary sense. In other contexts "racial balance" is used more reasonably to refer to the attempt to reflect in a school or workplace the exact percentage of each racial group in some relevant wider population (e.g., of qualified applicants), on the grounds that this would be a just and reasonable target. The Supreme Court has consistently found policies aiming at that goal unconstitutional. But sensible policies of an integrative or diversity-sensitive nature do not need to be, nor should they be in my opinion, cashed out in such a rigid way. As Louisville shows, school districts generally aim at a range rather than a strict percentage of different racial groups in each school. This form of "racial balance" seems entirely reasonable, as it did to the dissenting judges in the *PICS* cases.
39. Justice Breyer, in his dissent, notes that the harm to students not given their first choice of schools (or, to be more precise, not given the first preference of their parents) is significantly less than that suffered by a white student not being admitted to a superior institution because of an affirmative action program at that institution (a state of affairs defining of affirmative action programs and permitted by the *Grutter* decision) (Breyer, 47). By aspiration and, if the

district court's appraisal is correct, in fact, the consequence of not getting one's first choice in the *PICS* cases was that the student had to attend a school relatively equal in quality to the one from which he was excluded by the race-sensitive assignment policy. Affirmative action policy by definition involves a hierarchy of quality assessed according to widely shared standards. Such a value and prestige hierarchy with significant implications for the student's future prospects is not generally present in K–12 cases, although there may be qualitative differences between schools in the district.

40. Roberts, 5 in summary, citing *Brown v. Board of Education*, 347 U.S. 483 at 494, then (in the internal quote) *City of Richmond v. J.A. Croson Co.*, 488 U.S. 463 (1989). Here is a quote from *Brown* that seems to be what Roberts is referring to: "To separate [children] from others of similar age and qualifications solely because of their race generates a feeling of inferiority as to their status in the community that may affect their hearts and minds in a way unlikely ever to be undone" (6). It is obvious that the court has only black children in mind here, not white. The justices are obviously not making a race-neutral point about mere separation here as Roberts claims. The context is made more explicit a few lines later: "Segregation of white and colored children in public schools has a detrimental effect upon the colored children."

41. At one point, Justice Breyer explicitly uses the concept of asymmetry to express the spirit of his entire dissent: "I have found no case that otherwise repudiated this constitutional asymmetry between that which seeks to *exclude* and that which seeks to *include* members of minority races," 29 (emphasis in original).

42. Roberts, 40f.

43. Note that I am not taking a stand here on constitutional interpretation per se. I note, however, that Breyer cites a unanimous opinion in *Swann v. Charlotte-Mecklenberg Board of Education*, 402 U.S. 1 (1971) in support of both the civic significance of racial integration and the permissibility of school districts using race-conscious criteria: "School authorities . . . might well conclude, for example, that in order to prepare students to live in a pluralistic society each school should have a prescribed ratio of Negro to white students reflecting the proportion for the district as a whole" (16).

44. Roberts, 23. First quote from *Richmond v. Croson*, 488 U.S. at 498–499; second from *Wygant v. Jackson Board of Education*, 476 U.S. (1986) at 276. "Societal discrimination" is the court's term of art for, essentially, racial disparities that have multiple causes, the way educational disparities are due to a combination of income, housing, occupational, and prior educational disparities rooted in racial discrimination. Another way to put this point, as Roberts does, is that a governmental unit (like a school district) is permitted to correct *only* for racial wrongs (such as disparities or segregation) that it had itself brought about.

45. An important new affirmative action case, *Fisher v. University of Texas at Austin*, will be decided by the Supreme Court after I have finished this book. Because of changes in the composition of the court since the 2003 *Grutter* case (the most relevant here being Justice Alito's replacing Justice O'Connor), it is quite possible that the court will in its decision further restrict the use of race in higher education admissions. This would be unfortunate. As I have indicated, I think that the *Grutter* court's reasoning—that diversity in higher education is a compelling

interest, although rectifying a history of black, Latino, and Native American lack of access to higher education is not and cannot be part of the reason for diversity's value—is a shaky foundation for race preference policies. Unfortunately, given the composition of the court, there is no chance that the foundation for race-sensitive admission will be shored up with a recognition that society's stake in creating racial justice is morally compelling. Nevertheless, it is not likely that the current court will actually *deny* the educational and civic benefits of diversity articulated in the *Grutter* decision. Much more likely is that diversity will be demoted in its standing as a compelling governmental interest.

Such a demotion might have a minor ripple effect on the use of diversity arguments to support race-sensitive K–12 school assignment policies such as the Obama administration interpreted Justice Kennedy's opinion in the *PICS* cases as permitting. My guess is that most of those guidelines would survive the demotion of diversity. But we will have to see.

46. Orfield and Lee document the increasing racial segregation in schools; the judicial rulings (from the early and mid-1990s) that facilitated it; and the failure of public policy to reverse this trend. Gary Orfield and Chungmei Lee, "Historic Reversals, Accelerating Resegregation, and the Need for New Integration Strategies" (Los Angeles: UCLA, Civil Rights Project, August 2007). (The Civil Rights Project moved from Harvard to UCLA in 2006.) The Obama guidelines can be seen as a positive response to these unfortunate developments. A book published as I was finishing this one also speaks to both the need for and the possibilities of integrative initiatives in the post-*PICS* era: Erica Frankenberg and Elizabeth Debray, eds., *Integrating Schools in a Changing Society: New Policies and Legal Options for a Multiracial Generation* (Chapel Hill, NC: University of North Carolina Press, 2011).

47. All statistics are from Martha Minow, *In Brown's Wake: Legacies of America's Educational Landmark* (New York: Oxford, 2010), 9, and Breyer's dissent in the *PICS* decision, 4.

48. Gary Orfield and Chungmei Lee, *Racial Transformation and the Changing Nature of Segregation* (Cambridge, MA: The Civil Rights Project at Harvard University, 2006).

49. Wells et al., *Both Sides Now*, 9. The election of Ronald Reagan in 1980 was the beginning of an attempt at the presidential level to halt the push toward integration through judicial appointments (the elevation of Justice Rehnquist to chief justice, and appointments of Justices O'Connor and Scalia to the court). But during that period there was local prointegration momentum, resulting in something of a standoff during the 1980s. It was in the 1990s that resegregation really began in earnest. For documentation of this history, see Gary Orfield, "Turning Back to Segregation," in Gary Orfield and Susan Eaton, eds., *Dismantling Desegregation: The Quiet Reversal of* Brown v. Board of Education (New York: New Press, 1996), 16–18.

50. Jennifer Hochschild and Nathan Scovronick, *The American Dream and the Public Schools* (New York: Oxford, 2003), 6.

51. See Richard Weissbourd, *The Parents We Mean to Be: How Well-Intentioned Adults Undermine Children's Moral and Emotional Development* (Boston, MA: Houghton Mifflin Harcourt, 2009), chapter 3, 61: "Increasingly in recent years I have heard

stories about children in private schools and wealthy suburban schools who are strung-out achievement junkies and about parents who drive them relentlessly."

52. Tyack, *Seeking Common Ground*, chapter 1.

53. Breyer, 39–40.

54. Tyack, *Seeking Common Ground*, 157.

55. Powell and High, "The Common Schools Democracy Requires," 280 (internal quote from district court's decision, p. 854).

56. In 2010, the UCLA-based Civil Rights Project released a report claiming that on average, charter schools were much more racially segregated than comparable traditional public schools—70% charters compared to 35% traditional public schools have over 90% black and Latino students. Erica Frankenberg, Genevieve Siegel-Hawley, and Jia Wang, "Choice Without Equity: Charter School Segregation and the Need for Civil Rights Standards." (See also Adai Tefera, Genevieve Siegel-Hawley, and Erica Frankenberg, *School Integration Efforts Three Years After "Parents Involved"* [Los Angeles: UCLA, Civil Rights Project, June 28, 2010].) A study critical of Frankenberg et al. found a 10% gap in central cities and a 20% gap in metropolitan areas between charters and traditional public schools in the incidence of hypersegregated schools. Gary Ritter, Nathan Jensen, Brian Kisida, and Josh McGee, "A Closer Look at Charter Schools and Segregation," *Education Next* 10, no. 3 (Summer 2010). Without attempting to assess this controversy, it does seem to me that the degree of hypersegregation the latter authors defending charters find is still worrying. If Frankenberg et al.'s figures are closer to the truth, that is all the more reason for concern.

ACKNOWLEDGMENTS

Work on this book was supported by a grant from the Spencer Foundation's small grant program. It allowed me a semester free of teaching in spring 2010 that proved essential to my being able to turn my various writings into something like a coherent book. I am extremely grateful to the Spencer Foundation for this, and for the added support through a gathering of others with the same grant and the selection committee. I want especially to thank Harry Brighouse and Michael McPherson, who have been leaders in seeing the value of philosophy to education, and in embedding that value in Spencer's grant program.

Special thanks to all the people at Cambridge Rindge and Latin High School who supported the course and made me feel entirely welcome at the school. Betsy Grady put in place the administrative structure for the course, helped find students for it for the first two offerings, and provided a lot of initial support that made the course a reality. After Betsy retired (and even before), Wendell Bourne, the district social studies coordinator, was very supportive of the course and of me personally and helped to shepherd the class through its final two offerings. History teachers Larry Aaronson and Bill Tobin (twice) and English teacher Ed Hurley inconvenienced themselves by letting me use their classrooms to teach the course, and were gracious and generous in doing so. Larry was and is a political kindred spirit and his enthusiasm for the course its first time out was a special gift. Other teachers at the high school were helpful through allowing me to consult with them about particular students and general teaching issues, or to sit in on their classes. In this regard I want to thank Dionne Campbell, Jennifer Hogue, Carol Siriani, Cindy Weisbart, Jon Chen, and Betsy Bard, and anyone else I may have forgotten with the passage of time.

Quite a few guidance counselors got into the spirit of my course and sought and found appropriate students for it. I especially want to thank Yvon Lamour, Brian Downes, Norma Garcia-Turner, George Finn, Lynn Williams, Gordon Axtman, Lorraine Davis, and Kara Lopez. During her principalship, Sybil Knight embraced the course and my teaching of it. Chris Saheed was principal during most of the writing of the book and was always willing to see me and answer my questions. Damon Smith, the current principal and former coordinator of social studies, has also been very encouraging and helpful.

My four teaching assistants—Myriam Guerrier, Nakia Keizer, Woodly Pierre-Louis, and Vadeline Jules—were all wonderful partners in this teaching adventure. They carried out crucial and very demanding administrative tasks and, equally important, contributed their particular perspectives about specific students, class dynamics, pedagogical approaches, and how the course was going overall. Mary Casey, a friend and then postdoctoral student, sat in on a good number of the classes during two offerings, and also frequently conferred with me and the teaching assistant. I am extremely grateful to all these colleagues.

I also want to thank the UMass Boston administration and my colleagues in the philosophy department for recognizing the value of teaching this sort of high school course to the university's urban mission. I particularly want to single out Hubie Jones, at that time the vice-chancellor in charge of community relations at UMB, for supporting and facilitating my first outing, before the district of Cambridge took over financial support for the course.

At a later stage, Brian Halley, an editor at University of Massachusetts Press at UMass Boston, spent a great deal of time helping me put together a prospectus that made sense for a kind of publishing to which I was unaccustomed. And when I had reached the end of my own publishing ideas and wasn't sure the project would ever see the light of day, Brian came to my rescue and started me down the path that led to Harvard Education Press, which, at least from my end, has been a match made in heaven. All the folks at HEP have been wonderful and professional throughout.

In my memory, my friends and colleagues philosopher Rene Arcilla and UMass Boston anthropologist Tim Sieber were the first to suggest that I write a book about my experiences teaching this class, and I appreciate their providing that initial push. The philosopher David Hansen gave me advice about the world of educational publishing early on; his own work delineating the moral dimension of classroom interactions and the moral core of the teaching relationship inspired my own. My former UMass student Emily Currier typed most of my interviews, read some of my early attempts to write the book, and was very positive when I wasn't sure it was going anywhere. Christopher Lewis, a former UMass student of mine and now a philosopher working in areas similar to my own, gave me invaluable feedback on various aspects of the manuscript, dug up and summarized helpful material, and provided tremendously important personal support at critical times. The philosopher and African American studies scholar Tommie Shelby helped with the chapter on David Walker. My cousin Steve Schewel, a writer and public school activist in Durham, North Carolina, provided excellent feedback on several chapters. My sister-in-law, the writer Ellen Cassedy, offered terrific suggestions on a middle draft of the book. My old and dear friend and philosophy comrade David Wong gave me wise advice on some moral and presentational issues arising in some of the chapters. Meira Levinson, also a philosopher and formerly an urban school teacher, gave me incredibly penetrating feedback on a late draft. Larry Foster, Kathy Greeley, Kathy Brady, Alan Zaslavsky, and Noel Jette were willing to stop what they were doing and consult on issues as they emerged. Elizabeth Anderson and Erica Frankenberg generously responded to some scholarly queries in the final stages.

Two of my reading groups were particularly central to this project. Colleagues of divergent disciplines in my "moral education group"—Martha Minow, Rick Weissbourd, and Mary Casey—helped me think and rethink the project over several years, in the process of reading quite a few drafts of chapters. Rick also gave me excellent advice about writing and publishing. My race and education group of scholars and practitioners—Lisa Gonsalves, Nakia Keizer, Ann Ruggiero, and Nury Marcelino—read several chapters and gave me critical feedback from their classroom and school-based vantage points. I am also grateful to this group (including several former members and the newest members Danielle Wheeler and Chikae Yamauchi) for many years of conversations about racial and educational issues. Danielle also read the almost-final version and made some wonderful suggestions. In addition, Nakia, having been one of my teaching assistants for the course, helped me process teaching issues from his vantage point. I am particularly grateful to Lisa Gonsalves for her friendship and support of the project over many years.

My family were all greatly involved and helpful at many points in teaching the course and writing the book. My children, Ben, Sarah, and Laura, all attended Cambridge Rindge and Latin and helped me with "cultural translation" during and after the years I worked there. As I mention in the book, Ben taught at the high school some of the time I was also teaching there and was immensely helpful in thinking through pedagogical issues with me. I have learned much from him. Ben also read several chapters of the manuscript and gave me terrific comments. Sarah has taught elementary school for years and her penetrating insights about education over the years have profoundly affected me and my thinking. She also gave me vital feedback on chapter 8. Laura's time at the high school spanned some of my own and she helped me understand the school's norms and mores during those years. In addition, she typed up my rambling mini-cassette debriefs with incredible skill and sensitivity. I'm still amazed that she could do that, and it very much helped me get to a place where I could survey and organize the material to actually write the book. Finally, my life partner, Judy Smith, read the whole manuscript and gave me the benefit of her deep knowledge of American cultural and social history and her expertise in African American history and culture. In addition, I discussed many small and large issues about this somewhat unusual project with her, and her support and insightfulness have been unbelievably helpful and sustaining, regarding the book as well as our life together.

Finally, I am happy to give deepest thanks to my editor at Harvard Education Press, Caroline Chauncey. I have not had an editor with anything like Caroline's hands-on, skilled engagement for any of my other books. Caroline saw merit in my project when I was floundering. She has kept me going with absolutely terrific comments on various drafts, advice about all kinds of matters, and ongoing support I did not realize could be part of an editor's portfolio.

I am deeply grateful to all these people, but I want to give final and special thanks to all my students in the four classes I taught at the high school. It was the experience of a lifetime for me, and you changed me in ways that will stay with me always. Your uninhibited excitement and engagement with the course and the issues raised in it put me into a teaching zone I had never experienced before. I learned much from you, and dedicate this book to you.

ABOUT THE AUTHOR

Lawrence Blum is the Distinguished Professor of Liberal Arts and Education and a professor of philosophy at the University of Massachusetts, Boston. He has written extensively on race and racism, moral philosophy, social and political philosophy, philosophy of education, moral education, multicultural education, philosophy and the Holocaust, race and film, moral emotions, and other topics. He is the author of four books—*Friendship, Altruism, and Morality* (Routledge and Kegan Paul, 1980), *A Truer Liberty: Simone Weil and Marxism* (with V. J. Seidler) (Routledge, 1989), *Moral Perception and Particularity* (Cambridge University Press, 1994), and *"I'm Not a Racist, But . . .": The Moral Quandary of Race* (Cornell University Press, 2002), which was selected as the Social Philosophy Book of the Year by the North American Society for Social Philosophy. Blum has also taught at Teachers College, Stanford School of Education, and UCLA (in philosophy). He lives in Cambridge, Massachusetts.

INDEX

Page ranges in **bold** indicate the
relevant chapter page span.

Abdul
  race and ethnicity information, 205
  reflections on racial asymmetries in
    comfort level of the students,
    178–179
Adam
  African slave trade morality discus-
    sion, 80, 81, 82
  on being in a mixed-race class, 187
  concept of race discussion, 40
  origin and morality of race discus-
    sion, 29, 32
  race and ethnicity information, 205
  race and religion discussion, 143
  recognition of value of learning
    about ignorance and stereotyp-
    ing, 169, 170
  reflections on slavery and personal
    identity, 154–155
  symmetry question surround-
    ing pride in skin color for all
    groups, 138, 139, 140
African Methodist Episcopal (AME)
  blacks-only denomination, 96–97
African role in slavery, **77–88**
  economics as the basis of slavery,
    80, 119
  history of the slave trade, 77–78
  morality of slavery, 79–85
  morality of the African traders'
    actions, 78–79, 85–87
  seeing moral issues as having an
    historical context, 81–84
Allen, Richard, 96

American Anthropological
  Association's statement on race,
  25
Anna
  African slave trade morality discus-
    sion, 80, 81, 82
  on immigrant blacks versus African
    Americans, 70
  opening class exercise on stereo-
    types, 18, 19, 20, 21, 111
  race and ethnicity information, 205
  reflections on slavery and personal
    identity, 155–157
  symmetry question surround-
    ing pride in skin color for all
    groups, 143
Antonine, 2
  comments on Smedley and her
    work, 44
  concept of race discussion, 40
  discussion of popular culture and
    racism, 49, 51
  high expectations concept and,
    128–129, 132
  impact an authority figure had on
    her priority setting, 117–118
  introduction of a "bad hair" issue
    for blacks, 136, 137
  opening class exercise on stereo-
    types, 18, 20, 21
  origin and morality of race discus-
    sion, 28
  question about comfort and
    suspicion regarding race of a
    person, 34–35
  race and ethnicity information, 205
  race and religion discussion, 142